Emmanuel Lev

EMMANUEL LEVINAS

His Life and Legacy

SALOMON MALKA

Foreword by Philippe Nemo

Translated by Michael Kigel
& Sonja M. Embree

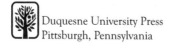
Duquesne University Press
Pittsburgh, Pennsylvania

Published in the United States of America
by Duquesne University Press
600 Forbes Avenue
Pittsburgh, Pennsylvania 15282

Library of Congress Cataloging in Publication Data

Malka, Salomon.
  [Emmanuel Lévinas. English]
  Emmanuel Levinas: his life and legacy / by Salomon Malka; translated by Michael Kigel & Sonja Embree.
    p. cm.
  Summary: "An in-depth biography of Emmanuel Levinas, twentieth century ethical philosopher and religious thinker, that details Levinas's life and his contributions to modern continental thought. Malka's journalistic approach includes personal accounts from Levinas's family, friends, colleagues, and students"—Provided by publisher.
  Includes bibliographical references (p.   ) and index.
  ISBN-13: 978-0-8207-0357-2 (hardcover: alk. paper)
  ISBN-10: 0-8207-0357-5 (hardcover: alk. paper)
  ISBN-13: 978-0-8207-0358-9 (pbk.: alk. paper)
  ISBN-10: 0-8207-0358-3 (pbk.: alk. paper)
  1. Lévinas, Emmanuel. 2. Philosophers—France—Biography. I. Title.
  B2430.L484M3413 2006
  194—dc22
                              2005030728

∞ Printed on acid-free paper.

CONTENTS

FOREWORD

For those who know Levinas's philosophy, Salomon Malka provides here the essentials of what needs to be known about his life. The book is clear, precise, gathers together a number of testimonials, and is filled with events and anecdotes, all the while giving a faithful account of the significant stages of the philosopher's life.

Malka recalls the places where Levinas lived or visited: Lithuania, France, Germany, Italy, Belgium, Holland, Switzerland, Jerusalem. He illustrates how Levinas, at a young age, came to live in France and how, having acquired French citizenship, he was always loyal to this country as a result of an unwavering rational and spiritual decision.

Malka retraces Levinas's family life, with the attractive and somewhat mysterious personality of Raïssa, his wife, and his two children, Simone and Michael, who speak passionately of their father. Malka also recalls the Jewish circle in Paris where the philosopher lived, the École Normale Israélite Orientale (Enio), of which Levinas was the director for a long time, and which was (and still is) a synagogue and center for studies. Salomon Malka is well situated to discuss this place, having been himself a student of the school and having lived (and suffered) under the iron rule of the stern director. He describes the Rashi course and the talmudic lesson that Levinas gave without fail each week throughout the decades and which people from all over Paris came to hear. Levinas's life was not limited, however, to the Jewish community. Beginning with his studies in philosophy at Strasbourg, then at nearby Freiburg-im-Breisgau on Husserl and Heidegger, and throughout his life, he regularly frequented philosophical and academic circles as well as, quite early on, ecclesiastical, Protestant and Catholic ones. Levinas, who was not a recluse at all but rather an outgoing and effusive man, charming and jovial in conversation, was also familiar with the most diverse of Parisian milieus, intellectual, artistic and even political.

One of the most interesting things about the book is Malka's particular focus on the philosopher's important encounters in these different settings, encounters with friends near and far, acquaintances or lifelong intimates, working class people or intellectuals, anonymous or famous: Maurice Blanchot, Edmund Husserl, Jean Wahl, M. Chouchani, Dr. Nerson, Jacques Derrida, Paul Ricoeur, Roger Burggraeve, Adriaan Peperzak, Enrico Castelli, up to and including Pope John-Paul II. Whenever possible (it is not always so), Malka demonstrates what role these encounters played in the development of the philosopher's thinking.

In the last, important section of the book, Malka carefully examines the reception of Levinas's work. He demonstrates how Levinas, who was fairly unknown up until shortly after the war, was gradually discovered first by academic circles, then by Christian ones where the author of *Otherwise Than Being* very quickly inspired passionate interest, and (with an altogether rather strange delay) by Jewish circles in France, America and finally Israel.

Throughout this trajectory, Salomon Malka takes care to relate, each time that interlocutors noted them, Levinas's words, thoughts and even his jokes, all those unwritten comments, seemingly without importance, that, thrown to the wind, would be forever lost if no one collected them from surviving witnesses, but that sometimes provide critical insight into such-and-such an aspect of his thinking and that assist, in any case, in better understanding his philosophical character. In order to bring together these words and other biographical details, Salomon Malka worked hard. He meticulously sought out the witnesses, family members, places, friends and colleagues, finding a great number and recording at length their testimonies and, equally often, their analyses and reflections. The teacher would have appreciated this modesty of the biographer, who naturally often makes known his own interpretation of things, but is more accustomed to being the spokesperson for other interpretations.

This concrete portrait of Levinas taught me an enormous amount. I realized that I knew nothing, in effect, about Levinas before reading this book. Despite the fact that I knew Levinas throughout the years (we lived one hundred meters from each other!), and that I had had numerous conversations with him, especially during the time we were working on our little book of interviews, *Ethics and Infinity*. But these conversations always took place within the realm of philosophy and theology, a realm in which he seemed to permanently live. If on occasion he politely asked me about my life, I never dared to ask him about his. All I knew was that he came from the Russian empire (as revealed by his distinctive accent), that he was Jewish, and that he had been a professor at the Sorbonne. At his home, I saw the little lace doilies, which would become a question several times in the book; I greeted his wife Raïssa and met his son Michael; I walked through the school to see him, a school about which I knew little in terms of what it was, who its students and teachers were, and what exactly was studied there. I must say that, when I met with Levinas, all of these concrete aspects were just meaningless details: the philosopher's thinking was so vast that it alone took center stage. Moreover, this thinking occupied so great a place in my own moral and intellectual development — it would gradually become throughout the years so constitutive of my own worldview — that I barely had time to concern myself with the concrete circumstances from which it was born. I already had done so much to grasp it intellectually, in the completed form where I discovered it. *Difficult Freedom, Totality and Infinity, Otherwise Than Being, De Dieu qui vient à l'idée,* the *Talmudic Lectures* are the books that one needs years to read. Salomon Malka's book suddenly discloses for me the other side of Levinas's work, the flesh that lived together with this mind. And I ask myself: What is the relationship between this mind and this flesh?

As Michael Kigel demonstrates in his insightful preface, a biography of a philosopher is always a paradox. A biography and a system of thought do not occupy the same realm. Biographies of political figures immediately make sense because, overall, the events of their life closely parallel those of history. On the other hand, the biography of a philosopher could, in the extreme, have no discernible relationship with his or her thinking, and the kind that presents the details of a philosopher's everyday life may be of no interest to someone who wishes to understand their philosophy.

Michael Kigel nevertheless perceives a relationship between the life and thinking of Levinas. For him, Levinas's work is organized entirely around a hidden referent, the Shoah. I think this hypothesis is illuminating and indeed explains the genesis of the work. Levinas's work would not have been so radical if it had not been informed by a dizzying reflection on such a unique event as the Shoah. Levinas said so himself: it is the Shoah that revealed, through the absurd, the emptiness of a merely "humanist" Western culture, which his teacher Leon Brunschvicg believed in, but which could not prevent the horror. In order to fill this gap, it is necessary to return to the "humanism of the other person," taught by the Bible alone.

But I notice that Levinas, once examining this main organizing principle, gave it a scope that surpassed all contingencies, even that of the Shoah. Indeed, evil has been present throughout the centuries, and it will continue to exist until the end of the world. Thus, there will always be the need to respond to the suffering of other people. In fact, Levinas devoted all of his spiritual energy, all of his philosophical genius, to providing an entirely universal form to biblical ethics. He restricted himself neither to theology nor to exegesis, but completely embraced philosophy, the language of reason. Like Philo of Alexandria and the church fathers of long ago, like a René Girard of today, Levinas transcribed in "Greek" terms (which is to say, scientific and moral, understood by *all* of thinking humanity) the altogether particular message of biblical ethics.

In uncovering the particular context within which Levinas's thinking was born, Salomon Malka's biography thus allows for a much better assessment, through contrast, of the miracle and the mystery of its universality. And it allows for being *surprised*, like Michael Levinas, who said to Malka, "I am talking to you about a man [my father] I saw [every day of our shared life] get up, pray, put on *tefillin*, call the Enio students, bawl them out, encourage them, grade, eat, tear up a book, and I see a work *that totally escapes all of that.* [. . .] At a certain point, the work *simply doesn't want to return to from whence it came.*"

I think that critics still have not grasped the full extent of the possibilities of Levinas's work. For historical reasons that are understandable, Judaism ceased very early on to be proselytized, while Christians set out "to teach all of the nations." The shared biblical message between the two religions is no less universal, universal without limits. Levinas never stopped being loyal to Judaism and nourished by the sources of the Bible and the Talmud. But his philosophical efforts consisted of articulating the revelation in such a way that no one can avoid them. He developed the concepts and even the vocabulary of his ethical philosophy in such a way that no one could say: that is good for Jews, that is good for Christians, but that is meaningless to someone who does not believe in these superstitions or who does not belong to this ethnicity, for someone who is only human.

In this way, it seems to me, Levinas's work "simply doesn't want to return to from whence it came." It is also for this reason that it is unclassifiable. His work has given the old biblical tree a new fruit valuable to all of humanity; it translates the Word of God into a new language universally understood by all. In fact, it is to all of humanity that God wishes to speak. Levinas, thus, ultimately served God well, better perhaps than certain sleepwalking disciples of previously constituted established religions. This is why Levinas will continue to be a voice crying out in the desert for a long time to come. And yet this is the fate of all prophets.

Philippe Nemo

Translator's Notes

Pressentiment / Souvenir

Although Emmanuel Levinas has left us with little advice on how to read his biography, except for one or two off-the-cuff remarks about the "stupidity" and the "pathos" of any methodical interest in his life, he did leave us with clear instructions for reading any *table of contents* of such a biography.[1] And even this bit of advice is not without value for those of us who take an interest in identifying the critical influences in the intellectual biographies of philosophers, notwithstanding Levinas's disapproval in his own case. At the beginning of "Signature," the valedictory chapter of *Difficile Liberté*, Levinas sets down the contents of a prospective biography.[2] It is the only chronicle of his life he considered worth writing down himself. In fact, he took pains to update it in the second edition of the book, thirteen years after its first publication in 1963; and not just to update it but, more significantly, to revisit it and revise it. Certainly in the context of a biographical study of Levinas such as the present one, this short chronology is worth quoting in full, and deserves close study:

The Hebrew Bible from the childhood years in Lithuania, Pushkin and Tolstoy, the Russian Revolution of 1917 experienced at eleven years of age in the Ukraine. From 1923 on, the University of Strasbourg, where Charles Blondel, Halbwachs, Pradines, Carteron and, later, Guéroult were teaching. Friendship with Maurice Blanchot and, through the teachers who were adolescents at the time of the Dreyfus Affair, a vision, dazzling for a newcomer, of a people who equal humanity and of a nation to which one can attach oneself by spirit and heart as much as by roots. A stay in 1928–29 in Freiburg, and an apprenticeship in phenomenology begun a year earlier with Jean Hering. The Sorbonne, Léon Brunschvicg. The philosophical avantgarde at the Saturday soireés of Gabriel Marcel. The intellectual, and anti-intellectualist, refinement of Jean Wahl and his generous friendship, regained after a long captivity in Germany; regular conferences since 1947 at the Collège Philosophique which Wahl founded and inspired. Director of the one-hundred-year-old *École Normal Israélite Orientale,* training teachers of French for the schools of the *Alliance Israélite Universelle du Bassin Méditerranéen.* Daily communication with Dr. Henri Nerson, frequent visits to M. Chouchani, the prestigious — and merciless — teacher of exegesis and of Talmud. Annual conferences, since 1957, on talmudic texts at colloquia of the French Jewish Intellectuals. Thesis for the Doctor of Letters degree in 1961. Professorship at the University of Poitiers, from 1967 on at the University of Paris-Nanterre, and since 1973 at the Sorbonne. This disparate inventory is a biography.

It is dominated by the presentiment and the memory of the Nazi horror.

Whatever interesting points of divergence emerge between this autobiographical text and the table of contents of the present biography, an essential difference assaults the reader with the invocation of something that no table of contents can contain: *the presentiment and the memory of the Nazi horror.* This is something that stands apart from the "disparate inventory." It is something that no biography can contain as a chapter.

Positioned by Levinas in a solitary sentence with a deliberateness that seems out of joint, this one sentence summarizing his life entirely recasts the meaning of the paragraph that precedes it. Does it not read like an afterthought? In fact, it is an afterthought. The sentence is not in the first edition of *Difficile Liberté;* it was added in the second edition of 1976. But unlike the other additions and emendations made to the text, this sentence is an afterthought in the fullest sense of the word: something that is thought of only well after the initial thoughts have had a chance to express themselves without being self-conscious, which means without an awareness of a truth that is too much to bear and too much to face in the initial expression. It is the afterthought that comes only when certain fears, perhaps a certain shame, have been confronted. Was Levinas afraid of what his readers in 1963 might conclude about this book, his first Jewish book? Perhaps they might decide that this was an *Auschwitz philosopher?* Perhaps the confession, and the concession to the narrow historicity of these "Essays on Judaism," was too much to lay bare in this early stage of his literary career. Still, even the addition in 1976 of the sentence about the Nazi horror seems to come with difficulty. It comes out of nowhere and leads nowhere. It seems to be written with a kind of dawning dread that an entire corpus of thinking suddenly stands naked before a mirror, and with a fatalistic resignation to grant the reader a glimpse of this nakedness, as well as a shame and modesty that quickly covers up what has been glimpsed, as if the writer did not mean it, as if it were a mistake. It almost comes as a needed corroboration when Levinas makes the same mistake again in an interview with François Poirié in 1986, when he asks, as if quoting himself, "Will my life have been spent between the incessant presentiment of Hitlerism and the Hitlerism that refuses itself to any forgetting?"[3] Again the afterthought, spoken with the same summarizing biographical reach: "Will my *life* have been spent . . .?"

Such afterthoughts, in any case, are not without appointment in Levinas's work as a whole. The latter of his two major works, *Otherwise Than Being* (1974), is dedicated to "the memory of those who were closest among the six million assassinated by the National Socialists, and of the millions on millions of all confessions and all nations, victims of the same hatred of the other man, the same anti-Semitism."[4] Again the inability, the impossibility, of saying something within the text itself. The text is written for all who would read it about what is otherwise than being. But in the afterthought that tells us, on the first page, *to* whom the work is written, this impossibility and inability finds full expression in a dedication. What does it mean for a work to be dedicated? What does this mean for the Saying in this work, if not for the work's Said? Whatever it means, to suggest that Auschwitz is the topic of *Otherwise Than Being* would not only be to fail to read the work; it would be a failure to grasp the limits of what can constitute a topic for Levinas.

FALLINGBOSTEL / BERGEN-BELSEN / AUSCHWITZ

The inventory in "Signature" is a table of what intellectual historians refer to as "influences" in the development of a thinker. The little boy reading *Chumash* with Rashi, Tolstoy and Pushkin, the idle afternoons spent with Blanchot in their favorite Strasbourg café, the Sorbonne, Monsieur Chouchani, and so on are all key influences in Levinas's intellectual development, and one may dispute how to rank them in order of importance. The more philosophically minded historian will be able to make use of biographical information to shed light on the transhistorical, universal ideas of the philosopher. Such a historical analysis can greatly enrich a philosophical understanding of these ideas because, for Levinas, the meaning of these ideas was intimately bound up with the historical idiosyncrasies of his life. The ideas themselves, to be sure, transcend the idiosyncratic, and to be able to effect such transcendence for his ideas is precisely one of the talents of a great philosopher. The ideas always await some kind of hermeneutic input from the reader in order to recover the meaning of these ideas, like milk powder awaiting rehydration with new water. But because this hermeneutic task is not always easy, the intellectual historian or biographer can facilitate our grasp of these ideas by telling the story, the native logos, of the life in which these ideas first came to be. All of this relates to the content of Levinas's autobiographical inventory, the influences on his thinking. The Nazi horror, the presentiment of this horror and the memory of it is something of a different order. It is not to be counted among the influences on Levinas's thinking. It cannot even amount to the "greatest influence" on his thinking.

The Nazi horror belongs to the order of catastrophe and trauma. It stands apart from the biography because the biography is subservient to it. Levinas says "dominated." An exacting choice of words. Does it not suggest a life of bondage to something that lords over an entire intellectual development? The daily life of Emmanuel Levinas survived the Nazi horror and continued to thrive for fifty years after the fall of the Third Reich. Hence, Levinas could even mention the "long captivity in Germany" within the biographical inventory among various milestones in a successful academic career. *But the life of the mind of Emmanuel Levinas came to a halt, to a sitting*

*position, in a POW camp near Bergen-Belsen, at the same time that
his family and his wife's family were gassed to death in Auschwitz —
and this mind endured for fifty years in this vigilant position.* As
he confesses two decades into the vigil, in 1966: "When one
has that tumor in the memory, twenty years can do nothing
to change it. Soon death will no doubt cancel the unjustified
privilege of having survived six million deaths. . . . — nothing has been able to fill, or even cover over, the gaping pit.
We still turn back to it from our daily occupations almost as
frequently, and the vertigo that grips us at the edge is always
the same."[5]

Why did Levinas write so little about the Nazi horror when,
according to his own confession, this *dominated* his entire
intellectual history and literary career? The task of characterizing the order peculiar to such intellectual trauma, in its
essential difference from the order of intellectual influences,
is never easy because of a characteristic silence that protects
it from analysis. Levinas's son, Michael, relates something
about the anxiety of writing and the profound solitude that
his father lived in, a solitude that even his own son, evidently,
could not penetrate. Besides the solitude that genius craves
as its natural residence, this is the solitude of a Jew surviving the Nazis, for whom silence is not a matter of noble discretion. The Said that would break this silence is more like
a logical mistake that the survivor cannot make because of
an extremely heightened logical sensitivity.[6] Levinas was not
stuck in the memory of Bergen-Belsen and Auschwitz because
he could not get on with life, with new events to put those
events behind him. He did get on with life. The silence commensurate to what took place in Bergen-Belsen and Auschwitz
from 1939 to 1945 indicates something other than an event.[7]
Strictly speaking, it never "took place" at all — a truth that,
oddly enough, Holocaust deniers intuit in its profundity,

despite themselves, despite the easy perversion of thinking whereby the unthinkable diachrony of the Holocaust is deformed and reduced to ordinary chronological terms that any dolt holding a calendar can cross out with a pencil. Auschwitz is "too much," even for their anti-Semitism. It is too much to believe, too much for time to contain. Levinas's frequent use of the numeric phrase "1939–1945" actually mocks the calendrical reality of the nontime of Auschwitz. Its temporality belongs to an "immemorial past," a past of which there is no memory, of which only a pure trace remains. It is not by accident that this formula so often invoked by Levinas to define the "trace" can be compared to the classical definition of trauma as a wound in memory.

So Levinas says little. However, to conclude from this infrequently broken silence that Levinas must have avoided the nonevent and nonplace called Auschwitz, as one avoids bad memories, would be a mistake. On the contrary, essential to the vocation of Levinas's thinking is the search for a language that can be dedicated to the memory of those who died at Auschwitz without naming Auschwitz as such and without making it a theme for discussion. This necessity of leaving it nameless is due, not to its parochial significance, its significance for Jews, but to the fact that "Auschwitz" actually fails to name this place which is no place, this event outside of time. This is what makes it the very "space" of Levinas's thinking.[8]

DESTRUKTION / DÉCONSTRUCTION

Reflecting on the early signs of Nazi tendencies in Heidegger, Levinas once remarked ironically: "In which moment was *Being and Time* a feeling of this pre-Hitlerian atmosphere? 'Destruktion!'"[9] What for Heidegger was still a project, namely the "deconstruction" of European metaphysics, became for Levinas's thinking an empirical datum, given in the Hitlerian realization of simple, literal *destruction*. To be precise, the destruction of every metaphysic of morals, empirically and ontically accomplished in Auschwitz, became the leveled ground and "space" of Levinas's thought.

Until Auschwitz, the job of formulating an ethics was left to a metaphysics that would establish the *authority* of moral imperatives. This was carried out by theology until the advent of German philosophy when Kant grounded such authority on the autonomy of the moral law, which was basically an internalized theology that equated itself with morality. Such metaphysical arrangements seemed to work for a while. "When the temples are standing, the flags flying atop the palaces and the magistrates donning their sashes, the tempests raging in individual heads do not pose the threat of shipwreck."[10] These structures were destroyed by Hitler. "Interregnum or end of the Institutions, or as if being itself had been suspended. Nothing was official anymore. Nothing was objective. Not the least manifesto on the rights of Man."[11]

With the collapse of all metaphysical authority for ethics, consequently, Levinas turned to the problem of describing or evoking the face of the Other in such a way that a non-authoritative moral "authority" in the Other's face could be seen. Was this a new turn in thought — or a return? Was the face of the Other not always there — before philosophy and before theology — making its claim, its accusation, without any authority? Was it not metaphysics and theology that, erecting great authoritative structures to protect this claim, had also stifled its still, small voice?

The destruction of authoritative ethics exposed the face of the Other in its utter nakedness and vulnerability, abandoned by every metaphysics, unprotected and open to any phenomenology that would now interpret the *weakness* of the face as a license to violate it. That is precisely what the philosophical labors (beginning with the pioneering efforts of Nietzsche, perhaps) that made Hitler possible as "Hitlerism," as a phenomenology,[12] were able to put in the place of the old authority, namely a new way for the murderer to *see* his victim, a new "optics" in which murder could be sanctioned with a clear conscience.

By means of the phenomenological interpretation of the Jew as subhuman, as an "ape," for example, or as a "carrier of germs";[13] by a reevaluation of the infinite value ascribed by the Jew to this vulnerability and the vulnerability of humanity — the naked face of the orphan and of the widow — Nazi hermeneutics were able to reduce the vulnerability of the face to an inferiority and an illness deserving extermination. How can one refute the new kind of *authority* wielded by Nazi philosophy? Auschwitz itself, the success of Nazi philosophy, made any appeal to a yet higher authority unthinkable. The God who, until Auschwitz, had always been invoked for this purpose was hanged on the gallows in Auschwitz, as Elie Wiesel says. "Did not Nietzsche's saying about the death of God take on, in the extermination camps, the meaning of a quasi-empirical fact?"[14] And not just the transcendent God of theology, but also the internalized, immanent divinity of all moral thinking after Kant. "Auschwitz" is another word for atheism, understood not as a credo, but as a fact. "Even now I ask myself if there is not a strange teaching — may God forgive me for saying this: a teaching of Auschwitz — strange teaching according to which the beginning of faith is not at all the promise . . . there would even be an offense in contradicting the despair of those who went to their death."[15] Their deaths were, in fact, meaningless.[16]

What ethics can emerge from this despair and meaninglessness? An "optical" ethics that is a phenomenology describing the claim made by the vulnerable face of the Other in nonauthoritative terms, not despite Auschwitz, but precisely within the apocalypse of all authority, within the same vulnerability of the face exposed by Auschwitz as the human condition. But such a revelation is the Jewish condition: "the fact that settled, established humanity can at any moment be exposed to the dangerous situation of its morality residing entirely in its 'heart of hearts,' its dignity completely at the mercy of a subjective voice, no longer reflected or confirmed by any objective order — that is the risk upon which the honor of humankind depends. *But it may be this risk that is signified by the very fact that the Jewish condition is constituted within humanity.* Judaism is humanity on the brink of morality without institutions."[17]

In this destruction, Levinas reclaims an old Jewish optics that sees the fragile face of the Other and, simply by seeing it, stands infinitely in its debt. Vulnerability as such is reclaimed as the source of all prescription, vulnerability as vulnerable; not by any inversion into authority, not by any power, but precisely by its powerlessness, by a passivity "more passive than passivity." Levinas calls the invisible force of this vulnerability the "trace" of the face of the Other. "A face is a trace of itself, given over to my responsibility, but to which I am wanting and faulty. It is as though I were responsible for his mortality, and guilty for surviving."[18] The face of the Other comes toward me from this trace. It emerges out of the trace. Apart from this emergence, the Other's face might well be adequately addressed as a "Thou" in whose countenance I might find great comfort and communion. "Through a trace the irreversible past takes on the profile of a 'He.' The *beyond* from which a face comes is in the third person."[19] It is because the "Thou" emerges out of the illeity of a "He" that I fall into infinite debt vis-à-vis the Other in a situation of utterly asymmetrical obligations. The trace of the Other is the borrowed presence of God. Levinas generally takes great pains to avoid such straightforward theological language;[20] indeed, the very metaphysics of signification subtending theological language is suspected and suspended by evocations of how traces work differently than signs. But the divinity of the trace is also undeniable: "the trace is not just one more word: it is the proximity of God in the countenance of my fellowman."[21] It is divine commandment without divine authority.

Where Nietzsche would have seen an inversion of the powerlessness of the Other, the cunning whereby herd mentality is able to appropriate for itself the power of the wild beast via myths of guilt, Levinas describes the originary inversion as happening the other way. Original "power," which is something ego-less, resides with the weak and vulnerable, and it is only through the cunning and atheistic myths told by the ego to itself that the divine forces of illeity, making their demands out of the vulnerable face of the Other, are pushed into oblivion in favor of discourses that signify without remainder and without trace and consolidate their totalitarian rule.

Lichtung / Clairière / Clarity

This reevaluation of vulnerability is the basic task of Levinas's thinking. But again, it is a phenomenology grounded in an optical situation established in Auschwitz, established not by Levinas but by Hitler. There is no uglier truth perhaps, but it needs to be said. *Levinas's phenomenology of the face of the Other in its ethical height receives its philosophical clarity in and from Fallingbostel, Bergen-Belsen and Auschwitz.* In the concentration camp, the "trace" of the face that, could it signify anything, would signify the divine commandment "Thou shalt not kill," becomes transparent in the clarity that only happens in an overcast afternoon. If the *grayness* that we associate with images of concentration camps is an issue for Holocaust representation and art, I would conjecture that this is because this kind of light is, in fact, the most conducive to clarity. Sunlight in a cloudless sky affords more light, but less clarity. If ethics attained a high degree of transparency and sharpness in the camps, it was because the camps were the absolute suspension of ethics, and not in spite of this. The camps were the proper *aletheia* of ethics; even as the truth of ethics is otherwise. Whether these optical conditions in the camps were grasped as the basic conditions for ethical phenomenology by Levinas or anyone else during their actual internment in camps, we do not know. But in the unearthly nontime where trauma and thought convene, where presentiment and memory are interchangeable, the face of the Other emerges, as if out of gloom and brilliance alike, into a Godless and worldless clearing to which memory and documentation assign names like Bergen-Belsen and Auschwitz.

What the remarkable preface of *Totality and Infinity* says about war in general applies to the camps. "Does not lucidity, the mind's openness upon the true, consist in catching sight of the permanent possibility of war? . . . In war reality rends the words and images that dissimulate it, to obtrude in its nudity and in its harshness."[22] Ethics is not the way of peace, war's contrary, which beats the sword into a plowshare. Peace is an eschatological postulate within the "vision" of ethics revealed in war. War destroys all ethics based on authority. But this is why the ethics that is older than any authoritarian thinking is revealed within the destruction.

BIOGRAPHY / PHILOSOPHY

A final note of clarification. Many scholars who take an interest in the works of Levinas also share some kind of recognition of Heidegger as the greatest philosopher of the last century — something Levinas himself acknowledged. Heidegger, more than any other philosopher in the last century, has given rise to the question concerning biography. Heidegger's *life* has given rise to this question (see chapter 10). Our interest in the life of Levinas might seem like a matter of innocuous curiosity in comparison with the anxious fascination devoted to Heidegger's life. Are we simply turning to something more cheerful than the life of Heidegger in the present biography?

The clarity achieved for ethical phenomenology in the German concentration camps in Germany and outside of Germany must not be confused with anything like an *academic* clarity. On the contrary, the clarity of thought achieved in academic philosophy in Germany, particularly by Heidegger, before the war and during the war, was not the antithesis of the clarity of horror in the concentration camps, but shared in the clarity of horror. Among other things, Auschwitz was also an academic exercise. This was its banality. Keeping this in mind will help us to understand, for example, Levinas's behavior during a defense of a doctoral thesis on Heidegger in Louvain (see chapter 10). It explains not just what happened after the defense, but Levinas's apparently innocuous remarks during the defense to the effect that he found the thesis to be "very scholarly" and "overly pedagogical."

The clarity of horror achieved in Fallingbostel, in Bergen-Belsen, in Auschwitz was a Nazi clarity that Levinas spent his entire intellectual life, in presentiment and in memory, refocusing into a *Jewish clarity* that can never be wholly academic.

Here, too, philosophy meets up with biography. Where purely academic thought easily offers up its truth without reference to the biography of the thinker, and where philosophical thought makes claims at times to a similar indemnity, Jewish thought finds such indemnity unthinkable, by definition. In this sense, *Jewish philosophy as such is thoroughly and essentially biographical.* The life of a Jewish philosopher, the *life* of Emmanuel Levinas, measured against the demands of the Torah, which tradition clings to as the very Tree of Life (Prov. 3:18), is the locus of the *truth* of his philosophy. Whatever this philosophy will be able to discover in the name of truth as *aletheia,* beyond or within the horizons of the Torah, depends directly on how the philosopher puts down his pen in order to pick up his phylacteries, or to fetch another dozen eggs for his wife from the corner store, or to hold open an elevator door and say "Bonjour!" The truth indigenous to Jewish thought has its first and last revelation in these deeds. As Rabbi Haninah ben Dosa used to say: "Anyone whose deeds surpass his wisdom — his wisdom will endure; anyone whose wisdom surpasses his deeds — his wisdom will not endure" (Avnot 3:12).

A biography that does justice to this kind of philosopher, accordingly, cannot be wholly academic in approach or temperament. The biographer too must stand in a relation of truth understood as trust (*emet* rather than *aletheia*) to the life whose story is being told. And this is perhaps the primary reason we may be grateful for the labors of Salomon Malka, who was, during the life of Levinas, and who remains, in the trace left behind by that life, a disciple deeply devoted to what the French call *maître,* in all the ambiguity of the word, and what Jewish students, with the greatest tenderness added to that ambiguity, call their *rebbi.*

Michael Kigel

Acknowledgments

My thanks go to Jean-François Colosimo, who wanted this book, supported it, understood in my worst moments of discouragement, and whose aid and assistance were indispensable to me. Michael Levinas, Simone, Georgie and David Hansel for their invaluable and constant help. Ausra Pazeraite for her support during my stay in Kaunas and Elena Bovo for her assistance with my research. Victor Malka for his brotherly advice and all the "alumni" of the Saturday classes for their collaboration. Father Maurizio Rossi for his friendship and encouragement. The former prisoners of Stalag XIB, so many of whom sent me their stories (I could only use a portion of them). The National Archives in Paris, the Kaunas Archives, the French Cultural Center in Vilnius, the Jewish community of Vilnius, the Archives of the United Jewish Social Fund and of *L'Arche,* the Universal Israelite Alliance library, the Sèvres Center library, the Sorbonne library, the André Néher library, the University of Louvain in Belgium, Loyola University in Chicago, the Hebrew University of Jerusalem. All those whom I could meet and who provided me with their accounts or their assistance: Émile Amzallag,

Paul Atterton, David Banon, Agnès Bastit-Kalinowska, Rafy Bensimon, Viviane Bensimon, Zev Berger, Christophe Bident, Lisette Blottière, Ami Bouganim, Dominique Bourel, Stanislas Breton, Henry Bulawko, Roger Burggraeve, Mendy Cahan, Bernhard Casper, Catherine Chalier, Fabio Ciaramelli, Ilana Cicurel, Gabriel Cohen, Haïm Cohen, Richard Cohen, Roger Cohen, Shimon Cohen, Françoise Collin, Alain David, Jacques Derrida, Alex Derczanski, Patrick Desbois, Emeric Deutsch, Patrick Donabedian, Bernard Dupuy, Fabien Durand, Edmond Elalouf, Simon Elbaz, Prosper Elkouby, Rafaël Elmaleh, Daniel Epstein, Didier Franck, Maurice de Gandillac, José Garzon, Claude Geffré, Roland Goetschel, Thérèse Goldstein, Jean Greisch, Michel Gugenheim, René Gutman, Jean Halperin, Daniel Harrus, Elias Harrus, Vaclav Havel, Simon Hazan, André Jacob, Léon Jakubovitz, Richard Kearney, Roger Laporte, Jacques Laurent, Dominique Laury, Hervé Legrand, Benny Lévy, Zeev Lévy, Anne Lifshitz-Krams, Fabrice Maindron, Rafy Marciano, Jean-Luc Marion, Ephraïm Méir, Paul Mendès-Flore, Gilbert Malka, Evelyne Méron, Barbara Meyer, Henri Minczeles, Stephane Moses, Marco Olivetti, Adriaan Peperzak, Marc Petit, Guy Petitdemange, Freddy Rafaël, William Richardson, Paul Ricoeur, Claude Riveline, Jacques Rolland, Shalom Rosenberg, François-David Sebbah, David Serfaty, Méir Shubas, Meyer Sisso, Simon Sisso, Serge Smulevic, Ady Steg, Claude Sultan, Xavier Tilliette, Anna-Teresa Tyminiecka, Frederic de Towarnicki, Claude Vigée, Jean-Jacques Wahl, Manek Weintraub, Shmuel Wygoda.

Salomon Malka

Departure

It took place at the Pantin cemetery during winter on a morning marred by unpleasant drizzle, wind and general grayness. There was a crowd of people exchanging nods and shuffling about in small, scattered clusters that kept at arm's length from one another.

One of these clusters was the synagogue membership, his first community, the small circle of those with whom he had prayed every *shabbat*, who knew very little about philosophy, perhaps nothing more than the appropriate opportunity to insert a "yes, yes," but who nevertheless had held a share in his life across the decades, had attended his classes right up to the twilight years, had lived in his neighborhood and had seen him raise his children. These were the ones who came to mourn for a familiar face from the *shul* benches who would be called up to the Torah in Hebrew by the name "Emmanuel son of Yekhiel the Levite," a member of this particular synagogue, this congregation without a rabbi, where he had held the unique post of teacher, landmark, and spiritual guide all in one. Everything had revolved around him, even if his presence was ever discrete. Especially toward the end, after he had relinquished his official duties as principal of the school (on which the *shul* depended) but still continued to give his traditional Saturday morning class in Rashi right after services. A community much like any other, consisting of ordinary people, where profound and time-tempered links were forged and fastened together, where the silhouettes in the hallways were familiar and made him feel at ease. The primary and immediate community, the near and dear, the place where, without effusiveness — he never came across as very warm — without abandoning his reserve — he was always in control of his gestures and words — he could allow himself to be himself.

Another cluster followed, this one made up of his former students from the Enio, L'École Normal Israélite Orientale, men and women who were once boys and girls, of all ages and grades, most of whom had kept in touch with him. He was their principal, their teacher, and, quite simply, their mentor. He would remember everything, attend every wedding he was invited to, recognize each face, each name, each story. And each one of these men and women now responded by being present, to follow, for a last stretch of road, the one who had made them who they are.

Finally, the last cluster, the circle of friends, colleagues, disciples, former students from Poitiers, Nanterre, the Sorbonne, rabbis, representatives from Jewish institutions, priests, and anonymous readers who came to say good-bye to the author of this or that book that had changed their lives.

This morning, Jacques Derrida delivered the eulogy in a blanched voice, barely audible through the wind. The family, Michael, Simone, sat demurely before the wooden coffin. Grand Rabbi Gutman officiated, inserting a personal recollection:

Among the seventy comrades of the forest commando unit
who had been taken prisoner to Fallingbostel near Hanover,
a camp for Jewish POWs that by a strange coincidence
bore the number 1492, the year of the expulsion of the
Jews from Spain, my father was by his side throughout
the five years. . . . How can we fail to recognize in him
one who endured suspended "between the living and the
dead," one whose thoughts after the catastrophe obliged
us to rethink the human as awakening, as insomnia, as
responsibility?

In the winter grayness, the absence of any official delegate,
university president or political or cultural representative was
regarded with nothing more than relief. All the same, the
obituaries in *Libération* featured his portrait at the top of the
page, France 2 reported the death during the eight o'clock
news, and *The New York Times* ran a lengthy obituary.

A philosopher has passed away in Paris on December 25,
1995, a day when Christians celebrate Christmas and Jews
conclude Hanukkah, the festival of lights. Henceforth, the
life of Emmanuel Levinas could be succeeded by the trace.

INTRODUCTION

Twenty years have elapsed since my first readings of *Difficile liberté, Totalité et infini* and *Autrement qu'être,* the major works of Emmanuel Levinas, and during that time I had not been able to resolve anew to write about him. I knew the man Emmanuel Levinas for much longer than that. I knew him since I was seventeen, when I was a student at the Enio. The small, energetic being, like a tight ball of nerves, who paced up and down the hallways, made a deep impression on us. He would lose his temper at times, such as when the girls at the boarding school plugged up the toilets with clumps of hair. Or when we were called up to the fourth floor to get chewed out. Or the anger when we wouldn't go down to the office. Then there were the invitations to his Friday night table, for the select few, when one might observe his eager manner of deboning a chicken, or the way he talked about the pastries from Chez Lenôtre. His walk, of course. His small jerky steps. His "n'est-ce pas?" at the end of every sentence. The copy of *Le Monde* under his arm everyday after lunch. His affectionate way of looking up at the tall frame of his longtime friend Dr. Henri Nerson, and the secrets they would whisper in each other's ear like two accomplices. The gaze that we would feel on the back of our heads when we would run off to the corner café in chattering groups or walk around the block silently. His philosophy, in which we immersed ourselves without really realizing the sort of attention it demanded, our desire to be noticed and acknowledged being something of which we failed to became aware amid the anxious questions of our youth. The first day he walked in for the first course on Plato and his definition of philosophy as the "science of naïvetés." His repeated expression that struck me so much at the time: "You've got to get in the game!" His first suspicions against me personally — the nickname "Sartron" he gave me, which I found rather perplexing until it finally dawned on me that I was quoting Sartre too often for his taste. For me as for others, all this might seem remote, a memory that might have been laid to rest, a fond memory of a school principal who was rather austere and about whom we knew relatively little, except that he busied himself elsewhere writing books that no one read.

For the most part we came from Morocco, some from Lebanon or Iran, the students namely. Studious, serious, ill mannered. We knew the prayers by heart. We knew how to decipher a comment by Rashi. The biblical world was familiar to us and there was really nothing anyone could teach us.

What could he have to offer us? It was difficult to appreciate at the time. In any event, nobody sensed it then, and it certainly was not an issue.

Then, a few years later, came the publication of *Difficile liberté*, which came down on us with a crash, a sharp departure from folklore, a breakthrough in thinking that took our "old" concerns seriously, a thinking that called up Martin Heidegger, Paul Claudel, Simon Weil . . . and measured them against the innermost dimensions of our texts. How can one express the astonishment standing before the height where this writing took place, this limpid writing that one would reread, underline, revisit again and again?

"We do not dissociate a lesson from the face that was the necessary interlocutor," Levinas used to say in recalling Husserl. Even less do we dissociate books from the places where they first seized us, the circumstances in which we first read them. It was in a small room of a student residence hall, on rue Guy-Patin in the ninth district of Paris, that I discovered *Difficile liberté*. Sitting at my work desk, dizzy with delight, I read with pencil in hand, underlining every line of these sumptuous pages which presented Jewish existence in all of its dimensions, in its greatness, in its poverty, in its everydayness, its liturgy, its source, its depths. All at once, Jewish life became a category of Being. All at once, it acquired new meaning. All at once, the origin was revived.

I had left behind me a grumpy school principal, whose French we made fun of because of its heavy Slavic accent, only to rediscover a sublime thinker. Was it really the same person? Sometimes I actually doubted it.

The years continued to pass. Then came the second shock, *Totalité et infini,* linked in my memory to one of the most beautiful places one could read a book, the ocean, not far from Montpellier. How could anyone read *Totalité et infini* at the beach? Before going on vacation, I had bought a copy at one of the philosophy bookstores at the Place de l'Odéon; this large book with its sky blue cover, its disconcerting price that was really too dear for my wallet, published by Martinus Nijhoff. I spent the summer reading it with ardor, without always or altogether understanding it, but surrendering to the waves that carried me away, with the conviction that in the end, after experiencing the flow of the same sentences rolling on the same shores, everything would come together and enter into connivance and clarity.

The life and the trace, therefore. What is a philosophical life made of? What does a philosopher's life look like? I desired to know more, revisiting Levinas twenty years after my discovery of his works, and thirty years after meeting the man.

In order to avoid the double danger of appropriation and paraphrase, I decided to look less into the works themselves than into the archives, the testimonies of others, the personal encounters, the mark left on places passed by, the memories in the classroom and of anyone who can bring him to mind and talk about him.

But I also wanted to know what became of the dead. Not unlike the stroll that Gabriel Marcel recalls in *La Dignité humaine* where, at the age of seven or eight, he would ask himself where do the dead go. We would like to think that death, indeed, transforms life into destiny. That it strips it of all pretense, that it is a filter, that it restores the truth to beings. That it is this very proof of truth. And that what the dead leave behind is a profound rapport that disappearance does not erase.

But at the same time everyone knows all too well that death is an abandonment.

No biography is complete. It is always personal, and therefore always interpretative. The posthumous one escapes — and becomes all too available. We can avail ourselves of him. He belongs to the world. He belongs to no one. Nothing is guaranteed by the posterity of a work. Everything requires going back again and again. And everything depends on the ability to keep the books open.

Childhood

Rue Michel-Ange. I deliberated about what to bring, flowers or chocolates. In the end I arrived empty-handed, somewhat intimidated, wondering if we were going to talk philosophy and whether I would be equal to the task.

They waited for me, he and his wife, at the door of their apartment. He in a lightly crumpled suit, with the ever-present white handkerchief in the breast pocket. She, for her part, a little wizened.

We sat around the table, bare but for a small embroidered doily on which the philosopher's wife tugs from time to time. He is pleasant, full of attention, asks me questions about myself. What do you do? How is life treating you? Are you still drawn to philosophy?

His wife compliments me on my voice. She once heard me leading prayers in the Yom Kippur service. "Are you a musician?" I respond that I'm not, to my regret. "It's like my husband," she says, "but he never had an ear for it, he has never understood anything about music." And she turns toward him sighing: "How could one be insensitive to music to such a degree?" — "It's true," he admits sheepishly, "except my son's!"

I engage them in conversation about their childhood, and they do so with obvious pleasure. They tell me how they met in Kovno where their apartments were adjoined. He draws the street on a piece of paper with a thick pencil line, and the face of his wife lights up: "Yes, that's it, exactly like in this drawing! How do you remember so precisely?" He gives a little gallant smile.

"Your family wasn't revolutionary?" "No, not at all!" she exclaims. "And your family?" I say, turning toward the philosopher. "All of that was very confused, you know, I was just starting to get interested in the life of conscience," he responded. Then, to push the issue aside, he adds: "This might interest a historian who would have the stupid idea of being interested in my life."

They grew up together, then they left each other, and then found each other again in Paris. By chance? "How so by chance? We were bound."

I sense that he's weary, that he feels like resting, that I have to leave. It would be the last time.

I. Places

1 | KAUNAS

In preparation for becoming Emmanuel Levinas, could there be a better place to be born than Kaunas, Lithuania? The city is situated at the confluence of the Neman and Neris (formerly Vilia) rivers at the border of Latvia and Russia, at the intersection of an extreme occident and the beginning of the orient, reposing under the implicit shadow of Vilna, once known as "Jerusalem of the East."

The city would not escape the great jolts of the twentieth century and would, in quick succession, experience Nazism, Communism, and then independence once again after 1989 and the fall of the Berlin wall.

Today, the Llaisves Aleja, the Liberty Path, is a pleasant pedestrian avenue bathed in sunlight, a row of trees on either side, cafés with terraces, ice cream merchants, and St. Michael's Church, surrounded by greenery, at its end.

Setting out in search of the earliest traces of Levinas amounts to retracing a lost world.

THE ABODE

Before the war, his father ran a stationer's shop and bookstore on this street at an address that numbered 25. During the Soviet era, however, the addresses were changed, without any apparent logic, anarchically, so that it is no longer possible to locate the store by its number. The only hint is that it was situated in a two-story building and was adjoined to the Conrad café, which was very well-known before the war. The older neighbors remember how, in the twenties, an orchestra would play there almost every afternoon. The clients danced the waltz, the tango and sometimes the Charleston. Later on, it became a meeting place for artists and intellectuals. The café is still there today, but the sign has been changed. It's called Tulpe, "the tulip," and, like the rest of Kaunas, it has surrendered its looks to a certain Americanization.

On the left, one sees a small boutique for women's clothing. The business is probably what took over the stationer's shop of Yekhiel Levinas.

The Levinas family didn't live there, even though it is the address Emannuel gave at the time of his French naturalization. They lived a little further away, on the banks of the Neman, at 1 Kalejimo Street. This narrow and short street owes its name to the adjacent prison. The future wife of Levinas, who started out as his neighbor, recalls being quite surprised as a child at some of the conversations that took place between passers-by and the political prisoners behind bars. Today the prison is gone, and the name of the street has been changed. It is now called *Spaustuvininkus,* "printers' alley." All the way up, facing the old prison and perched on a promontory, with the Neman River below, one comes up to an enormous old house laid out in two wings, with a garden in the middle. And a tree that still stands there.

One of the wings was the residence of the owners of the property, Chaim Volpe and his wife, Chaya-Lina, together with their daughter Frida Volpe-Levy and her husband, the parents of Raïssa, the future Mme. Levinas. The other wing was occupied by tenants, Yekhiel Levinas, his wife Dvora, and their three sons, Emmanuel, Boris and Aminadav.

At one point, the owners had a large public bathhouse, well known to everyone, installed in the middle of the house and named after the river, "Nemunias." The venerable Professor Shubas, from the University of Vilnius, remembers going there in his childhood. It admitted men and women on separate days and you couldn't make a mistake. Ausra Pazeraite, a young teacher in the department of history of religion and a translator of Levinas, reports that this public bathhouse still existed during her own childhood and that her family made good use of it.

Since then, however, one of the wings of the building was entirely reconstructed. It is a modern building that houses an imposing department for the taxation police. The sign makes you smile. Something fortuitous: the archives of Kaunas contain dozens of letters from the Volpe family and heirs, in which they complain endlessly about being harassed by property taxes, canalization taxes, the price of water, how difficult it is for them to find tenants because of the proximity of the prison and because public baths are declining in popularity as people are taking more baths at home. The situation is bad enough by the beginning of the thirties that Raïssa's parents leave the country altogether and relocate in Paris, whereupon the Levinas family moves down a number of streets to Mickevicious.

One has to visit Kaunas in order to grasp how Emmanuel Levinas spent a part of his childhood and adolescence on this narrow lane, the walls of a prison to one side, a public bathhouse enterprise on the other, below, a green landscape traversed by a river, and, perhaps most significantly, how the one who became his wife, the landlords' daughter, lived on the other side of the wall.

FIRST LOVE

Emmanuel Levinas was born on December 30, 1905, according to the Julian calendar, which was in use in the Russian empire at that time; it corresponds to January 12, 1906, in the Gregorian calendar. Kaunas was no longer the temporary capital of independent Lithuania, which is what it officially became in 1918. Belonging to what was still czarist Russia, the city was the administrative centre of a *Gouberniya*.

The father, Yekhiel, was himself born in Kaunas, like his parents and grandparents. As mentioned, he ran a bookstore with a line of stationery on the main street of the city that, at that time, bore the name "Prospect-Nicholas." Without employees, he worked by himself to sell books and school supplies, and took pains to secure the best education for his children. The three boys, Emmanuel, Boris and Aminadav, had a private Hebrew tutor at home from a very young age. The family was basically traditional in its religious observance. They attended synagogue. They ate kosher. They observed *shabbat* and the Jewish holidays. It was a religious environment, not excessively religious, but certainly in accordance with the widespread Lithuanian tradition where Judaism marked time for daily life.

The mother, Dvora, né Gurvitch, was born in Tilsai into a family that was well known in this northwest Lithuanian city, near Zagor, itself an important rabbinic center. From the photographs, we see how Emmanuel resembles her feature for feature. The fine lines. The protruding cheekbones.

The thick eyebrows. She is the one who imparted the love of books, of literature, who read Pushkin to him, helped him discover Turgenev, shared his enthusiasm for *premier amour*. On the dining room cabinet lay a translation of Cervantes's *Don Quixote,* a beautiful edition that she received as a prize at the Hebrew school she attended as a child where instruction was carried out in Russian. But these are only to name a few. The family library, according to witnesses, held a very impressive collection, too large to count. The aunt, Yekhiel's sister, moreover, was director of the Russian library in the city of Kovno.

At home, mostly Russian was spoken. Levinas liked to recall how as a child he learned to read almost on his own, by deciphering the letters on the cocoa box during breakfast. In any event, literacy came quickly. And with it, the discovery of Russian literature. Pushkin, of course, the national hero, the only Russian poet who still has his bust in a Vilnius public garden. Then, very early, the works of Dostoyevsky, to which Levinas remained ever loyal and which he continued to read and to cite until the end of his life. Tolstoy, whose obituary notice he kept since that critical childhood experience of losing someone who seemed to be a close relative, a bereavement in the family. Gogol, particularly novels like *The Nose, The Coat,* and so on. And finally, to round out this early *Bildung,* Chekov and Lermontov.

"Between Lithuania and Russia there is a unity of language and culture," he said. "All things considered, while the czarist regime was an unjust regime which did not meet the needs of human existence, Russian literature enjoyed an immense prestige. We maintained a great interest in that culture, and in that sense there was quite a bit of assimilation. Yet for all this curiosity, this interest accompanied neither the abnegation nor the negation of Judaism."[1]

In fact, from the age of six, in tandem with this Russian literacy, he began to learn Hebrew and to read the Bible with his private teacher.

SOUND AND FURY

At the beginning of the twentieth century, Kaunas, or Kovno (its Russian title), was a city torn between Germany, Poland and Russia. Each hope of emancipation was duly smashed by a succeeding domination. And before long it would find itself caught in a vice between the First World War and the Communist revolution.

Once war was declared in 1914, the Levinas's family vacated Kovno, emigrating to Russia after the German invasion, and eventually settling in the Ukraine. There the young Emmanuel frequented a state school for a while. But it was soon evacuated, and he had to transfer to a high school in Kharkov at the age of eleven, where he was admitted despite the severe *numerus clausus* in effect. He was one of only five Jewish students granted admission to the school, a reason for celebration in the Levinas household. This first exile, however, also held a first return in its wake.

In 1920, the family took advantage of an opportunity to return to Lithuania. It had become an independent state since February 1918, after the Lithuanian Council, the *Taryba*, amid the chaos of revolution, managed to proclaim a republic. The father regained his stationery shop, and the young Emmanuel enrolled in the graduating year of a Jewish high school. It was from there that he received his high school diploma.

In this school, built in 1920 on the ruins of a school of commerce, the languages of instruction were Russian in the large classrooms and Hebrew in the small classrooms.

Beginning in 1925, Hebrew took over as the only language. The principal was Dr. Moshe Schwab, who later emigrated to Israel and taught at the Hebrew University in Jerusalem, eventually to be nominated dean of the philosophy department, and then rector. The philosopher would pay him homage in an anthology dedicated to the "honor of teachers."[2] This admirer of German culture, a Goethe enthusiast, made a deep impression on him. Emmanuel Levinas would one day send him a copy of *De l'Existence à l'Existant,* published in 1947, with an enigmatic inscription inside, a quotation in English without an author: "I woke up one day and knew I was a European." Most likely a memory from the classroom in Kovno.

The quotation exemplifies an ideal of *Bildung* and of emancipation through education, which was popular among the Jews of the time. But it also concurs with the aspirations of the Russian intellectuals who so much desired to participate in European culture. From this perspective, the nineteenth century signaled a remarkable awakening. And if Slavophiles and Occidentalists stood in opposition, it was over the manner, and not just the necessity, of such a confrontation. As early as the 1830s, Ivan Kirievski had returned from a long trip to Germany and France with the newfound conviction that he was a European Russian, or, better still, a Russian European. His disappointing encounters with Schelling and the great German thinkers had brought him to a critical conclusion: Russia was entrusted with the sacred mission of reviving the religious intention at the heart of philosophy. Dostoyevsky had also been working on this, in his own way, by illustrating the primacy of transcendence in his romantic works. And this was the basic mission of religious philosophers like Nicholas Berdyaev and Leon Shestov, first during the revolution and then after emigrating to Paris.

Such was the intellectual climate in which the young Emmanuel Levinas grew up. It had an urgency to it that could only become sharper and clearer by a round-trip to the Ukraine, a Russian land in full revolutionary turmoil as well as a literary and artistic turmoil erupting in the Age of Silver. However, it was from his own tradition, Judaism, that he would find the motifs of inspiration.

FROM TRADITION TO MODERNITY

Kovno is also a city where all the currents of modern Jewish life run together and intersect: the temptations of assimilation and the nostalgia for tradition, the passion for scholarship, the rise of Yiddishism and the renaissance of Hebrew, aversion to the injustices of the czarist state and the lure of Russian culture. All of these elements coalesce in a Jewish society bursting with diverse and often opposing sensibilities. In one camp, for example, we find the adherents of orthodoxy and the long legacy of rabbis whose influence extends over all the Ashkenazi regions and who head the prestigious *yeshivot,* like the great yeshiva of Slobodka, which attracts students from every neighboring country. Opposing them are the devotees of the *Haskalah,*[3] the Jewish Enlightenment that drifted into Lithuania from Germany, prompting a rejuvenation of the Hebrew language and a flourishing in letters, arts and theater. Friction between these two camps was a daily affair. The *maskilim* were considered heretics, agnostics and sinners, while the Orthodox were branded ignorant, obscurantist and superstitious.

Between Zionists and Bundists, the controversy is no less lively. The former militate for a return to Zion and the rebirth of a Jewish society in Palestine; the various currents are represented in Kaunas: the socialist Zionists of HaShomer

HaTzair, the religious Zionists of Mizrahi, alongside generic Zionists. The latter endeavor to organize the Jewish proletariat around Socialist ideas, particularly the members of the Bund,[4] a working-class movement born in Vilnius in 1897. Touching elbows with the Bund, moreover, we find the Folkists, a sister movement with a special interest in promoting the autonomy of Jewish culture.

To say nothing of the Homeric war waged between the *hassidim* and the *mitnagdim*. Hassidism, a pietistic movement of religious and mystical rebirth, founded by the Baal Shem Tov in the eighteenth century in the Ukraine and Poland, was maligned since its inception, under the authority of the Gaon of Vilna, by a resolute and active opposition to anything suggesting ecstasy, fervor and the cult of emotions, in the name of a Judaism more squarely rooted in study, rigor and sober observance.

Revolting against Hassidism, what is called *Litvak* culture — named after the area that was consolidated from a grand duchy since the Polish-Lithuanian Republic — stood for the love of knowledge, familiarity with texts, and a certain stiffness, which bring to mind the manner and philosophy of the talmudic schools scattered throughout the world in the diaspora.

At this turn of the century in which language, religion, and the question of nationalism are found at the center of the debate, when the vague pangs of emancipation are felt everywhere, when a cultural effervescence agitates the spirit, Kovno, like the rest of Lithuania, lets all these currents flow together into a single pool. And this conflux is reflected in the diversity of schools of thought spanning from the religious to the lay and including the Zionist and the Yiddishist. This spectrum of sensibilities gives the city, like the whole of Lithuania, the particular stamp described by Yves Plasseraud in apt and simple terms: "The Litvaks represented a Jewish constituency that was simultaneously the most deeply imbued with external culture and the most deeply imbued with internal Jewish culture."[5]

LITVAK

At the start of the century, just when Emmanuel Levinas was born, Lithuanian society was open and heterogeneous. Jews and non-Jews lived together on friendly terms. There was neither a ghetto nor even a Jewish quarter in Kovno. The young Emmanuel enjoyed a happy childhood, in the bosom of a warm family, in well-to-do surroundings that did not leave him with any memories marked by anti-Semitism. There was no fresh memory of pogroms in Lithuania in general.

Zev Birger, director of the international book fair in Jerusalem, who recalls a similar childhood in his memoirs, reports that he had heard the cry *Zydas!* "Jew!" in the streets on occasion, but adds: "Anti-Semitism in Lithuania didn't have a political or propagandistic character. It was strictly a pedestrian matter. The official Lithuanian circles didn't display any negative attitude, and the government was genuinely liberal in relation to the Jewish minority."[6]

In the registers of the Kovno *Gouberniya* we find records of an intervention in 1905, the same year the philosopher was born, made by a communal delegation of Jews and Orthodox Christians near the Russian authorities. Rumors of pogroms were circulating in the city — this was shortly after the pogroms in Kishinev in Russia — and this ecumenical initiative succeeded in calming the people and possibly evading any outburst of anti-Semitism.

If one goes back even further, the chronicle reports that in August of 1886, in the municipal garden of the city — the same one in which, one century later, a nineteen-year-old student set himself on fire in protest against the Soviet regime — and at the initiative of the officiating minister, Rabinovitch, cantor at the synagogue Ohel Yaakov, a public concert was staged with Handel's *Judah the Maccabee* on the program. In the audience, where both Jews and Christians could be found, one of the spectators stood up at the end of the concert and struck up an anti-Semitic tune. A brawl ensued. The next day, the pest was asked to leave the city within three days, and a policeman who had taken his side resigned from his post.[7]

Still earlier, in the year 1761, one finds mention of a Jewish pogrom in Kovno. The inhabitants of the city set fire to Jewish homes and the *Bet Hamedrash,* the house of study. For the most part, the survivors took refuge in the suburb of Slobodka. Then the Jewish community of Slobodka quickly mobilized to file legal proceedings against the mayor of Kovno. They finally won their case after twenty years. The tribunal pronounced its verdict: the Jewish residents were authorized to return to their city, their rights were reinstituted, and the mayor was condemned to pay for the legal process, over a period of two years, as well as for the indemnities of the victims. He was also incarcerated for two weeks. Thereafter, the entire ordeal was recorded in a "Megillah of Kovno" composed by Rabbi Shmuel the Younger, known for his intelligence and humility, and was commemorated every year on the day after Purim in the old synagogue of the city.[8]

This tradition of tolerance shows up again and again in a long history. The first Jewish *litvaks,* it is said, were captives brought back from the Crimea by the grand duke Vytautas (1392–1430) after his war against the Tartars. Among the prisoners there were Jews and Karaites whom he brought to Lithuania for the sake of developing commerce, according them privileges, direct protection, and a complete autonomy over their internal affairs. This veritable charter would subsequently provide for the status of Jews in Lithuania who ended up immigrating by the thousands from the Occident, particularly from Germany. There were unhappy times of course. Dark periods — most notably the Cossack massacres of Bogdan Chmielnicki — but the tradition of the multicultural grand duchy of Lithuania was perpetuated until the beginning of the Great War.

With the advent of this war, the Jewish community numbered forty thousand souls, enjoyed an intense cultural life, and could boast of several playhouses in Hebrew and Yiddish, as well as an ethnographic society. It had its own journals: the *Blater* (the page), the *Briker* (the bridge), and also a journal in Lithuanian advocating the independence of Lithuania, *Apsvelga* (panorama). The Jews reflected the proclivities of their society. A minority had a penchant for communism. The Bund continued to have its followers; it was, in fact, in Kovno that the second congress of the movement was held in 1898. The Haskalah penetrated the Jewish schools where, on the whole, the curricula resembled those of other establishments, except that Bible and Jewish history were taught as well. Abraham Mapou, the first Jewish writer of Kovno, published historical novels written directly in Hebrew on his street in the old city, right across from Zamenhof Street, so named after the founder of Esperanto. Zionism was present in all its varieties. Herzl had a good number of admirers, and in 1903, when the train that brought him from Vilnius to Vienna crossed through Kovno in the middle of the night, two thousand people waited on the platform of the station in the hopes of catching a glimpse of the bearded prophet. In the end, Kovno remained, as it always was, an inexhaustible reservoir of rabbis, of talmudists and educators, all stemming from the glorious crown of *litvak* Judaism, the Vilna Gaon, whose statue stands in front of his house in Vilna, notwithstanding his demure tomb in the cemetery of the city that is a place for visitors and pilgrimage. Is one conscious of the influences to which one is subject? A specific comparison within Lithuanian Judaism naturally lends itself for consideration and may shed light on the development of Levinas. Ausra Pazeraite, my guide in Kaunas and its archives, takes a special interest in Mussar literature, a movement in which she sees one of the profoundest innovations of Judaism. Originating in the nineteenth century around Rabbi Israel Salanter, it was a unique intellectual and religious phenomenon of the modern period that arose from the very heart of orthodoxy, hostile to both the driftings of Hassidism and the temptations of the Haskalah, and with the positive agenda of rejuvenating this orthodoxy from within.

THE HERITAGE OF SALANTER

Mussar has various meanings in Hebrew: morals, ethics, education, edification, sermon, homily. In the writings of Salanter, the term is employed to describe the human effort and the psychological means that are needed for the attainment of ethico-religious perfection, self-control, ascesis, inner discipline.

Israel Lipkin, known by the name of Salanter, was born in 1810, in the city of Zagor, a district of Kovno, into a family of rabbis and within a *mitnagid* setting. He carried out his studies in Salant, the religious center of the era, where he met Joseph Zundel, who was among the disciples of Rabbi Chaim Volozhin, a pupil of the Vilna Gaon. The genealogy is evident, as Immanuel Etkes describes it very well in a biography of Israel Salanter.[9] Etkes perceives the relations among these four personalities as a single chain where each link is a transmission from master to disciple of a tradition reinvested and transformed.

The Gaon (genius) of Vilna, Rabbi Elijah ben Solomon Zalman (1720–1797), the central figure of Lithuanian Judaism, is legendary for his virulent opposition to the Hassidic movement. It was under his influence that Vilna became a bastion of *mitnagdim* (opposers). Against the pursuit of *devekut*, the mystical communion with God, against pietism, he defended the primacy of study, of intellectual rigor, and the effort of the human spirit. Recalcitrant to *pilpul*, the "casuistry" practiced in the *yeshivot*, the talmudic institutions of Poland, he paved the way to a more substantial approach to texts, one closer to literary interpretation. Renowned for his humility and his austere manner of life, adept at ascesis and temperate retreat from the world, he conceived the service of God as resting on three pillars: *Torah*, "the Law," *Mitzvot*, "the commandments," and *Middot*, "human character traits, or virtues." A Kabbalist, but in a style of his own, he was preoccupied with education and created his own *yeshivot*, beginning with that of Volozhin.

Rabbi Chaim of Volozhin (1759–1821) was considered by his contemporaries as the closest disciple of the Vilna Gaon. His major work, *Nefesh HaChaim, The Soul of Life*, was intended as a response to Hassidism, but a response formulated as a positive system of thought, not a polemical denunciation. As firm as he was in his mastery of doctrine, he proved himself supple in its application. In the spirit of the Gaon, he saw Hassidism as nothing less than a heretical sect bent on upsetting tradition and breaching the limits of Judaism, and therefore something that needed to be battled at all costs. For Rabbi Chaim of Volozhin — it is true that in the meantime the Hassidic movement had significantly gained in strength — good intentions were not in question. The bottom line was that the Hassidim were mistaken.

Rabbi Zundel of Salant (1786–1866) was an intermediary figure. To him we owe the development of notions like the *yetzer harah* and the *yetzer hatov*, the "evil inclination" and the "good inclination," which became key terms in Mussar literature. The encouragement to abandon *pilpul* and to study the Torah in the pursuit of truth, as well as the quest of a personal discipline, found resolution in three decisions: not to serve in the Rabbinate, not to write books, and not to study Kabbalah.

And the contribution of Rabbi Israel Salanter? It fell to him to establish the movement proper as a social phenomenon. He took the Mussar system out of books and brought it into everyday life. Mussar, for his predecessors, emerged from the "fear of God." But beyond that, how was one supposed to live? What was to be done on a daily basis? The Vilna Gaon lived in isolation, entirely absorbed in study. Salanter wanted to be more open to society. He extended the system into normative Jewish society and blazed new paths within it that were better suited to the generation and conditions of the contemporary era. To the precept of the Haskalah, "Be Jewish at home and human outdoors," the mastermind of Mussar was said to respond: "Be Jewish and human everywhere."

His references? Ibn Gabirol, Bahya ibn Pakuda, Moshe Chaim Luzzato. His approach? To convince Orthodox Jews to put moral life and the development of human character traits at the center of their concerns and actions. His aim? To promote an educational system that placed the emphasis on this moral dimension just as much as on study. The Torah, yes, but in the truth, for the truth.

His major work, *Or Israel, The Light of Israel,* a classic work in the Mussar movement, was published in 1900, only after his death, through the efforts of his student Rabbi Israel Blazer. It was to the field of education that Salanter first attached his name. He began by establishing a school in the suburbs of Vilna, in Uzuis. In 1848, a cholera epidemic compelled him to leave Vilna and settle in Kovno, where he once again founded a school and gathered *ba'alei-batim,* "masters of the house," to wit, laborers, craftsmen, common people, into houses of learning across the four corners of the city. This manner of study that included common folk remained one of his trademarks. The movement began to soar. Then, suddenly, Salanter decided to leave Lithuania in order to live in Germany. The reasons that have been given for this sudden departure vary widely. A sense of failure? Bad health? Depression? He offered his own explanation: he compared Lithuanian Jewry, traditionalist yet subject to attacks by the Haskalah, to an unbridled horse working to pull a wagon up a slope. He went from one physician to another in Koenigsberg to raise money for his schools, and finally settled there for twenty-five years, nurturing a number of projects that all came to dead ends. He tried to start a Mussar journal that was also to be a forum for translating the Talmud from Aramaic to Hebrew and into European languages, and for elaborating methodological principles for studying the Talmud. He sought to introduce his teachings into the university at one point, only to be declined. He stayed in Paris for two years where he set out to work for the Russian and Polish immigrants, without really succeeding in establishing himself. Finally, he died in Koenigsberg in 1883, without family, without any disciples present, in the company of a housekeeper whose wages were paid by the local Jewish community. One of his biographers, Hillel Goldberg, evokes the final hours of the venerable rabbi, recounting how he took it upon himself to console his housekeeper and explain to her that she had no reason to fear spending a night with a corpse, namely his own.[10]

Goldberg also shows how the Mussar movement was both an attempt to reestablish and regenerate current orthodoxy and a testimony to failure. It is true that the efforts of Salanter in the 1840s and 1850s did not have a strong, immediate impact. But the impact would be felt in time. In 1870, his students created a *kolel* in Kovno, a school for the training of Mussar masters. In 1881, the great Yeshiva of Slobodka, founded on the Mussar movement, was built in the suburb of Kovno.

The deep impression made on Jewish orthodoxy by this neglected school of thought, at the beginning of the century in Eastern Europe and beyond, reached further than might first appear. How necessary is it as a biographical beacon? The Levinasian ethic is very far from the Mussar school, and Rabbi Israel Salanter's concern with moral edification has little to do with the work of the philosopher. But Ausra Pazeraite is right to underline the dynamic tension between the cosmopolitan environment and the quest for an open identity that was embodied in the Mussar movement. If we want to properly gauge the atmosphere of the age, we cannot forget the profound impact made on traditional Judaism by this movement that sought to extract ethics from the domain of theology in order to introduce it into conceptual, psychological life, and into life in general. With this, Israel Salanter, like Chaim of Volozhin, remains a significant point of reference in the life and the work of the philosopher.

2 | STRASBOURG

Emmanuel Levinas arrived in Strasbourg in 1923. Why Strasbourg? Because of its prestige in France. And because it is the French city closest to Lithuania.

Bestriding several worlds, a longtime symbol of Franco-German antagonism, it had last been regained by France at the end of the First World War. Alsace and Lorraine were bristling with patriotic sentiment, but without compromising the uniqueness of their fusion culture. As part of the republic, Strasbourg benefited from the old Concordat regime, which protected every constituted religion and school within civil institutions. The Jewish community was significant and well established. Still something of a stopover on the road to Paris, the capital of lights, provincial Strasbourg did not yet enjoy the European status that would be conferred upon it on the morrow of the Second War. But for the young Emmanuel Levinas, it would serve as an excellent airlock chamber in the adjustment to the new barometric readings of this exile, his first exile, and, although he did not yet know it, his definitive exile.

LITERATURE AND PHILOSOPHY

The routine of student life commences far from home. Levinas hunts down a flat in the city, finds one, then moves, repeatedly changing districts. His father regularly sends him money for room and board, supporting him for the entire duration of his studies.

He begins by perfecting his French — "Languages were never a problem for him," says his grandson David — and he enrolls in philosophy. The choice may seem surprising. He falls prey to a single intellectual fascination, pushing aside every material preoccupation. It corresponds, one might say, to an imperative.

Whence the sudden attraction to philosophy? As he explained to François Poirié in an interview: "I think that it was first of all my readings in Russian, specifically Pushkin, Lermontov, and Dostoyevsky, above all Dostoyevsky. The Russian novel, the novels of Dostoyevsky and Tolstoy, seemed to me very occupied with fundamental things. Books shot through with anxiety — with an essential, religious anxiety — but readable as a search for the meaning of life."[1] The answer to Poirié's question explains the passage from literature to philosophy, since he arrived at one through the other. He said it even more explicitly to Miriam Anissimov. "Have you read Russian literature?" she asked. He responded: "Russian literature was my preparation for philosophy."[2]

The French philosophical scene of the time was far from propaedeutic. Nevertheless, it was experiencing an analogous fermentation. Perhaps because of a certain sense of inferiority in the shadow of the great German systems, Paris had opened itself up to diverse influences. If the academic legacy of the nineteenth century, the positivism of Auguste Comte, or the still-present epistemology of Cournot, or Léon

Brunschvicg, maintained its hopes of resuscitating republican thought by means of a neo-Kantianism of law and order, new concerns pushed themselves to the fore nonetheless.

On the one hand, the status of the humanities was entirely revindicated, be it psychology with the debate generated by the first translations of Freud, or sociology with the methodological revolution proposed by Durkheim from the height of his chair at the Sorbonne, or linguistics with Saussure and ethnology with Mauss. On the other hand, religion and spirituality were again regarded as fields for theoretical reflection and historical investigation. The impact of Bergson's work in this respect is undeniable, but we must also remember the renewal of Christian philosophy, through the speculative endeavors of Jacques Maritain, and the scholarly labors of Étienne Gilson with his rediscovery of medieval thought by way of the *Summae* of Thomas Aquinas.

In this division between the old and the new, which was not free from ideological stakes, the university of Strasbourg had chosen its camp. Its reputation lay with the preservation of the classical role of philosophy, which meant that philosophy, to begin with, must attend to studying its own history. This ascetic commitment to transmission, this respect for the great masters, this rumination of foundational texts was enough to win over the mind of the young Levinas. He gave himself to the discipline of the tradition in much the same way that one might take up piano or the Talmud, first by playing scales and then moving on to interpretation.

THE PROFESSORS

The initial charms came from Maurice Pradines, professor of general philosophy, whose courses unfailingly disclosed the rapport between morality and politics. He was rather aloof, but made an impression on the young Lithuanian student by citing the Dreyfus affair as an illustration of an ethics that triumphed over politics. He also published an autobiography bearing a title that did not displease the child of Kovno, *Le Beau Voyage: An Itinerary from Paris to the Borders of Jerusalem.*[3]

Then there was Charles Blondel, professor of psychology, an anti-Freudian, a disciple of Brunschvicg, who, in his ironic style, liked to put psychoanalysis in its place. "There is no social science," he writes, "from the science of religion to the history of art, including linguistics and ethnography, about which psychoanalysis doesn't have some word to say, even if it doesn't itself believe that it has said the final word. . . . My task would be, the hour permitting, to signal without prolixity but without fear, the unique fantasies whereby, as the poet says, the pig that sleeps exposed at the heart of every man would, by an additional effort of psychoanalysis, be made into a sad pig."[4] Another impressive figure was Maurice Halbwachs, a sociologist who would be appointed to the Collège de France a few months before his deportation to Buchenwald where he perished in 1945. Finally, there was Henri Carteron, professor of ancient philosophy, who died prematurely in 1927, to be succeeded by Martial Guéroult, an expert in Descartes and Spinoza.

Levinas would often pay homage to his teachers in Strasbourg, as he did, for example, in his farewell speech at the Sorbonne in 1976 upon his retirement. Yet for all that, it cannot be said that he followed in any of their paths. What he emphasized is how in Strasbourg he was brought back "to the importance of the Holy Scriptures by a passion brought to medieval studies which had developed in my Catholic friends from contact with Henri Carteron." And he adds, "My interest in Jewish studies was revived in the course of my research plan, which was, in fact, altogether exterior to Judaism, properly speaking."[5] It was to Carteron that he dedicated his first book on Husserl.

The symbolic value of this linkage must not be downplayed. It is possible to be at once loyal to one's religious identity and to the broad theoretical exigency of philosophy. Like the Russian novel, the research of the neo-Catholics served as a good example for Levinas, even though it was in other texts that he would find his first motifs of inspiration, namely, in the works of Henri Bergson and Edmund Husserl.

TWO AWAKENINGS

Bergson at that time was at the height of intellectual fashion. There probably is not a single *baccalauréat* exam from the period that is not riddled with quotes from him. And it is also around this time that Husserl began to be spoken about.

Even more than with his great themes — foundational intuition, the freedom of the spirit, memory and endurance, the *élan vital* — Henri Bergson came to influence the young Levinas with his bearing and attitude. Here was a philosopher who, against the prevailing materialism, did not hesitate to defend the metaphysics of Plotinus or the spiritualism of Ravaisson, and whose influence could be felt in writers like Proust and Péguy. The young Lithuanian also had a sense of the latent debt to Judaism in the future Nobel laureate who, after a period of attraction to Catholicism, explained in 1937: "I would have converted had I not seen the formidable wave of anti-Semitism which broke out over the world taking shape over the years. I wanted to remain among those who would be persecuted."[6] Very much in sympathy with the fierce patriotism of Bergson, moreover, Levinas's own love of France made him write in 1939: "We are therefore called to fight for France. I cannot do otherwise! All my life I have asked myself how I might repay this country to which I am indebted, to which I owe everything."

And there is always Levinas's discovery of *Les données immédiates de la conscience,* which he repeatedly claimed to admire. He would often cite the book as something to be counted among the five or six major works in the history of philosophy. In the preface to the German edition of *Totalité et infini* he would avow "a fidelity to the revolutionary work of Henri Bergson."

As for Husserl, his writings circulated among a few rare students. In this case again, the attitude was decisive and the parallel appropriate. Likewise a reader of Plato, Husserl wanted to open up consciousness once again to the spirit, to renew the contemplation of essences by means of intentionality, all in the name of reestablishing philosophy as a rigorous science.

A Jew as well, but converted to Protestantism, the founder of phenomenology similarly found himself on the side of the persecuted, chased out of the university by the Nazis, his unedited works saved in the eleventh hour from an *auto-da-fé.* Levinas was not just the translator of Husserl, or, better still, his initiator into France. His entire work, in a sense, represents a response to the work of the master from Freiburg.

LAUREL AND HARDY

In Strasbourg in the 1920s, the academic atmosphere was somewhat stiff. The students would address one another formally as *vous* rather than *tu.* The dress code called for ties. Some would even walk around with a silver-knobbed cane, in the manner of the royalist supporters, or more simply by way of dandyism. Among the latter, a certain Maurice Blanchot stood out, a student of philosophy and German. Already a taciturn young man, he felt no calling for a teaching profession in academia and preferred journalism instead. He was two years Levinas's senior. He had not yet written anything, but was seductive enough in speech.

The two men bonded very quickly, yet their friendship seemed improbable. One was a Russian emigré, enamored with the France of Captain Dreyfus and Abbot Gregory, steeped in Jewish culture. The other came from a bourgeois family, preferred to move in Maurrasian circles and did not hesitate to collaborate with journals on the extreme right. They were as far apart from each other as possible. So what was the attraction?

In a photograph from the era, we see them standing shoulder to shoulder. Blanchot is pale, slender, hieratic. Levinas is round, cheerful, disheveled. In handwriting that belongs neither to Blanchot nor Levinas, someone has scribbled on the back: "*Doublepatte et Patachon,*" the classic precursors of Laurel and Hardy. Another way of saying: "Because that's him, because that's me"? No doubt it sums it all up.

"From the outset I had the sense of an extreme intelligence, of a thinking that proffered itself as an aristocracy, very distant from me politically at that time — he was a monarchist — but we had very quick access to each other."[7] This is how Levinas would describe the early acquaintance with the friend of his youth. Blanchot made him read Proust and Valéry. In his traditional affiliations in literature, in his personal tastes, in his references, drawn equally from Russian as from French texts, Levinas is classical. When he calls upon literature, it is with a ready ear for Corneille and Racine. Similarly, when he speaks of painting, he thinks of Joconde. Through Blanchot, he gained access to more modern works. Would he have discovered and come to love Proust without his friend from Strasbourg? Probably not. Levinas for his part made Blanchot read Tolstoy and Dostoyevsky, spoke to him of Husserl and Heidegger, both of whose courses he followed in Freiburg, Germany. From Levinas, too, the influence would be lasting. Against all odds, a deep friendship and an intellectual complicity were born between them.

Recalling the years at Strasbourg in a letter to *L'Arche,* Maurice Blanchot would write: "I think everyone knows what I owe to Emmanuel Levinas, today my oldest friend, the only one who lets me call him *tu.* It's also known that we met in Strasbourg in 1926, where we studied a more than mediocre philosophy from so many great teachers. Did our meeting happen by chance? One could say so. But friendship is not something chancy or fortuitous. Something very deep drew us together. I wouldn't say it was already Judaism, but apart from his cheerfulness, it was some kind of solemn and fine manner of considering life profoundly and without the least bit of pedantry."[8] In another letter where he revisits this period, he speaks of "a friendship immediately affirmed: a personal friendship, an intellectual friendship. In the meantime, or perhaps already by then, Emmanuel Levinas had been in Germany where he attended the courses of Husserl. This name, what it represents, and later that of Heidegger, came back into our conversations day after day. We must not forget that it was Levinas who truly opened French philosophy to an understanding of Husserl with his thesis on intuition. We met again in Paris. I will not add anything else."[9] Still elsewhere, he would say that he found in Levinas a philosophy "of life itself, of youth itself."[10]

A friendship for life? Indeed. With a give-and-take from one to the other. A nearness of works. A circulation of themes and concepts, to the point of producing a sentiment that persisted and harmonized. A kinship not without style, but with the intonation, the manner of always going to the edge of the precipice, of holding itself within modernity yet without yielding to it. Each would continually write under the gaze of the other. And continually write to the other. But after the Strasbourg period — a crucible for both of their creative evolutions — even though the connection persisted, the encounters would be spaced further apart.

THE FRACTURE

Levinas obtained his bachelor's degree in 1927 and defended his doctoral thesis in the third year of graduate studies in 1930. He left for Paris, where he attended the courses of Brunschvicg at the Sorbonne and became a director at the school of the Alliance Israélite Universelle. Blanchot also moved to Paris in the same year and completed a thesis on skepticism in graduate studies at the Sorbonne before definitively orienting himself toward journalism.

The two men saw each other less and less. This was the period in which Blanchot was involved in radically right-wing environments. He was close to L'Action française, regularly collaborated in the *Journal de Débats,* where he was an editor, wrote for *L'Insurgé,* for *Aux Écoutes,* for *Rempart.*

Blanchot thus participated openly in a certain fascist "romanticism." Convinced, like so many other young intellectuals, that the old world was at an end and that a new human being was about to be born, he worked to precipitate the "Great Night." In this respect, editing *L'Insurgé* was exemplary. Robert Brasillach and Thierry Maulnier were his seniors. He crossed paths with Lucien Rebatet and Claude Roy. All of them were disappointed with the Maurassian wait-and-see policy and called upon the Sorelian myth of violence, dreaming of a national revolution.

In November 1934, Levinas sent him a piece he had written for the journal *Esprit* entitled, "Some Reflections on the Philosophy of Hitlerism," in which he writes: "It is not this or that dogma of democracy, of parliamentarianism, of a dictatorial regime or a religious politics that is in question. It is the very humanity of the human being."[11] This best expresses the fracture in their relationship. For Blanchot, in the meantime, had professed his aversion to democracy, parliamentarianism, capitalism and communism. He developed a very violent rhetoric on these themes. At the beginning of 1936, the ink ran like blood with an animosity that targeted Léon Blum, a prototypical democrat, a symbol of the popular front, and an example of the "cosmopolitan Jew."

Christophe Bident, a biographer of Blanchot, who recounts the ferocious attacks on Blum in *L'Insurgé*, writes that, nevertheless, "anti-Semitism never intervened in this discourse except as an added bit of eloquence. An easy way to get to Blum, a controlled slip of the pen, rarely employed, which poorly masked the embarrassment in which his friend Emmanuel Levinas, or Paul Lévy and Georges Mandel, suddenly found themselves, as he grappled with his own inner contradictions, in this right-wing circle from which he would divorce himself before long."[12]

The fact remains that he did not take notice of how "the friend Levinas" lived through this "rhetoric" which, however you read it, must have been insufferable.

At the beginning of 1938, four years after his arrival in Paris and one year before the war, Blanchot continued to collaborate with the *Journal de Débats* and *Aux Écoutes* on literary columns, but the polemics came to an end. There are no more political texts from this date onward. Nothing more about the *Anschluss*, about Munich, about the immanence of the conflict.

Maurras himself, weary of his excesses, brought about the suspension of *L'Insurgé*, too deviant for his tastes from his own doctrine. Amid all of this youthful agitation, the defeat of France and the German occupation came to deal a new hand of cards. Lucien Rebatet would opt for collaboration, while Claude Roy joined the resistance and the communist scene.

EXODUS AND RECONCILIATION

The fact is that Maurice Blanchot was to help Levinas's family hide during the war. "We left Strasbourg for Paris nearly at the same time, but despite the fact that the contact was never exhausted, it took the misfortune of a disastrous war for our friendship, which could have slackened, to be tightened again. Especially since, initially held prisoner in France, he entrusted me, by a kind of secret request, with the task of watching over his loved ones whom the perils of a detestable politics threatened."[13] Another gesture: Blanchot would title his second work, which appeared in 1942, after Emmanuel Levinas's younger brother — Aminadav.

It is the one visible victory of friendship over the ideologies of the age. But it is not the only dimension of a retreat from this clamorous century, which would become ever more voluntary. At the beginning of the 1950s, Blanchot entered into a long silence which he would leave only intermittently. Sickness, voluntary solitude, a writer's decision to efface, the struggle for anonymity, writing as an intimate adventure, the book as refuge — these are possible reasons for the retreat, but none of them are really satisfactory explanations. This retreat would come to know advances and reversions. Blanchot stayed in touch with the times by means of publications, articles, timely opinions. He would sign the Manifesto of 121, and would participate in the Committee of Writers and Students of May 1968. Most significantly, after meeting Robert Antelme, he would publish the first texts on Auschwitz, on the question of Judaism, with his two books, *La conversation infinie* and *L'Écriture du désastre,* which were written under the mark, or in the wake, or on the trail of Levinas. The correspondence between these works and the early works of Levinas is, in fact, quite visible, almost explicit. In 1947, in a critical note on *De l'existence à l'existant,* Georges Bataille observes a great proximity between the two of them with respect to the notion of the *il y a,*[14] and somewhat later Christophe Bident also came to speak of a "common brainwave."[15] And this is something that did not desist over time. It would continue to be emphasized on one side or another, although it eventually became less pregnant with meaning, and, instead, simply faithful to certain common intuitions and the profound inspiration of a shared youth.

The friendship persisted, but was more distant. The two men maintained a steady epistolary liaison. They called each other often, keeping each other abreast of the ups and downs of their lives, sharing news of the newly hatched and the panics characteristic of telephone conversations with Levinas, but the face-to-face encounters became rare, altogether rare.

Laurel and Hardy? To be sure, a kindred esthetic sensibility brought them together in Strasbourg, a common taste for literature and philosophy. But is friendship not also nourished simply by itself, by encounters and the memories of youth? There is another photograph characteristic of the period in which Emmanuel Levinas can be seen perched on a Citroën. Marie-Anne Lescourret recounts the history behind this photographic cliché.[16] There are five of them — Blanchot, Rontchewsky, Madeleine Guery, Suzanne Pentilles and Levinas — posing on the hood of a car before they got into it and drove off to the home of their professor, Charles Blondel. The five students were invited to dinner. The young Lithuanian asked if it might be arranged that his meal be prepared according to the precepts of *kashrut* to which he had adhered since his childhood. Blanchot and he are standing side by side. Levinas in a double-breasted suit, the white handkerchief already in the side pocket, smiling, scrutinizing the horizon with his eyes slightly squinting. Blanchot, with cane in hand, his chin resting heavily on the other hand, pensive, a sorrowful pout, the eyes half-closed.

Allô

Allô? — His "Allô" was a tall order. You would call to chat and hear what was new, and what you would get on the other end of the wire was an "Allô" that was urgent, out of breath, jerky. The "Allô" wasn't there just to set off the conversation. It recurred within the conversation to punctuate the topic at regular intervals as if to confirm that the nature of the dialogue hadn't changed, and as if to say that a telephone exchange was hardly appropriate. It was repeated in a disquieting tone as if to solicit the interlocutor to listen, to verify that he was still there, that the connection had not been lost, that there was no interference in the transmission. . . . This man who had written admirable pages on the virtues of technology fell into utter panic before the simplest media device: a telephone, a tape-recorder, a camera. . . . The anxiety was there without awareness, without explanation, and could disappear at any moment.

One can sometimes catch an echo of his favorite expressions among some of his disciples. "Enough to make the stars cry"; his "in a fashion" instead of "in a way"; his "It's like . . .," as if metaphor were the most appropriate way to say things. But the "Allô" belonged exclusively to him and can hardly be imitated. If anything, it was very much like the constant "n'est-ce pas?" Be it in the classroom or in a private conversation, the "spa" would come with every four or five sentences in search of approbation. "Spa? Spa?" He needed it in order to advance his reasoning, or in order to find the right word, the perfect adjective. A heritage of his native Russian? Or perhaps a souvenir of the young man who arrived from Lithuania and went on to make French his language for philosophizing?

3 | FREIBURG-IM-BREISGAU

Regarding the two semesters he spent during the summer of 1928 and the winter of 1928–1929 in Freiburg-im-Breisgau, Germany, Levinas often said: "I came to see Husserl, and what I saw was Heidegger."

It would be hard to find a more apt description of a crucial intersection in the history of twentieth century philosophy, and, in a more profound sense, in the history of the century itself. The closure, the critique, the renewal of metaphysics effectively hinged on the advent of Nazism. For the time being, Husserl had yet to be chased out of the university, and Heidegger had yet to deliver his famous *Rektorat* address. Better still, the former was the teacher of the latter, and the conceptual rupture between the two thinkers had yet to be consummated, at least officially. The important thing, for the time being, was how each of them, in the eyes of the young Levinas, would leave his indelible mark on the universe of ideas. He came across both of them as contemporary teachers who made philosophy a living exercise, taking on the duties of disciple and interpreter to each one in turn. Without knowing it, though, he was already heading toward his own thinking, as he rather precociously stepped into one of the great rendezvous points of the century, a place at the very hub of the contradictory destiny of the era.

HUSSERL'S HERALD

Levinas came to this Swabian city, a few miles from the Swiss border, in order to prepare a thesis that he had to defend in Strasbourg on "The Theory of Intuition in the Phenomenology of Husserl." He was rather young, twenty-three years old, but already up to date with the Husserlian revolution known to some in Strasbourg. Gabrielle Peiffer, a young woman he had met at the Philosophy Institute in the faculty — whom he always addressed as "Mademoiselle Peiffer" — had recommended Husserl and had prompted him to read *Logical Investigations* in German. There was also Jean Hering, a professor in theology at Strasbourg, who had studied with Husserl in Göttingen, and who had just published an introductory primer in 1925 called *Phénoménology et philosophie religieuse.* The intuition behind it was significant. Hering had already grasped the original dimension of the debate, which would not fade away, and poured out so much ink on the subject that he ended up making a tour in the 1890s throughout France on this one point of contention: Did the reform proposed by Husserl succeed in establishing a radical science, or, on the contrary, did it establish the rights of theology? Levinas himself would not respond to the question and bypassed it one way or another, but, undoubtedly, being the student that he was, he could hardly retreat in indifference from such a clear opportunity to articulate the heritage of the Bible in a conceptual manner. Still in the same emerging movement, Hering, who had made this very suggestion to him, initiated Levinas into Heidegger. The former student of Husserl one day offered the young Lithuanian a copy of *Sein und Zeit*. "But there's no Husserl in it!" exclaimed Levinas. To which Hering responded: "This one goes further than Husserl."[1]

Like the encyclopedists of the eighteenth century, le siècle des Lumières, the philosophical circles of twentieth century Europe in the years between the wars indulged in a communitarian dream. Exchanges, trips and meetings abounded. Levinas himself would reminisce about his Swabian sojourn with great satisfaction, but not so much about the city of Freiburg itself and its surrounding countryside, which seems to have made little impression. Thinking back on it, in fact, he would remember "crossing streets that themselves remained almost unnoticed."[2] As if phenomenology was the unique event of this period in his life. The city was agreeable enough, with its rose-colored cathedral at the center of pedestrian roads, and its green landscapes on the city outskirts, even though his own residence, which was far enough from the university at the city core, was a little room on Colmarer Strasse in a somewhat dismal neighborhood.

At the time he took up his studies in Freiburg, Husserl was in the process of retiring. He was offering his last courses. The grandeur of the master was in decline, and the nascent glory of Heidegger could be seen dawning on the horizon with the publication of his magnum opus in the preceding year, *Being and Time*.

In this summer of 1928, Levinas was still an auditor in Husserl's courses and seminars, but the old master quickly adopted him. In a letter to Ingarden, dated July 13, he writes: "Hering has sent me a very gifted Lithuanian student."[3] He often received him in his home, at 40 Lorettostrasse, where they would discuss philosophy. And when an invitation arrived from Paris to a series of conferences at the

Sorbonne — which was to give birth to the *Cartesian Meditations* — Husserl asked Levinas to give private French lessons to Mme. Husserl to help her brush up on her language skills before the trip, which the master regarded as a watershed moment in his career. These lessons, which took the form of conversations, left Levinas with rather mixed memories of the old matron of Freiburg. Many years later, in a discrete note at the foot of a page, he recounted memories of wounded feelings provoked by strong language from his French student — Malvina Husserl — which verged on anti-Semitism, and which were quickly corrected by her embarrassed spouse: "Never mind, Mr. Levinas, I myself also came from a home of shopkeepers. . . ."[4]

A FRENCH AFFAIR

Returning to France, Levinas published an article in *La Revue Philosophique de la France et de l'Étranger* on "The *Ideen* of Mr. Husserl." This is his first known publication. Jacques Rolland notes that he may have previously put out a few poems, but nothing of a philosophical order. The translation of the *Cartesian Meditations* followed.

A truly remarkable initiative. When he arrived in Strasbourg in 1923 at the age of eighteen, Levinas spoke very little, if any, French. He knew Russian, German and Hebrew. Six years later, he was professionally translating an author who was known for his obscurity. The translation was a collaboration with Gabrielle Peiffer, and the text was revised by Alexandre Koyré. "Mademoiselle Peiffer," as it happens, ended up taking more credit for the parenthood of the work than Levinas would have granted her. But at least the essential part of the project, the discovery of Husserl's thought, the grasp on the ideas and their transcription, was his.

It was with this translation, and afterwards with the indispensable treatise, "La Théorie de l'intuition dans la phénoménologie de Husserl," which assumed the form of an introduction to accompany the translation, that Levinas made his entry into the French intellectual scene. It would be through these two texts that Sartre, Merleau-Ponty, Ricoeur and Derrida would have the first contact with the movement of thinking that was destined not only to enjoy good fortune in France, but also to witness some of its most fertile possibilities come to fruition.

According to Jean-Luc Marion, a neighbor and friend of Levinas who followed in his tracks by succeeding him initially at Poitiers, then Nanterre, and finally at the Sorbonne, "it must not be forgotten that Levinas would still have been counted as one of the great philosophers even if he had died during the Second World War, simply by virtue of having done two absolutely extraordinary things in 1930. First, he published the translation of Husserl's *Cartesian Meditations,* which appeared in France twenty years before it appeared in Germany. And second, in the same year, he authored a text on the theory of intuition which is an extremely well-crafted and profound introduction to Husserl's concept of intentionality and, in fact, to the whole of phenomenology."

In 1929, Husserl delivered a series of conferences at the Sorbonne that served as the original material for the *Cartesian Meditations.* The German text was carefully reworked and developed on the return trip from Paris to Freiburg and sent off to Levinas for translation. Husserl supposed that the collection would appear very quickly in Germany, which it did not. The original German text would not see the light of day until after his death, in the *Husserliana,* after the war.

It was only thanks to Emmanuel Levinas, then, that the *Meditations* came out so early in France. But with the event of this publication, the whole of phenomenology found itself emerging into the topography as something not to be circumnavigated.

"We must keep this well in mind," continues Marion. "He imported and acclimatized phenomenology almost in real time, almost in the moment that it came to be. He was therefore at the origin of this utterly extraordinary grafting which, by now, has succeeded in making phenomenology a philosophical movement that is more alive in France, it seems to me, than in many other countries, perhaps even in Germany. In terms of duration, both quantitative and chronological, this movement is at least as much French as it is German. And this we owe to Levinas."

In the 1928–1929 academic year, then, the first influence for Levinas was Husserl. It was from him that he acquired the phenomenological method. It was to him that he owed the use of fundamental concepts — intentionality, constitution, reduction. Just like Heidegger, who was Husserl's disciple, Levinas could say: "He gave me eyes to see."

The second influence then followed immediately on the heels of the first, for his arrival in Freiburg precisely marked a period of transition between Husserl and his disciple. Heidegger had come from Marburg, the place of his first professorship, and was in the process of unseating the master. In the autumn semester, the great auditorium of the university was packed. Students stormed into the courses. And each one had to reclaim his seat anew the next day. Levinas was victim to the shock and to the charm. *Being and Time* was a monument in his eyes, obliging all of philosophy to pass before its eyes henceforth. And he would never renounce this first infatuation, even after the discovery of the subsequent Nazi involvements of the philosopher from Todtnauberg, and still even after the polemics over this involvement.

This issue too would be a French one, in a way. As with Husserl, the fate of Heidegger in Paris, his reception at the university and beyond, outstripped his fortunes in Germany. And again as for Husserl, Levinas was the one standing at the crossroads. What new perspective did Heidegger open up for him during 1928–1929? To be sure, the revelation of existence as a new departure for philosophy, the resonance of the verb "to be" — as he often said — with which he would educate an entire generation of thinkers. But not only this, for there was also something like a similarity, however distant, between his own journey and that of Husserl's disciple. Martin Heidegger came from a religious world as well, namely traditional German Catholicism buttressed against the temptations of the twentieth century. He began as a student of theology, was familiar with seminary studies and devoted a first thesis to Duns Scotus, the medieval Franciscan thinker of infinity. But Heidegger burned his bridges. In 1919, he writes: "I believe in my inner vocation as a philosopher, and I believe in doing my utmost for the eternal destination of the inward man — and for this end alone — by accomplishing this vocation in research and in teaching, and I believe that I will thus justify my life and my activity before God himself."[5] This profession might have been made by Levinas, who similarly agreed that philosophy had an a priori suspension of claims regarding God and was essentially "atheistic," in the sense not of a denial but rather of a condition of its freedom to speak. Contrary to Heidegger, however, on the subject of what could be said concerning the Bible, the "unthinkable debt,"[6] Levinas, on his own path of thinking, rediscovered the question of transcendance, which was also destined to characterize the philosophical debate in France in the decades to follow.

Freiburg signified Husserl and Heidegger, therefore. But this city, rich in challenge, held something else in store for Levinas. To be sure, he never met Franz Rosenzweig. But his shadow hovered over the city and showed itself to be just as decisive for him.

THE STAR AND THE CROSS

Present-day Freiburg on a windy spring morning. The city has not changed very much over the years. The cathedral is still rose-colored. The corner of Colmarer Strasse, where Levinas lived, is still dismal. And the city even now carries a weight of history and myth. One can nonetheless be enthralled by the summits of Feldberg in the distance, especially when seen from the balcony of Bernhard Casper. The hut in Todtnauberg is not very far, still occupied by Heidegger's son and, I have been told, subject to a recent "pilgrimage" by Derrida in the Black Forest. Casper, who was a friend of Levinas, a resident in the city and a specialist in Rosenzweig studies, tells me the story of how *The Star of Redemption* was written in Freiburg.

At the end of the Great War, the young Hegelian from Kassel is sent for convalescence in a nearby barracks after being stricken with malaria on the Macedonian front. Still in uniform, he sometimes checks into a local hotel. Due to the cold in the barracks, and again in the hotel, he regularly runs for refuge to the local taverns, his papers under his arm. The general gossip about the pale young man in military garb who can be seen in all the bistros is: "He's writing a book on the war," which is not altogether wrong. The loose papers of *The Star* must have been brought together into a treatise in seven months, from August 1918 to March 1919, the same period during which he was posting one letter a day to his beloved.

It was only six years apart, then, that these two men — Levinas and Rosenzweig — sojourned in two corners of the same city, across from each other, as it were. After his stay in the hotel, Rosenzweig lived in a house in front of the famous cathedral (as noted on a plaque on the house), two minutes away from where Levinas resided. Their lives crossed paths just as their works crossed paths — at a distance, and yet in a certain communion nonetheless.

Levinas never heard of Rosenzweig while in Freiburg, of course. It was later, in Paris, that he read *Der Stern,* which appeared in Germany in 1921. The work was recommended to him by a friend, Marcus Cohn, who came from Strasbourg and taught at a rabbinical seminary on Vauquelin Street. Cohn would later say: "It was reading Rosenzweig that kept him within the tradition."

The itinerary of the child of Kassel, raised in a family nourished on German culture and cut off from religious sentiments; his tortuous path to faith on the eve of his conversion, on the night of Yom Kippur in a small synagogue in Berlin; that "road to Damascus" that brought him back to Judaism, to the "tradition of his fathers" — all of this could hardly leave the young Lithuanian student unimpressed.

Although Rosenzweig himself never spoke of this experience explicitly, it is at the heart of his major work, *The Star of Redemption,* in his analysis of the relationship between Judaism and Christianity, which assigns to each one its own vocation and concludes that both are "revealed in the same truth."

According to Paul Mendès-Flor, who is currently the director of the Franz Rosenzweig Institute in Jerusalem and has been working for a number of years on a biography, the Jewish identity of Rosenzweig was affirmed since his childhood, but he didn't know exactly what to do with it, he didn't know very well how to express it, what direction to give it. He was encumbered by it, and he hesitated to scoff at Christianity, as his friends did, because of this same problem of identity. He sought out a voice, a reason, a pretext for not converting. And this is where that crisis-experience on Yom Kippur intervened, in which he discovered that Judaism is not empty, that despite the assimilation, despite the urbanization, it retain in itself something strong, alive, vital. The conversion was no longer necessary, no longer possible. There was a phenomenon of superimposition amid his religious, spiritual needs which became for him the essence and necessity of preserving his Jewish identity.

The origins of Levinas and the solid Jewish culture that he had absorbed in his childhood shielded him from these types of mutations. Nevertheless, this vigorous thinking that penetrated into the depths of the Jewish texts but came from the universal and the human, this new manner of seeing Judaism as a path of truth, made an impression that was more profound than any other. As did this vision of an encounter between Judaism and Christianity: two parallel voices that nevertheless did not converge, a symbiosis that was not a synthesis but rather a coexistence, a common life, a veritable experience of a path. Levinas would often come up against this question in his commitment to Judaism, and in dialogue with Christians, during which he was demanding and without concession.

But all of this was yet to come. In Freiburg, what mattered for the time being, what predominated above all, was the discovery of phenomenology and all the possibilities that it contained.

One episode marks this period more clearly than any other: a kind of "victory prize" won by Martin Heidegger in the town of Davos.

HEIDEGGER IN DAVOS

Well before becoming the rendezvous point for great international economists and the symbol of globalization, Davos, the small vacation town situated in the Grisons in the Swiss Alps, was for a brief moment bound up with the history of philosophy. In mid-March of 1929, a series of academic meetings were organized for the second time (the first year had been inaugurated by a lecture by Albert Einstein). The event was financed by an association of local shopkeepers and hotel managers who hoped to animate this holiday spot during the intermediate season between winter and summer. One guiding purpose of these meetings, moreover, was to host a *rapprochement* between French and German intellectuals, on the neutral territory of Switzerland, in the spirit of the Locarno peace treaty of 1925. In fact, Jean Cavaillès, mentor of a small group of French college students who were invited to participate, gave a report on the "beneficial influence of the spirit of Locarno" and of a "Locarno of intelligence."

There were about a hundred French, German and Swiss participants, spread out over several inns in the village, and this entire little world would assemble for the plenary sessions and the conferences in the halls of the Grand Hôtel. The duration of the colloquium — three weeks, from March 17 to April 6 — was proof of the seriousness of the enterprise, as much as it confirmed the quality of the delegations. Among the French, one could count Brunschvicg, Schwob, Boivins, Cavaillès, Schuhl, Gandillac, and finally, a young Lithuanian from Strasbourg, Emmanuel Levinas. Among the Germans, two celebrities stood out: Cassirer and Heidegger. The general theme, "What is man?" was to open and to pull together the anxious questions born in the Great War.

Ernst Cassirer, the great neo-Kantian philosopher, heir and

disciple of Hermann Cohen, illustrious representative of the Marburg School, had just been named rector of the University of Hamburg and would remain the only Jew known in Germany to hold this post. He was scheduled to speak on the "fundamental problems in philosophical anthropology." Heidegger, who had just published *Sein und Zeit,* planned to evoke Kant's *Critique of Pure Reason* and tackle "the task of a foundation of metaphysics."

These two sessions constituted only one part of the program. But before long the entire conference came to focus on the dialogue between the two philosophers and the confrontation between the two paths of thought. The sessions were planned as debates. Each one of the two protagonists was to share his thoughts on the work of the other, and the interpretation of Kantianism was to be the culminating point of dispute.

Written accounts of this colloquium are extremely rare, and Heidegger's family has banned access to all archived documents. But we do have Pierre Aubenque's introduction to the proceedings of the debates: "A strange dialogue. One of them was irenical, the other had a neophyte's fury and iconoclasm. In one corner, a personage that one observer described as 'olympian,' heir to a cosmopolitan culture that came from his big-city lifestyle and bourgeois origins; in the other corner, a provincial, still young and already famous, but timid, stubborn and tense, whom Mme. Cassirer compared to a peasant boy who had been suddenly shoved into the inner court of a palace."[7]

The terms of the debate? For Pierre Aubenque, it was two philosophies that clashed: "One reclaimed the European tradition of the eighteenth century philosophy of the *Lumières,* the other, announcing a new beginning, didn't hesitate to proclaim the destruction of what was still the foundations of Western metaphysics (Spirit, Logos, Reason)."

In memoirs that were edited after the war, Tony Cassirer, the spouse of the professor from Marburg, would write a bitter account of the encounter in Davos, not hesitating to suggest that the violence of the Heideggerian language of 1929 was a foreshadowing of the attitude of the author of *Sein und Zeit* after 1933: "Thereafter one could see quite clearly on which path this man would set out."[8]

One of the participants at Davos, Maurice de Gandillac, came away with a different view of the Cassirer-Heidegger debate. He is one of the last witnesses — in France, in any event — of this confrontation. As he remembers it, reenacting it in his mind, the confrontation was much more attenuated than has been suggested.

> It remained a civilized dialogue between the elegant professor who symbolized the humanistic and liberal tradition, and Heidegger, who brought with him an entirely new outlook. Mme. Cassirer was speaking of a real scene between the two of them. But if there was something there, no one registered so much as an echo of it. The students were far from the holy of holies. Certainly Cavaillès, who was our cayman, and who directed the general rapport in the session, gave an extremely positive summary of the exchange between the two men. Many among us, myself included I must say, felt closer to Cassirer, but Heidegger interested us as something new. In other words, the tone of the polemic was, again, extremely courteous. I was not struck by any particular tension. Besides, had there been a great tension, Levinas would have stepped in as the interpreter.

But what was the Levinas of that time like? How did he behave during the colloquium at Davos? How did he react to the confrontation between the two German philosophers? In a photograph from the time, we see him standing between Eugen Fink, Husserl's assistant, and Ludwig Bulnow, with a snow-capped mountain in the background. The face refined, a double-breasted jacket already decorated with the white handkerchief, he is standing very erect, with one hand behind his back and the other holding a slender cane he must have borrowed from Maurice Blanchot. "We were seduced by this lad," recalls Gandillac, "because of his French. He was very much at ease. He had already made his choice."

On the same day that the Cassirer-Heidegger confrontation took place, between the morning conferences at the Grand Hôtel and the evening session which concluded the debates, the participants were free for the afternoon. This little world was dispersed along the main slope toward the lake of Davos. The French group found itself clustered around Emmanuel Levinas, who recounted his discovery of *Sein und Zeit.* Gandillac described the scene in a book of memoirs: "How could one forget this beautiful afternoon in which he translated, and commented on, a number of pages from *Being and Time* for a group of French participants? Little by little the sun melted the heap of snow on which Emmanuel sat, dressed in urban clothes with court shoes and rubber galoshes. When he got up, we noticed that, like the biblical Job, but this time without having reason to question his God, it was on a heap of ashes that he had spoken to us of 'being-there' and 'care.'"[9]

Gandillac has no doubt that, at the time, Levinas considered himself a fervent disciple of the Swabian philosopher: "He spoke to us of Heidegger with reverence, revealed to us all the meanderings of a thinking that was already familiar to him. At that time he did not have that distrust that came upon him later." Gandillac hastens to add that, even at the end of his life, after all the horrors were uncovered, Levinas was not among those who took up a sectarian attitude toward Heidegger, like Koyré, for example, who put his mind to devalue both the man and the work, philosophically, from the day he found him politically disgraceful. But certainly in the beginning he showed no less reserve than Levinas.

This is Gandillac's testimony. Is it true to the philosopher's sentiments during that period? According to other testimonies, Levinas was never fooled, not even at the beginning, and not even at the height of his admiration for the work. "He always held Heidegger to be an anti-Semite," says his daughter Simone quite bluntly. All the same, it is worthwhile to resituate Davos in its era. Gandillac recalls: "At Davos, in 1929, we were still far enough from the atmosphere that would prevail much later, in '32, in '33, in '35 with *Kristallnacht* and the first synagogues to be vandalized. A year earlier, I had made a trip to Germany. You didn't see any Nazis. You heard of marches and even of acts of violence, but the Germans we spoke to would say: these are small groups of no importance. No one was aware of what was being prepared. It was still believed that Fascism was Mussolini. No one had read *Mein Kampf*. Heidegger was already involved, mainly because of his wife, but we did not know of it. We never saw Mme. Heidegger during the seminar anyway. Him we mostly saw alone, in a skiing outfit."

According to Jean-Luc Marion, who belongs to another generation, a younger one, and who knows of Davos only through books and a few conversations with Levinas,

> it was an episode that remained painful and troubling for everyone who participated. It was a very ambiguous meeting, and I think that Levinas experienced it that way. But I don't think one can experience twentieth century philosophy without being imbricated in ambiguities that were not only political, but were the very ambiguity of the end of metaphysics. There was a moment when a number of benchmarks tended to disappear, for motives that were, for that matter, often rational and arguable. But when

these benchmarks disappeared, at one moment or another, there was a price to pay, and the whole world was gripped in ambiguity. Even for Levinas, it was not easy to have a simple, entrenched position.

LAUGHTER AND TEARS

Was there a personal encounter, was there any discussion, between Levinas and Heidegger at Davos? No, says Gandillac. And Levinas himself never mentioned such an event. According to some witnesses, though, it would seem that it was Heidegger, whose classes he attended at the time, who notified him about the colloquium at Davos and who even facilitated his getting an invitation, Levinas being otherwise one of two students selected by the University of Strasbourg to participate. The conditions for an encounter, apparently, were out of place at Davos. But it is also true that the professor from Freiburg did not socialize with the group. We see this, for example, on the day after the confrontation, when the participants were all invited to an excursion in the Grisons. The French participants and some of the Germans, Cassirer among them, took a detour on the way to visit the house of Nietzsche at Sils Maria. Heidegger did not join them. As was his habit, he kept to himself.

At the end of the stay at Davos, a typical variety show was staged in the spirit and style of those satirical presentations found in most colleges. The professors were caricatured by the students, and everyone put on a real performance. No one was spared. Boivins acted out a Brunschvicg, who, sporting a blue, white and red headband emblematic of pacifists, exclaimed: "As for me, I don't have a tricolored brain!" The task of mocking Heidegger was entrusted to the future professor Bulnow. In the French group, Levinas was the one who had mastered the most German, so the task of mimicking Ernst Cassirer fell to him. At the time he had a shock of black hair, so talcum power was sprinkled on his head to make him look more like the venerable guardian of neo-Kantianism.

"Cassirer was not easy to caricature," Gandillac continues.

> It was done with such perfection, such fluidity. I had never seen anyone speak such a pure, such a clear language. Levinas really pulled it off. With Heidegger, it was simpler. I don't recall if Bulnow had that rather harsh, somewhat peasantlike, voice that had so struck us. In an article in *Temps Modernes* after the war, I compared it to Hitler's voice. This was a bit unjust, I was wrong to say that. It was somewhat subjective, due possibly to the moustache. But the voice was not the same.

The diverse perspectives of three ages, suggestive in an implicit manner, cannot fail to strike us as significant: the frivolity of youth in the era between the two wars, the polemical indignation upon liberation, and the truly critical turn today.

"It must be noted," adds Gandillac, "that we hardly imagined we were experiencing a historical event. We simply felt that we had something in common with Cassirer, while Heidegger was the great curiosity." Who could see, during the innocent distraction on the shores of Lake Davos, that only four years later Ernst Cassirer would abandon the rectorship at Hamburg to go into exile in Sweden, while his interlocutor would take hold of the rectorship at Freiburg and deliver a discourse of servitude to the Nazi powers?

Levinas spoke little of Davos, and still less of this final variety show. When he did, it was always with sadness. For him, as I witnessed on several occasions when I was in his company, all of this was a painful memory.

What weighed upon him most heavily was the fact that

Mme. Cassirer died without his being able to express his regrets in person[10] for having shown his preference for Heidegger over Cassirer at Davos, and for the role that he took in a frivolous stage production, ignorant of the perils that were approaching. He knew that she would have liked this coming from him.

Rosenzweig was not present at Davos. Already very sick, having fallen prey to the disease from which he would die a few months later, he nonetheless heard of the Cassirer-Heidegger confrontation from an account given in the *Frankfurter Zeitung*. He responded in the form of a small article entitled "The Reversed Front" in which, curiously, Rosenzweig, without reservation, came down in favor of the successor of Hermann Cohen to the chair of philosophy at the university of Marburg and against the principal disciple of Hermann Cohen.[11] That is to say, like Levinas, he sided against Cassirer and for Heidegger, in a supposedly new dawn of philosophy, to which history nevertheless promptly caught up, as on the laughter of Davos were presently superimposed tears of grief.

4 | Paris

During the years between the two wars, France provided safe haven for the economic, political and intellectual refugees who were streaming in from the rest of Europe, and its ministry was not only cultural. In the eyes of Jewish immigrants in particular, France represented a model of emancipation and an ideal of integration. Becoming French meant entering into a contract of language, civilization and values embodied by the republic, coupled with the demands of a general humanism. Emmanuel Levinas was no exception in this regard and freely adopted the entire legacy from Pope Gregory, through the Napoleonic Consistory, to the Crémieux Decree. He even took pains to see a profoundly ethical seriousness in it. A Frenchman as well as a Jew, it was in this nation that he would find new roots, a new life, with the experiences of marriage and paternity, but also a language that was no less philosophical than German, the language of Descartes and Pascal, to which he would make his own contribution, eliciting from it a distinctive beauty and sonority and refracting through it the colors of his own heritage.

HISTORY OF AN EXEMPTION

"Sir Minister of Justice, I have the honor of soliciting from your great benevolence the favor of French naturalization. My name is Emmanuel Levinas. I was born in Kaunas (Lithuania) on December 30, 1905. I have been living in France for two years now without interruption, and I lived here earlier from December of 1923 to May 1928. I graduated in the Arts with a doctorate from the University of Strasbourg. I hope to receive an *agrégation* degree in philosophy. My residence is in Paris, 59 rue d'Auteuil. I am a bachelor. I would also ask to be exempted from the acquisition of an official seal due to the insufficiency of my means."

The request was handwritten by Levinas on October 18, 1930. After the completion of his studies in Strasbourg and the two-semester sojourn in Germany, in Freiburg, the young man arrived in Paris on June 1930. He made a brief trip to Lithuania for a three-month vacation, and upon returning he resolved to settle down in the French capital.

A university doctor, author of a brilliant thesis recommended with a very honorable mention, a bachelor, without children, a man enamored with France — "a nation to which one can attach oneself by spirit and heart as much as by roots," he wrote[1] — French naturalization nonetheless required his initiative. Faced with an influx of immigrants and refugees that did not let up until 1939, the Third Republic made the process of absorption increasingly complicated.

The dean of Strasbourg in his official capacity had sent a letter to the Guard of Seals (lord chancellor) with a warm recommendation: "Mr. Levinas left all of his professors with the memory of a powerful and well-ordered performance, and a most vital intelligence that plays with remarkable ease when directed toward philosophical problems. We readily predict a brilliant future in philosophy for Levinas." And he concludes: "It would be advisable, therefore, in my opinion, to naturalize this young man; on one condition, however, which it is perhaps unnecessary to mention. Levinas proposes to embark upon the difficult course of attaining an *agrégation* in philosophy. It is thus desirable that he assume all the responsibilities that will eventually befall his colleagues, and in particular that he not be released from the military obligations that they will have to satisfy." Formulas typical of the era: the excellence of the claimant is underscored without any request for exceptional status, in the name of republican discipline.

The naturalization dossier contains a number of other recommendations.[2] One of them is from Sylvain Levy, who was president of the Alliance Israélite Universelle at the time, and who signs with the title of vice president of the Foyer Français and professor at the Collège de France. There is also a letter on letterhead from Enio, École Normal Israélite Orientale, from the director, Mr. Navon, certifying that Mr. Levinas is officially employed at the institution in the capacity of general director. Finally, a note from the prefect confirms that he is an educational director, that he earns five hundred francs per month in addition to room and board, and that he, the prefect, would be happy to answer any further inquires.

Solicited for his opinion — the process of naturalization was not only long and fastidious but downright nitpicky, especially in light of concerns for state security — the French Secretary in Kovno addressed a note dated February 2, 1931:

> Except for a six-month stay in Freiburg-im-Breisgau, the applicant has continuously lived in France for more than seven years. He was recommended to me by Mr. Tronchon, professor at the University of Strasbourg, who held him

in high esteem and judged him to be a young man who matched his talent with hard work. I am certain that Mr. Tronchon would be quite ready to repeat at length everything that he told me concerning Mr. Levinas. The aforementioned, after brilliantly passing the requirements for a doctorate in philosophy at the University of Strasbourg, returned to Lithuania for a while. But he felt expatriated there and sensed that no interesting career options were available to him. This is what caused him to return to France in order to take the *agrégation* tests.

He concludes:

There is no question in my mind that the information I possess about Mr. Levinas is excellent in every respect, and I have no doubt that the young man will make an excellent recruit. His parents run a small shop in Kovno that is both a bookstore and a stationery shop for office supplies. It is a very humble operation that does not even hire employees to serve customers, and his parents have made difficult sacrifices to ensure the success of their sons' studies. I mention this because I think that the fees for the rights of naturalization would constitute a heavy financial burden for them.

The fees for the seal were waived, although waivers and exemptions of fees were rarely granted. It was done only for the best recruits to the republic, which was the case with Levinas.

With emphasis that all of the letters of reference were very favorable, and the list of information obtained about the applicant drawn up, the well-rounded proposal was recommended to the Bureau of Seals: "It would seem clear both from the dossier and equally from verbal inquiries made from Mr. Levinas's professors that we are dealing with an extraordinary individual. In such circumstances, the naturalization of Mr. Levinas presents a positive interest for France."

The style is rather unusual, as it was generally sufficient

to conclude with something like "It seems not inconvenient," or "It is suggested. . . ."

Among the various documents, though, we do find the following note — no doubt highly characteristic of its time — from the head office of seals to the minister of justice, which we cannot read without smiling: "Mr. Levinas, who did his secondary studies in his country of birth, claims to be well versed in the history of France from Louis XI onward. He is equally familiar with the whole of French literature after the Middle Ages. By contrast, he has ignored the geography of France." But the writer adds: "Mr. Levinas seems honest and sincere."

RAÏSSA

"Build a house, plant a vineyard, and get married," says the Talmud. The young doctor of philosophy had become a French citizen. In 1932, equipped with his new passport, he returned to Lithuania to betroth to Raïssa Levy, his neighbors' daughter.

He had known Raïssa since childhood, as she lived two paces away from him in Kaunas, on Kalejimo Street. A musician gifted with a wonderful voice, she learned to accompany her singing with piano. She had been influenced by her grandfather, Samuel Levy, in a love of music. Family legend reports that, at the age of three, she heard a young prodigy play piano and burst out sobbing. She went on to do her studies in Vienna, then in Paris where she became a student of Lazare Levi at the Conservatory. It was there that the two youths met up again after having fallen out of touch for so long.

With her high cheekbones, penetrating blue eyes, her profound glance, and the delightful Slavic accent with its rolling *r*'s, Raïssa was a number of years his junior. They spoke Russian together, understood each other without having to say anything, and had an immense mutual respect that anyone who knew them could testify to. She accompanied him on all of his job transfers. Her reserved yet always attentive presence was a constant reassurance. Those who worked closely with him at the Enio are full of praise for her manner of listening, her memory for commonplace details, her regular inquiries after the family of this person or that one. Warm, even-tempered, she was rarely seen to lose her calm. The only mood shifts that were ever noticed happened around the visits of the legendary Chouchani[3] — after the war, at rue d'Auteuil — when she felt dispossessed of her house and her husband.

Music was not her only passion, although she placed it above all others. Almost all of her energy went into the education of children, especially that of her son, whose musical vocation she encouraged and whose progress she watched over from day to day. She was interested in literature, read novels, was curious about everything, but made it a principle never to show off her culture and made sure at every moment to remain the discrete and attentive spouse of the philosopher.

At the time of their reunion and of their marriage, Raïssa was still a young girl, carefree, cheerful, passionate about music. She had just discovered Debussy and was enchanted by the life that awaited her in Paris on the arm of a young man who was promised a brilliant destiny.

THE ALLIANCE

Emmanuel Levinas then fulfilled his military duties. He was assigned to the Forty-sixth Infantry Regiment in the tour of

Auvergne, took the requisite classes, was made corporal and completed a course in interpreting Russian in order to finish as chief master sergeant.

In 1934, eleven years after his arrival in France to study at the University of Strasbourg, he became administrative assistant in the education department at the Alliance Israélite Universelle, the president of which, Sylvain Levy, was a specialist on India and a professor at the Collège de France.

The schools of the Alliance — the first of which was established in Tétouan, Morocco, in 1862 — had expanded across the entire Mediterranean basin and as far as the Near East with the purpose of propagating French culture. Its students numbered more than forty thousand in total throughout France, Morocco, Bulgaria, Greece, Syria, Palestine, Iraq, Egypt, Turkey, Iran and Algeria. The students received a solid, religious education and benefited from French academic curricula that were taught in French. The AIU brought any student from the Orient who wanted to come to the Enio in Paris, where the teachers of the future were made. Levinas was appointed assistant to the secretary general of the Alliance, Mr. Halph. He was mostly busy corresponding with the students and the teachers, a rather marginal function. He was confined to administration and had an office where he received future students and teachers. "He was extremely esteemed and admired," says Ady Steg, current president of the AIU, "but I always harbored a certain bitterness, a sadness that he could not be given the appropriate respect. At the central committee of the Alliance, if you go today and consult the documents from that time, you will find accounts of staff reunions that mention all of the members and then add parenthetically, 'also present was Emmanuel Levinas.' I truly resent that! He should have been placed at the head, if they took account of his personality and the responsibilities that fell to him. But that's how it is, that's tradition. I don't think he was hurt by it."

The pen was used as readily for writing texts as for giving accounts of recent projects in the monthly journal of the AIU, *Paix et Droit.* In April 1935, the review published a dossier on the eighth centenary of the birth of Maimonides. The Spanish government organized an official celebration in Cordova, and the chief rabbi of Paris, Julien Weil, delivered a speech that was published in the journal. Following that was a text, the first to be signed by Emmanuel Levinas, called "The Actuality of Maimonides." Faithful to the title, he writes, "The truly philosophical aspect of a philosophy is measured by its actuality. The greatest homage we can render it consists in mixing it into the preoccupations of the hour. The preoccupations of our time are particularly poignant. They concern the very essence of our existence both as Jews and as human beings. Judeo-Christian civilization is being called into question by an arrogant barbarism instated at the heart of Europe." And he adds, "Never before has the folly of the misguided been so large." This address, which doubled the regular size of the dossier, was supplied with a touching foreword: "This is the response of Jewish genius to its denigrators. It is also a reminder that, despite the disturbances of the moment, humanity has preserved intact its lucidity, its clairvoyance, its sense of true grandeur."[4]

A few months later, Levinas wrote a second article for the journal on "the religious inspiration of the Alliance," where the anxieties of the hour again burst through. "Racism," he writes, "constitutes a test that one must overcome rather than a problem that requires response. It is not worthy of refutation."[5]

MARITAIN AND ROSENZWEIG

Leafing through the numbered issues of *Paix et Droit* from these years, one notices how untrue it is to say categorically that the Jews of France were passive and powerless in the face of the rising peril, that they refused to see the dangers, or worse, that they wanted to hide their heads under the table. But it is true that they continued to have hope, and that they continued to believe in a kinship with Christians, Levinas in particular.

In October 1936, in a review of a book by Joseph Bonscriver, *Juifs et Chrétiens,* published by Flammarion, Levinas broached the subject with the line: "The antagonism between the monotheistic religions has subsided since Hitlerism threatens their common patrimony."[6]

In May 1938, he devoted an article to Jacques Maritain in which he repeats that Judaism and Christianity are equally caught in the sights of the Hitlerian enterprise.[7] One year later, in March 1939, in a text on the death of Pius XI, whose career he retraces as "a moment of human conscience" on the eve of the war, he dares to write: "In an increasingly hostile world that is being covered in swastikas, it is to the cross with its straight and pure limbs that we often raise our eyes."[8]

Levinas's encounter with the work of Jacques Maritain is significant. Initially taken in by Bergson and then, in a break with the master, Maritain converted to Catholicism at a young age after his encounters with Charles Péguy and, more importantly, with Léon Bloy, who went on to be his patron. The ambivalent patronage of the great pamphleteer of the end of the nineteenth century, whose tormented conscience is evident in a work such as *Le salut par les Juifs* (salvation according to the Jews), found a voice in Maritain. An antimaterialist, Maritain collaborated with l'Action français and participated in the *Revue Universelle* until Charles Maurras and the royalist movement were officially condemned by Rome in 1927. Preferring his religious ties to his political attachments, Maritain made a definitive turn toward Thomism and initiated a reflection on a social Catholicism that approached that of Emmanuel Mounier. In his work *De la philosophie chrétienne,* published in 1933, a fateful year, he attempted to derive an existentialism based on humanistic foundations from the theology of Saint Thomas Aquinas.

The possible dialogues with Levinas were therefore numerous. A note of trivia: Jacques Maritain also, throughout his life, was assisted by his spouse, who likewise converted to Christianity, was descended from Russian Jews and was also named Raïssa.

It was during the same period, around 1935, that Emmanuel Levinas discovered the Jewish German philosopher Franz Rosenzweig, who played a decisive role in his intellectual journey, as he came to explain. In Levinas's earlier works, few explicit references are to be found to this great older contemporary, few direct citations, even in *Totality and Infinity,* which otherwise situates itself quite clearly under the inspiration of the philosopher from Kassel. As Stephane Moses noticed, the similarities and the correspondences between the foreword of this book and that of the *Star of Redemption* are profound, echoing one another as variations on the same theme. And yet Levinas limited himself to saluting his precursor on the other side of the Rhine as "too often present in this book to be cited,"[9] which sounds a bit like what people say when they are fumbling for a handy introduction or when the subject is delicate and they say something like "too well-known to be worth mentioning."

Rosenzweig embodied a paradoxical destiny. Doubly an

heir of the Enlightenment, both the European one and the Jewish *haskalah*, he would develop a universal concept of the Jewish ethic, adapted to the times of the diaspora. His philosophy of anxiety, combined with the study of Jewish texts, revisited the essential question: What message does Israel have for humankind vis-à-vis Greek philosophy, particularly in light of this covenant, which the non-Jew does not know yet that he can no longer ignore? A tragic destiny, to a degree that neither Buber nor Levinas would know. The existential dimension of Rosenzweig's thought, redoubling its conceptual exigency, explains his rediscovery. No doubt the young reader of Husserl found a confirmation of his own Jewishness, together with a strong sense of human history. The debt would always be mentioned, even if it is always formulated in general terms, as if the personality in question were rather inhibiting. He was otherwise quite loath to dissimulate. The innermost motivations and motifs of the approaching works on the horizon, the basic motives driving the evolution of Emmanuel Levinas's own philosophy — the rapport between philosophy and religion, the approach to Judaism, the vision of the relationship between Judaism and Christianity — all of these were already there in the *Star of Redemption*.

We can hardly doubt, in any event, that this work made a deep impression on the young reader of that era, one of the very first readers in France who had access to the original German, and hence to the work altogether, since it was translated sixty years after its appearance in Germany.[10] This was a book that opened by invoking death, the cry of anxiety before immanent death, uttered by a soldier on the front in Macedonia in 1914, and that closed with the word "life" — a book that Levinas discovered just as another war, still more cruel and more devastating, was announced.

5 | Captivity

Europe, and France in particular, put its trust in the Treaty of Versailles even as the growing dangers began to assert themselves. Munich was a kind of crowning ceremony for Hitler, heralding the abysmal folly to come. For Emmanuel Levinas, who had chosen Paris as his refuge, the lessons were to flood in. No generation can hope to be exempt from all knowledge of bloodshed, but his generation came to know absolute horror. He might believe that he had chosen freedom, but he would come to know, firsthand, the experience of the camps, even if it was only a prisoner camp to which he was deported and not an extermination camp. Imprisonment and barbarity became unspoken elements, negatives, but, precisely as such, elements surviving in his philosophy. The heroic effort that demanded a repudiation of fatalism would, in a sense, remain the silent source of everything else.

The task of investigating the war years of Emmanuel Levinas, of describing them and transcribing them, faces a twofold obstacle: those who did not experience the camps are made sick hearing about it, those who did experience the camps are made sick talking about it. Between them lie the testimonies, and the trace, at times invisible or almost invisible, which never cease to haunt the work.

Six years after his arrival in Paris, Emmanuel Levinas, a noncommissioned officer in reserve, was mobilized to the front, like everyone else, comfortless but intent on doing his duty. He found himself among the hundreds of thousands of French soldiers who fell en masse into the hands of German soldiers and were transported, from bivouac to bivouac, to the frontiers of the Reich before being transferred to Germany and detained in a prisoner-of-war camp — victims of a collapse.

The battle of the Somme, on June 5, 1940, was lost within two days. General Rommel was in Rouen by June 9, and the Tenth Army, to which Sergeant Emmanuel Levinas belonged, was encircled and forced to surrender on June 18.

The previous day, Marshal Pétain asked for an armistice and declared on the airwaves: "It is with a heavy heart that I tell you: we must give up the battle." Without responding to the request for an armistice, the Germans made use of this declaration to push the French troops into surrender.

Four months later, at Montoire, Pétain would shake Hitler's hand and accept a collaboration. At the behest of the Germans, he declined American protection for French POWs in favor of the support of the Vichy government.

Raïssa's Letter

On October 24, 1940, Mme. Levinas addressed a letter to the president of the Commission of Revisions of Naturalizations, which amounted to a biographical resume, particularly for the years 1935–1939:

> "Mr. President," she writes,
> In anticipation of the implementation of the decree of revision of naturalization of foreigners pronounced after

the law of 1927, I have the honor of calling your benevolent attention to the case of my husband Emmanuel Levinas, naturalized on April 8, 1931, and presently a prisoner of war in the camp at Marne à Rennes, Transstalag (133). Born on December 30, 1905, in Kaunas (Lithuania), he arrived in France in 1923 in order to study philosophy at the University of Strasbourg. Receiving his Bachelor of Arts degree and then his doctorate at the University of Strasbourg, he obtained the status of a French citizen on April 8, 1931. He completed one year of military service in the 46th Infantry Regiment (1931–1933), as was taken into consideration in 1935 in the course of his admission to the corps of military interpreters in reserve. He was nominated Interpreter in Training by a ministerial decision on July 12, 1935, a rank comparable to that of master sergeant. In this capacity he carried out two calls of duty in 1937 and 1939. Mobilized on August 27, he was transferred in May 1940 to the 2nd bureau of the headquarters of the 10th Army stationed on the Somme, and was taken prisoner on June 18 to Rennes. We were married on September 11, 1932, and have a daughter, born on February 28, 1935, in Paris. My husband is a specialist in the study of contemporary German philosophy and has devoted a work on the subject (recognized by the Institute in 1932) as well as various studies in philosophical reviews.

Mr. Maurice Halbwachs, professor at the Sorbonne, who knew my husband as a student, has been good enough to send you a note on this matter. I should like to beseech from your high benevolence the favor of adding this note to his dossier, as well as the present letter. In the hope that the Commission of Revision of Naturalizations would readily recognize that my husband is a French citizen, which is something he has always been careful to honor, I remain very respectfully yours . . .

It is signed Raïssa Levinas, followed by her address, 29 rue Lemercier, Paris XVIIe. This letter, found in her husband's dossier of naturalization preserved in the National Archives, appears to be the evidence of anxious legal proceedings. Was there a real danger, then? Was Levinas at risk of losing the French citizenship that he had acquired six years earlier? Probably not. The POWs were protected under the Geneva Convention, even when they were Jewish. But Mme. Levinas, frightened by the discovery of the existence of revisions in naturalization, wanted to make sure that her husband would not end up among the deported, that the Geneva Convention applied to him, too, even though he was a Jew. She was worried because, upon being taken prisoner to Rennes on June 18, 1940, with the Tenth Army, Emmanuel Levinas was initially detained in France for a few months and only later transported to Germany for incarceration in Stalag XIB in the region of Hannover, where he remained until the end of the war.

IN THE STALAG

A few months after the collapse, Levinas and his comrades were brought to the frontiers of the Reich. Crammed into trains, surrounded by the Wehrmacht, the POWs were sent to Hitler's Germany to help him mobilize the German farmers and workers in preparation for the conquest of the USSR and Great Britain. There were 1,600,000 French POWs (4 percent of the population) in Germany spread out over more than sixty stalags and twenty oflags throughout the country.

Levinas was allocated to the camp at Fallingbostel, between Bremen and Hannover. Above the iron entrance hung the inscription "XIB," the name of the stalag. And a number, "1492," which he would always remember, the year of the expulsion of the Jews from Spain.

The camp, judging from the photographs, appears as a large central area with rows of wooden barracks on each side.

A German soldier would hand out a wooden placard bearing a number to each of the inmates. This was the prisoner's reference number for the duration of his captivity. He was to wear it constantly, on a little chain around his neck. Then they would take away each inmate's belt, leaving him his cap and military uniform. They would proceed to have their bodies and clothing deloused, their hair and the armpits shaved, and from there they would go to the showers. The prisoners were naked throughout these procedures.

Next, they were transferred to the barracks; each prisoner had to fall into line around a central corridor with rooms on each side. Every room contained, on each side of the door, a row of five triple-deck bunk beds, so that thirty inmates occupied each barrack. In front of the barracks, the German eagle presided, or sometimes the swastika. And one German soldier was posted to every barrack all day long, morning and night, completing the feeling of confinement brought on by the barbed wire, the watchtowers and the armed sentinels surrounding the camp.

Stalag XIB housed 32,000 French prisoners. "It was like the hippodrome of Longchamp," says Jacques Laurent, one of the many witnesses — veterans of the camp — I was able to interview.

In the central camp were the POW commandos. A hundred commandos were stationed there, appointed to the factories and the farms within an area of fifty square kilometers in the region of Hannover.

Regarding the farms, Mr. Evariste-Promez Cesarus, taken prisoner on June 12, 1940, near the village of Beaumont in the Ardennes, close to Sedan, explains: "Each prisoner had a reference number. The numbers were written on pieces of paper and put into a hat. Then, each farmer was asked how many prisoners he'd like to take with him. For example: You, how many do you want? Answer: two. So take two numbers out of the hat. The two numbers drawn were called out, and they would leave with their new boss."

Under the cover of a French uniform, protected by the Geneva Convention, the Jewish POWs were spared the lot of civilians. Their status as soldiers was respected in the collective. But this was not without actual discrimination. The Jews were set apart in the barracks, and among the commandos. Such was the case with Levinas, who was designated to a group of sixty-six Jewish inmates split up into two barracks, all of whom were appointed to be woodcutters.

A DAY IN THE CAMP

How did Levinas endure these five years of captivity from day to day? What was his life like? How did he withstand the pangs of hunger? The lack of freedom? The submission to the arbitrary? The separation from home? The monotony of the days and the nights? The anticipation of liberation? The bombardments of the last months?

Yves Durand, author of *Histoire de la captivité*, recounts the life of a woodcutter in Stalag XIB during the war: "A hard existence. The work in the forest was sometimes very hard, especially during the extreme cold of the continental winters in Germany. . . . A brutal wakeup at 6:30 A.M., regrouping at 7:30; the distribution of axes and saws; then an hour or two of marching in the winter dark to get to the worksite. At the site, a small fire is lit for keeping warm during the day. A feeble glow; a guttural yell: it's the foreman who gives the signal to work. Every day is the same: chopping, sawing, felling trees, the hands swollen in gloves that have to be carefully patched up again at night in the barrack if you don't want to lose your fingers to frostbite."[1]

André Monnier, today a resident of Petit Quevilly, interned in Stalag XIB until the end of the war, first in a work camp and then on a state farm, recalls: "The daily menu never varied. A bowl of soup per day and a loaf of bread weighing about 1.5 kg for seven prisoners. Two slices of sausage, a small cube of margarine. A few vegetable peelings found on the farms supplemented the menu. Of course, a small food parcel sent by the Red Cross was very welcome."

The inmates were allowed to send one letter per month, subject to censorship. The authorities supplied them with one sheet of paper with two flaps, one for the prisoner and the other for the response. Moreover, the prisoners were allowed to receive parcels, as well as K-rations from the American army delivered by the Red Cross. Until D-day, in any case. After that, the parcels stopped and the mail came less frequently.

Yves Durand notes: "At Stalag XIB, a refractory officer once refused to take his hands out of his pockets during a search session. Threatened by a sentinel, he chuckled to himself. He was shot and killed on the spot by a German officer."[2] He also reports how, during a typhus epidemic that broke out after the arrival of the first Russian POWs, the Jewish physicians were systematically rounded up to care for them, without being inoculated themselves beforehand. Finally, he mentions the testimony of a Red Cross delegation that had to protest against the fact that about fifty French soldiers and officers had the word *Jude* inscribed on their uniforms in indelible characters fifteen centimeters in height. It is true that this took place only in Stalag XIA, however, an isolated case.

Reveille. Roll call. The march into the woods. Return at 18:30 hours. Roll call again. Then each one is left to himself.

Reading for some — Levinas read Hegel, philosophical texts, Proust, Diderot, Rousseau — for others, playing at cards, makeshift games, chatting until lights-out at 21:30. All talking forbidden, of course. Small grease lamps were lit with long wicks dipped in oil or in margarine.

In a very rare text about this period, Levinas recalls the friendship of a dog lost in this prisoner's life in which nothing but a "small inner murmur" subsisted.[3] Bobby and his cheerful barks welcoming the exhausted inmates returning from work — something that lasted for a few weeks until the sentinels decided to chase him out of the camp — left the inmates with a fond memory. One of the veterans of the stalag, Bertrand le Barillec, captured at Rosporden, near Rennes, like Levinas, evokes this momentary distraction: "The *Posten,* the German employers, came to select the prisoners of the forest commandos in the mornings and brought them back to the camp in the evening. This is how Levinas could have known Bobby, who belonged to a German soldier in the guards' barracks on the other side of the barbed wire. . . . A dog, as everyone knows, loves his friends. Deprived of affection, the prisoners looked for this friendship anywhere. Dogs may be German, but not Nazi."

Levinas expressed this somewhat differently, paying homage to Bobby as "the last Kantian in Nazi Germany."[4]

To Resist

Every once in a while, the prisoners were rounded up in the central camp for a medical or dental checkup, or to go see the counselor. At Stalag XIB, the counselor was Father Pierre, of no relation to the founder of Emmaüs, who eventually became a worker-priest. Afterward Levinas would come to evoke his name, to family and friends, with recognition and gratitude. Likewise, he also paid homage to Father Chesnet, a Catholic priest, chaplain of the camp, who one day prayed over the grave of a Jewish comrade whom the Nazis wanted to bury like a dog. "Prayers," says Levinas, "which were in the absolute sense of the term, Semitic."[5]

All the testimonies of the veterans concur: Father Pierre was held in high esteem by his comrades. At first he was with the commandos, in the central camp, where he served as spokesman for the POWs to the Germans. He was known only by his first name. A man with heart, with a strong temperament, he knew how to stand up to the Germans. It was not long before he became undesirable, and was transferred to another camp.

Raymond Méril, from Saint-Brieuc, recalls: "There was Father Pierre, a bearded man, at the beginning of the captivity, who was called the *Deutsch Fresser*, the 'German-gobbler.' You see, they had to deal with him as the counselor of the camp, who fervently defended the prisoners. I think I remember that he was liberated quite early, because they wanted to get rid of him."

Bertrand le Barillec confirms this: "There were men in the camp who had resolved to fight to the maximum against the spirit of abdication and submission to the enemy. To begin, Father Pierre, the first counselor recruited near the International Red Cross in Geneva, who constantly inspired this will in all the commandos." And he adds: "Because I knew the kind of man he was, it makes me think that Levinas could have been the spokesman in the group."

On the whole, in fact, Stalag XIB was, according to many testimonies, a breeding ground for resistors. It was there that a group called the "screwball club" was born, around André

Ullman, Charles Bonnet and Michel Caillau, which initially brought together POWs interested in questions of philosophy and literature and made up the matrix of what became the RMPWD, the Resistance Movement of Prisoners of War and Deportees.

Michel Caillau, a nephew of General de Gaulle, who was made secretary-interpreter to a German physician at the camp infirmary, relates the story of this movement, which was hatched "in Germany itself, in the bowels of the enemy, in Stalag XIB in Fallingbostel, between Bremen and Hannover, by three French POWs."[6] He reports that at Fallingbostel, the camp and the commandos alike, because of their recruitment among political hawks, was made up of few Pétain supporters. The Vichy propaganda was not well received. Escapes were numerous, more than three thousand. And the majority of the inmates were rebellious "against the defeat of June 1940 and its causes, against the abandonment of the armistice, against the captivity, against Pétain and his government of collaboration and treason, against the German enemy and Nazism." Yves Durand also notes that there were frequent escape attempts at Stalag XIB.

All the same, the prisoners lived in the heart of Germany, witnesses to what happened between 1940 and 1945, and in close contact with the local population. As they were relatively protected, they could observe Nazi methods, especially on the Russian POWs. Did they know what was taking place elsewhere, fifty kilometers away, in the camp of Bergen-Belsen, or further, in the camps of Poland?

Jacques Laurent is clear about it: "We knew about the existence of four crematoria. When there was fat in our food, jokes were cracked, in bad taste, about where this fat must have come from."

A Community of Deportees

According to the testimony of some of the camp veterans, the captivity presented an opportunity for the prisoners to deepen their spiritual and religious life. This was true for the Catholics and the Protestants, and no doubt also true for the Jews, except that, for them, religious practice was completely forbidden by the Nazi administration. Services were sometimes celebrated by the priests who were present, masses took place in the open air, although of course they had neither a religious space nor religious articles. For the Jewish inmates, this was altogether out of the question.

Ernest Gugenheim, in an address given in the autumn of 1945, during the first reopening ceremony of the Séminaire Israélite de France, of which he was the director, recounted his experience as a "Rabbi in the Stalag." He writes:

> Neither the war nor the captivity interrupted or overturned the course of life, and our conduct didn't in the least follow the new principles. Only the traits that habit or the varnish of civilization had little by little effaced were exposed with piercing clarity. The best sentiments, but also the most base, ceased to hide away. In this life where material preoccupations forcefully took up a more than preponderant position, egoisms frequently came up against acts of solidarity and devotion. And it is understandable how a Jewish commando was no different from a Jewish community transposed onto the plan of captivity. This was a society of human beings similar enough to any human society placed in the same conditions of life, no doubt with a more sharpened sensibility that would take a longer time to blunt, and an intellectual curiosity that would require a longer time to disappear. It was likewise the moral image of a Jewish community with its rare qualities and all of its faults.

He adds nonetheless:

Often the ardent prayers of the Jewish commandos would ascend to the God of Israel. And this is one of the many memories cherished in a rabbi's heart, to have seen a growing number respecting *shabbat* by at least refraining from smoking. No doubt you will say this is an act of faith and of heroic will. . . . The laws of *kashrut* were not done away with by everyone. But above all I remember with emotion all those holidays that, like points of light, illuminated the night of our long captivity. I remember the first Yom Kippur that, in a dismal barrack in a foul stalag in Eastern Prussia, brought together more than one hundred prisoners in fasting, tears and prayers. And another Yom Kippur when the hard labor intensified the greatness of the fasting and sacrifice. I also saw the Hanukkah light in the copper menorah that, in the most somber days of our captivity, our gaolers scoffed at. Finally I think back on the last Passover seder in which we relived the liberation of our ancestors from a country of slavery, and when we could see, within reach, the breaking of the dawn of our own liberation.[7]

René Gutman is the chief rabbi of Strasbourg. His father, arrested in 1940, was detained in the same stalag as Emmanuel Levinas. Gutman keeps in his possession a map of the camp drawn in pencil and brought back by his father. He once brought a copy of it to Levinas, accompanied by a letter in which he asks: "Is this the face of evil?" And the response of the philosopher, in characteristic manner, was: "Evil has no face."

Like the others, like all the others, René Gutman's father had little to say, except to relate an inmate's nightmares, the perpetual feeling of being pursued (he had attempted to escape on one or two occasions). Brief allusions, on the night of Pesach, when he came to the verse from Hallel in the Haggadah: "He raises the poor from the ashes and removes the filth from the wretched" (Ps. 142). Terrible memories of a Yom Kippur when the inmates were forced to act out a wild boar hunt and made to walk around on four legs. Images of an exhausting life whose story is never told, but whose details can be guessed at. The prisoners had the right to one day of leave in which they could have a tooth removed in the infirmary. And Gutman's father returned without a single one of his teeth.

One more testimony: some inmates managed to maintain a certain faithfulness to religious tradition. Gutman's father took care to wash his hands before eating bread.

The only detail recalled about Levinas, is that the two men once studied a few passages of Talmud together. This is how it was reported — without further elaboration, without knowing what form this study could have taken.

Camille Ajenstein ran a barbershop in Belleville before the war, and in Stalag XIB he was "Figaro" to everyone. During his five years of internment (he was taken prisoner in Dunkirk in 1940), he was in Levinas's barracks in the bed next to him.

"My father was a woodcutter, like Levinas and the other inmates," recalls his son, Dominique Laury. "But he spoke some German, in a broken way mixed in with Yiddish, so he served as an interpreter at one point. He was pretty resourceful: he received books and newspapers from Switzerland, and he managed to go to the toilets with his newspapers. He could stay there for hours. This was his way of tuning out."

Ajenstein became more "highbrow," more philosophical. Was this the influence of Levinas? In any event, it fell to them to collaborate on theatrical activities. One was a writer, the other an actor.

Dominique Laury is a journalist. He worked for the political segment of France 2 for a number of years. When Jean-Pierre Lustiger was named archbishop of Paris, Laury worked for the news segment of the channel and was assigned to make a report on the theme "Ashkenazi and Sephardic Jews in France." He remembers ending up at Levinas's place on Michel-Ange, and being received rather coldly — evidently the subject did not interest the host, who looked for polite ways to get rid of the strange visitor, not to mention that he was literally panicked upon seeing the camera — until the reporter revealed his identity: he was the son of Camille Ajenstein, his mate in captivity in Stalag XIB. Immediately Levinas's face lit up and he called out to his wife: "Raïssa, it's the son of Figaro!"

The interview never took place. The couple went off in search of photographs. Little cakes were served. "I was no longer the journalist from France 2, I was the son of Figaro, and I was being given a private party."

"Figaro" sent letters in which he spoke of an "illness" during the deportation. "I hope that the illness will not reach you," he wrote. He returned from Germany one fine morning, practically on foot, with hemorrhoids.

Léon Jakubovitz turned ninety when I met him. This was the only direct witness, still alive at the time, who was a companion in Levinas's barracks. I went to see him in a retirement home located in the twentieth district of Paris. He was arrested in Brittany, close to Coëtquidan. A soldier in the artillery unit of the foreign legion, he, too, spent five years in Stalag XIB.

The recollections were blurry, the memory failing, and the faces became jumbled together. But the images of the time were vibrant. "We got up at dawn, went out with a peeler to peel the trees, and a hatchet for cutting them. We were in groups of five. Wilhem, an old German, would lead us."

At noon, the group of prisoners would stop to get a piece of bread, and then go back to work until around six in the evening when they were handed a bowl of soup. "We stopped working, we didn't do anything at night."

He recalls that a shoemaker in the group became attached to Levinas and always ran after him. That Levinas had a little notebook in which he'd scribble now and then. That he would sometimes read to them from texts that would make little sense to them. That he was a bit withdrawn, keeping to himself somewhat.

After the war, they seldom saw each other again. Except once. When Léon Jakubovitz's son married Danielle Schul, daughter of Chief Rabbi Schul, it was the latter's cousin, the philosopher Pierre-Maxime Schul, who served as one of the witnesses to the marriage. Consequently, Léon Jakubovitz remembered his old comrade from the stalag, who was also a philosopher, and asked him if he would be the second witness. And it was yet another comrade, Chief Rabbi Gutman, who officiated the marriage.

Why did these men, who lived without any privacy from each other for five years, who could do nothing but recall their misery, not keep in touch?

No doubt, says René Gutman, the reason was a desire to rebuild. To forget those days.

VISION OF THE ABYSS

Throughout these years of captivity, Levinas received letters. He knew about the role played by the Monastery of Saint-Vincent de Paul, near Orléans, in rescuing his daughter, and then, on a second occasion, his wife.

Raïssa, who remained in Paris, stayed in an apartment lent to them by Maurice Blanchot for a while, and then moved in with the Poiriers, pharmacists at Rouen. She sent postcards regularly to Simone in Paris. "I have very good news about your papa," she writes, "He asked me to tell you he

loves you very much. I hope you're being good. I'll be seeing you soon."

She rejoined her daughter in 1943, and both of them
remained in hiding in the monastery under the names
Marguerite and Simone Devos. The maternal grandmother,
Frida Levy, was less fortunate. She was denounced and
deported, but not without sending her daughter a postcard
from Drancy: "I cannot write to you today. They told us that
we are to be deported to an unknown destination. . . . I'm
not afraid. . . . I hope that you too will be strong and take
courage." This was her last letter.

Nineteen forty-four. The invasions of Normandy and
Provence. This was the final period that revisited the exhaus-
tion and discouragement of the beginning. The period of
the Allied bombardments, the return of hunger with the brutal halt to parcels, the end of all contacts, the interruption
of all mail. Discipline was tightened again. More frequently,
the Germans left the POWs without protection against the
bombs (the shelters were reserved for the Germans).

On April 18, 1945, the vanguard of the Second English
Army (General Demrey) arrived in the village of Keshevaya.
The Allied tanks advanced and the Germans began to retreat.
The German officers raised a white flag over the Komman-
dantur, and the English made their entry into the Fallingbostel
camp and the barbed wires were demolished. This was the
German collapse. It was liberation, and the final exodus.

The POWs were cast onto the roads, thrown anew into
trucks. Exhausting marches under the bombardments, with
machine-gun fire from Allied planes and the difficulty of getting fresh supplies. For all of the POWs returning to their
country and their homes, the term of the ordeal was served.
The start of a normal life, the joy of reunion.

For Levinas, the return from captivity also meant the discovery of horror. His whole family in Lithuania had been murdered. His father, his mother, his two brothers. All of them were executed by machine-gun fire in Kaunas.

Levinas never spoke about it. A few discrete lines, placed in the dedication of *Otherwise Than Being*, which appeared in 1974, mention the mute pain, the absence of consolation and the tumor that cannot be cured: "To the memory of those who were closest among the six million assassinated by the National Socialists, and of the millions on millions of all confessions and all nations, victims of the same hatred of the other man, the same anti-semitism." And below, in Hebrew, like an epitaph on a gravestone that his family members could not have: "To the memory of my father and master, Rabbi Yehiel son of Abraham the Levite, my mother and guide, Dvora daughter of Rabbi Moshe, my brothers Dov son of Rabbi Yehiel the Levite and Aminidav son of Yehiel the Levite, my father-in-law Rabbi Shmuel son of Rabbi Gershon the Levite and my mother-in-law Malka daughter of Rabbi Chaim." And just below that, the traditional acronym for the usual religious expression, "May their souls be clutched in the link of life."[8]

The experience of captivity was nevertheless decisive for Levinas: the encounter with the most simple things, the ordeal of loss and of liberty, the sensation of time, deliquescence, misery, absolute passivity, fragility, precariousness — everything that continually tormented his work.

"Busy with the labors of the day, we were no longer existents, but living beings," writes a veteran inmate of the camp in Munster.[9] Levinas's first book, published in the aftermath of the war, was called *De l'existence à l'existant*, "Existence and Existents." It had been partially written during his captivity, with its compelling pages on the *il y a,* on the anxiety before Being and the horror of Being.

LIKE A REVELATION

To explain Levinas's relationship to captivity, we again turn to someone who did not know the philosopher, never saw Stalag XIB, but whose testimony is penetrating.

Vaclav Havel is a playwright and essayist, a veteran spokesman of Charter 77, founder of the Civic Forum, and president of the Czech Republic since the revolution of 1989.

In October 1979, the tribunal of the city of Prague put the signers of Charter 77 on trial and condemned them for their subversive actions against the state, which they had committed by disseminating texts that were considered harmful by the court. Vaclav Havel was himself condemned to four years and six months of imprisonment.

From June 1979 to September 1982, from the depths of his prison cell, Havel sent letters to his wife, Olga. On several occasions he refers to reading an essay by Levinas that was sent to him — in photocopy form — by his friend Yvan, "a magnificent essay like a revelation." He writes: "In Levinas, I sense not only the gathering of spiritual traditions and the millennial experience of the Jewish people, but also the experience of a man who spent time in prison. It is perceptible in every line, and this may also be the reason that this essay touched me so strongly."[10]

Havel did not say which essay was in question, but how did he guess that Levinas had experienced captivity? What made him feel this so strongly? How is this work marked by the seal of prison so clearly that it is immediately recognizable as familiar by the inmates of prisons in Ruzyne, in Hermance and in Plzen-Bory? He writes to Olga: "Levinas's idea that 'something must begin,' that responsibility establishes an ethical situation that is asymmetrical, and that this cannot be preached but only upheld, corresponds in every detail with my experience and my opinion. In other words, I am responsible for the state of the world."[11]

In a text titled "Nameless," which consisted of a collection of homages to his friends, those near to him, those with whom he felt an affinity and a dialogue (Agnon, Buber, Celan, Derrida, Blanchot, Jabès), Levinas writes:

> We must henceforth, in the inevitable resumption of civilization and assimilation, teach the new generations the strength necessary to be strong in isolation and all that a fragile consciousness is called upon to contain at such times. We must — in reviving the memory of those non-Jews and Jews, who, without even knowing or seeing one another, found a way to behave amid total chaos, as if the world had not fallen apart — remembering the resistance of the maquis, that is, precisely a resistance having no other source but one's own certainty and inner self; we must, through such memories, open up a new access to the Jewish texts and give new priority to the inner life.

This text, which opens up like a terrifying cry over the abyss — and wherein we recognize accents familiar from Primo Levi — ends up with an ardent appeal to the "heart of hearts," to "the obligation to lodge the whole of humankind in the shelter — exposed to all the winds — of conscience."[12]

The trace

There are words that remain attached to him that one can no longer evoke without the feeling of venturing into his domain, jumping into his universe, being in the world of his work.

The trace. A notion that is all the more fascinating in his thinking because it places itself between metaphysics and the police detective. Someone has passed by, has left a trace behind and is eclipsed. Someone, or something, or nothing definite. Nothing but a trace of something that did not happen. The sign of a passage that never had a place. An imprint that is always "already there" and that escapes the power of memory, eludes every reminiscence and evades every attempt to reinstate its origin.

A trace that comes from who knows where. A trace without a past. Or yet a trace whose past can never reveal a presence, but only testifies to that which can never be said. A trace like a retreat. A trace like an ancient promise. A trace that one can feel only as that which has always been missing.

Whence was it drawn, this notion that is so strange and beautiful?

From Proust, perhaps, and the passage of the "missing Albertine" where the memory of forgetting itself becomes suffering?

Or rather, as one might suppose, from the beginning, from Exodus 33, where God is manifest in his trace alone? "Show me your glory!" beseeches Moses. And God responds: "You will see my trace. As for my face, that is not visible."

6 | THE ENIO YEARS

"After Auschwitz, I had the impression that in taking on the directorship of the École Normal Israélite Orientale I was responding to a historical calling. It was my little secret. . . . Probably the naïveté of a young man. I am still mindful and proud of it today."

It was on a single occasion that Levinas admitted to others this secret; he would make a confession. It was in 1986, during a dinner put on at the Community Center in Paris marking the philosopher's eightieth birthday. Edmond Elalouf had organized a reunion for a group of alumni from the Enio. The guest of honor was at the center of the tribute, at ease, joyful, a bit nostalgic. It was the first time he spoke about his earliest years as principal of the school, about what he had tried to accomplish, the space he had wanted to create, the life he had wanted to introduce there. "To be Jewish," he said simply. "Not the pride or the vanity of being Jewish. That is worth nothing. But an awareness of the extraordinary privilege of undoing the banality of existence, of belonging to a people who are human before humanity."

The participants remember in particular how at the end

of this address a tiny piece of paper folded in four was produced, as often happened with him. It was a sublime variation on a Talmudic theme, a commentary on the word "thanks."

What do people say, asks a Talmudic sage,[1] when the leader of a minyan, a quorum of men at prayer, recites the well-known blessing of *modim* (a saying of grace that appears in the eighteen benedictions of the thrice-daily prayer): "We acknowledge that you are the Lord our God and the God of our fathers forever, the rock of our lives, the shield of our salvation from generation to generation. We give thanks to you and proclaim your praises, for our lives that rest in your hands, and for our souls that are entrusted to you"?

While the *hazan*, the leader of the quorum, pronounces these words of recognition and bows down, the others recite a "little *modim*" that is similar to that of the leader (on the page of the prayer book it appears side by side with the leader's *modim*) but with some key differences. If the intention of the major *modim* is clear and the object of acknowledgment explicit, the minor one seems to lack an object altogether. It can only be said to have an object if one follows the opinion of Rav, according to whom one must continue to the end of the text where everything becomes clear. "We give thanks, O Lord our God . . . for giving you thanks."

An exercise in gratitude, in short, for the simple ability to say thanks. Thank you, my God, for this possibility that you have given to us to be able to thank you. Thank you for letting us be in your presence, in a relationship that consists of giving thanks. Basically, one cannot give thanks without first making oneself thankful in this manner. This homage paid by the former principal to his students is something that all of those who were present still carry around with them.

A COMMEMORATION

Guy Petitdemange relates a telling incident. The day after he took part in a tribute to Levinas at the Sorbonne — a tribute organized one month after his death, under the auspices of the United Jewish Social Fund — he went to his usual barber in the rue Mouffetard quarter in Paris who complimented him on his presentation. "Ah, you were there?" "Of course I was there!" "So you knew Levinas?" "Are you kidding? He was a Moroccan Jew like me!"

At the community center in Paris, on boulevard de la Fayette, in 2000, five years after his death, another reunion of Enio graduates was organized by Edmond Elalouf. There were about thirty men and women of middle age, for the most part Moroccan in origin, who had been students at the school during Levinas's time. They came together to reminisce and share anecdotes about the man they had all followed, respected, feared, admired and sometimes loved.

The students addressed him as "Monsieur Levinas." In their memory, he had an air about him that was rough, severe, austere, with a side that was paternal, affectionate, at times joking. Very transparent at times, and at other times very opaque. Certainly elusive.

Many of those present at this small reunion had been members of the very first class, the one right after the war, the first years with Levinas. The school was still located on rue d'Auteuil. The girls were not in the same building; they had lived in a student residence in Versailles, arriving each morning and departing at night by bus, which was something that regularly provoked the legendary anxiety of the principal, who was stationed by the school entrance, his arms waving. One striking observation that could be drawn from the various recollections of the alumni, stretching across the years from 1946 to the end, is just how little the physiognomy of the institution had changed over the years. Everything was set in place at the beginning, and permanence prevailed: the Saturday course on Rashi; the Friday evening discussions of current events, which spilled over into Saturday afternoons (until cake made by Miss Blum, under the direction of Mrs. Levinas, was brought out); the omnipresence of Dr. Nerson; the invitations to the principal's *shabbat* table.

Everything had been set in place at the beginning except that the first years had been years of apprenticeship for him as well. He was not an educator by training; he had to learn to become one. Chance had placed him there. Chance, or rather, as one of the participants said, a kind of providence.

At first, there was only he, his wife, and Miss Blum the bursar. In the absence of a secretary and an administrator, he had to manage everything himself, which also meant that he was much closer to the students. As for the very first class, it numbered no more than thirty or so registered students.

We can imagine the encounter between this Lithuanian Jew and all those dark-haired children coming from a country he knew very little about. He had met Jews from Morocco during 1938–1939 when he had worked at the Alliance. But the class before the war was very different from the one that came at the beginning of 1946. These young people were not only fervent in, but also quite keen in every area of Jewish practice. Levinas was particularly impressed by how any one of them, it did not matter who, could easily lead the prayers. They knew all the Psalms by heart, they were adept at reading the *sefer torah* (the parchment roll of the Pentateuch) with the proper vowels and cantillation, also known by heart, and they could divide the day-long Rosh Hashanah or Yom Kippur service among four or five *hazanim*. There was a core group among them, moreover, that prayed regularly and conscientiously. Their manner of prolonging the songs, of taking their time to articulate everything, would bother him to some extent, and he was often known to jump into a lesson even before the *hazan* was finished.

An Ashkenazi among Sephardim, a philosopher in charge of a denominational school, a man approaching maturity plunged into a nucleus of youthfulness. It is something of a wonder that the role of this institution, which was to ensure the perpetuation of Sephardic Judaism by giving it the wherewithal to confront modernity, was not completely effaced — even if Emmanuel Levinas was completely besieged.

"Apart from the somewhat paternal aspect he invested in the role of principal," Edmond Elalouf recounts, "I think he was conscious of his post as an influence in the formation of the future ranks of the Moroccan Jewish community. We were not just students, we were not ordinary pupils, we were the future teachers in the schools of the Alliance. And he was very attentive to the formation of our character, with the initiation into the Parisian world, into Western culture, that awaited us, we who came from Morocco."

Prosper Elkouby, originally from Meknes, was also in the first class, before he went on to become a supervisor in the school. What he remembers most fondly is the Rashi course on Saturday mornings: "You had the sensation of a discourse being constructed before your eyes. His thought would visibly grow with each sentence he spoke. For my part, I grew up in the Jewish traditions of my grandfathers, but at that time I was in a phase of rejection. We were stuck on the letter of the text, we didn't go beyond it. And there, suddenly, this knowledge that I thought belonged to another era found itself validated, actualized. In any case, it spoke to me. It took some time. But he had a more positive view of our rabbis, a reconciliation that was stylish. Our history was accelerated.

Levinas played a very important role. He allowed us to reconnect the lines with the past."

Might Levinas, then, be described fairly as an educator or pedagogue? On that account, the assessments show some divergence. According to Simon Elbaz, a retired real estate agent who belonged to the class of 1948–1952, Levinas had a clear instinct for teaching. "I have a very specific memory. He had this anxiety over not having yet written something substantial. And he would speak to us of his future projects. He had a plan: not only to be principal of the high school, but to open up a teaching institute as well. He said: being principal does not interest me that much, at some point I should like to head a teaching institute. He was confident of his abilities as a teacher, therefore." Roger Cohen, a lawyer from the class of 1946–1950, remembers this a little differently. "It was known that he was a prefect before the war, and when the school opened, he was given this position. He thus manufactured a persona for which he was probably not prepared. My memory is distinctly that of a philosopher in the making. He regretted not being known yet, at forty, as Kant had already been at this age. But he added, by way of consolation, that Kant did not write his *Critique of Pure Reason* until he was sixty-six, which meant that he still had a few years ahead of him." For Simon Hazan, a computer scientist from the much later class of 1963–1965, and possibly because of this time interval in between, the distinction is really necessary, "It struck me that this was a truly great thinker, a philosopher, who, in the aftermath of the war, by pure chance, found himself placed by the Alliance at the head of a school. But everyone knew he had never been an administrator, and I wonder to what extent one can really speak of him as an educator."

THE CODE

It is true that the philosopher and educator did not always succeed in administration. The fact is that Emmanuel Levinas had difficulties communicating, both with students and with teachers. He often lacked self-restraint, was easily irritated. When a boarding student did not come down to the morning prayers, he would conclude: "He must have stayed out all night!" When someone arrived late, he would become enraged, he would get so choked up that he would be unable to speak.

He also dreaded rebellions. On one occasion, a small, subversive wind, a breeze, blew into the school dining hall because of a strange cheese soup that had been served. So the kids decided to sing the *Internationale*. Levinas came down the stairs, panic-stricken. Prosper Elkouby, a supervisor, had to calm him down: "But Mr. Levinas, taste must be acquired, it cannot be imposed." Elkouby reflects on this incident: "This being a small group, it was of no great consequence. But he certainly could not have managed a large institution in this manner."

Another time, there was an uprising among the students because they were served — again a gastronomic sedition — couscous boiled in water, perfectly tasteless. A petition circulated. All but one signed. Levinas exploded, and marched up and down the hall in front of his office. At the end, passing by the nonpetitioner among the boarding students, he shot at him: "Well, Mr. E —, don't you believe in solidarity?"

Some of the old students came to hate him for a long time, and even much later they still reproached him, in absentia, for his roughness, his moods, his unpredictable side. One day he expelled a boy from the school who had been caught in the supermarket on rue d'Auteuil with a stolen record album among his belongings. This was a relapsed thief, to be sure, but the boy was only sixteen. They tried to make the principal reconsider his decision, to no avail. The adolescent had to buy a return ticket to Tangiers. Discipline, for him, was not to be tampered with.

At the same time, Levinas took special pains to find the best teachers for his school, both for general studies and Jewish studies. When a student expressed a desire to learn Greek, or Latin, or Italian, he would hire a private teacher just for him. This happened time and again. The difference between the purely intellectual task at hand and the broader issues of education was quite clear in his eyes. Resourcefulness for one, discipline for the other.

With regard to religious practice, ritual and participation during prayer, everyone at the commemorative gathering agreed that he was exacting, on others and on himself. This was the rule, but it was possible to bend it. No one was asked to believe, no one was asked to do as others do. Roger Cohen explains: "When it came to respecting rules and tradition, I had the feeling, but maybe it was wrong, that he always kept a certain distance in relation to what was taking place before him, the prayers, the liturgical responses, the genuflections. It seemed to me that he was somewhat estranged from all this." This "distance" was also noticed by Emile Amzallag, a university professor from the class of 1946–1948: "The image I have in my mind of Emmanuel Levinas during the daily prayers is of him with a Bible or the Talmud in hand. While we were busy with our ritual recitations, he was immersed in study. One might well wonder whether the love of learning was not more urgent for him than religious practice."

Simon Sisso, retired, a big fan of Andalusian music and hiking, administrator of a synagogue in a Paris suburb and a member of the earliest class of graduates, remembers more his joyous mood during the festivals in contrast to his seriousness in study: "Pesach is a wonderful festival. We could invite whomever we wished so long as it was two or three days in advance. *Succoth,* also. We would build the booth together. I would see Levinas across from me, beaming, very happy. Just as he was happy after services on *shabbat,* when he would sit down at the table, when he would make *kiddush,* and when he would dunk a morsel of bread into his café au lait bowl. Mrs. Levinas would say to him: Watch out, you're on a diet! And he would grumble: Yes, Yes. But he would taste everything. He would eat everything prescribed by the diet, and then some extras on the side." Perhaps this agrees with the summary judgment of Gabriel Cohen, veteran supervisor, today a physiotherapist: "Levinas was religious and he wasn't religious. It was curious, because he never missed a service. He could have been anywhere, but at five o'clock on the nose, he would be there for *minha* or *arvit.*[2] At the same time, he had certain behaviors that were rather disconcerting." Due to the inevitable religious and cultural differences between the principal and the students, there nevertheless remained, intractable, a certain freedom that was properly his.

"He did not cover his head outside services," recalls Prosper Elkouby. "Had he been Sephardic, it would not have mattered. But for the Ashkenazim, this was fundamental."

To which one might add — minor sins — that Levinas took the elevator on *shabbat,* and drank nonkosher wine. About the wine, he held that the prescript was part of the commandments linked to *galut,* the present period of exile. But he would never tamper with those commandments in ritual matters that he did observe. To Fabien Durand, in charge of discipline at the Enio, he apparently once said, "The Torah — it's this!" and made the gesture of rolling phylacteries on his arm.

PATER FAMILIAS

No less important was the other Levinas, a good-natured principal, a family man who enjoyed a good joke, especially imitations. That is what really made him laugh. He would provoke them, without taking offense, when they were on the verge of being disrespectful.

Simon Sisso recalls, "I would often imitate the teachers, especially during Hanukkah and Purim. He loved this, because in my imitations he could perceive a bit of the life of the school. I remember one of these holidays. Michael was two or three at the time, he was always at the table with us. And his father would make him say: Sisso! Sisso! So he would sing out, with thick lisp: Thitho! Thitho! I had no choice, this would immediately get me going, and this always made him happy. Once, we put on a skit in front of the students. Levinas was giving an exam, he was talking about Kant. Says the examiner: Kant is all you need, think of him as your Bible. The students respond: Right, sir, it's the Bible; see, 'Kant' read backward spells 'Tnak,' *Tanakh*, the Bible! And I could see Levinas in the first row, busting out in laughter!"

Sisso recounts another revealing anecdote about Levinas's sense of humor. Climbing up to the dormitory, Levinas heard someone say "*merde*." He turned toward Gilbert Malka, a supervisor at the time, who was blushing and mumbling excuses. So he assured him, "No, no, don't worry, Mr. Malka, you don't say it often, and when you do say it, it's always in quotation marks." And before leaving the room he added, "Unfortunately, one cannot hear the quotation marks."

Levinas's affectionate side, the attention that he gave to relationships, which morally sustained the boys who stayed at 59 rue d'Auteuil, and the girls residing in Versailles, the way he was careful not to contradict, not to prohibit, his anxious but attentive manner, that's what really struck Roger Cohen:

> There was a fairly mundane episode that nevertheless made an impression on me. We were seventeen or eighteen. I met a young girl on the street, and I was supposed to meet her on a Sunday. Because we couldn't leave without some explanation, I put together a fictional invitation to a family gathering. But the stationery on which my girlfriend wrote "We are delighted to request your presence, etc. etc." was blue, I think it was even perfume-scented. He did not fall for it, but he said to me with half a smile: "Fine, alright, go ahead." I had permission to go.

This way of being delicate with people was part of his legacy, and it cropped up in daily affairs, seemingly mundane, as Edmond Elalouf also remembers:

> The first years after the opening of the Enio, he had asked Chief Rabbi Jaïs to be our Jewish history professor. Chief Rabbi Jaïs responded: 'I'm afraid I can't, but you know, you can ask so-and-so. This literally sent him into a frenzy. He said: "Think about it, not only did he refuse, but he proposed someone else, which I didn't ask him to do, and he gave me his name. This puts me in a terrible position. What if this person finds out tomorrow that I don't want to take him on? He'll be upset with me." I found this rather remarkable. This way of putting things, this kind of reaction, is something we often experienced. I am Levinas's pupil more in this respect than with respect to any theory of alterity. Unless you consider that, basically, they're the same thing.

Viviane Bensimon knew Levinas for only one year. She came to Paris to do her one year of teacher's training and took the courses at Molitor in preparation for her CFEN (high school certificate), all the while lodging in Versailles and commuting to rue d'Auteuil every morning and for *shabbat*.

"Levinas was not my philosophy professor, but he was the principal of the school. I very much liked and respected him. When I arrived at the Enio, from Morocco, I was a young girl, a bit spoiled. I had some difficulties fitting in. Mr. Levinas immediately took notice of this, and he often invited me into his office. I remember having discussions with him. I also remember it was the first time I had ever seen a fireplace. It was in his office. I had no idea what a fireplace was. He was like a father to me. He comforted me when he saw that I was upset. I often confided in him, even little anxieties of different kinds."

Ariel Wizman, today a television producer and animator, spent two years at the Enio, in 1978 and 1979, as a member of the last class, and knew the Levinas who was coming into notoriety. More relaxed, less anxious. More open to conversation with, if not to confiding in, a young man with an aptitude for philosophy who was something of a rebel.

"We were adolescents," he says, "we did all kinds of stupid things. These youths coming from Morocco, or people like me who were looking for some direction, found a paternal dimension in him."

Levinas then became a professor at the Sorbonne. But his presence at the school remained strong. What struck the young Ariel Wizman, like those before him, was the austerity, even severity, and the degree of strictness, and how this was mixed in with a good dose of humor and sensitivity that made dialogue continually possible: "He never spoke in a light manner. He set a high standard for responding to whoever happened to be the interlocutor. He responded to a student exactly as he might have responded to Cassirer."

The out-of-breath speech in search of just the right word, the labor of thinking so evident in his work, always unfolding in a succession of awkwardness and illumination, like the opening of a clearing, a concrete vision of the psyche, as if one could take it up with a material approach, and then an instinctive and brutal reticence before every show of pride — all of this came together at once. "At no moment," says Ariel, "could we show pride or self-satisfaction. His very presence made this utterly impossible. He himself never showed it. This was a person untouched by any aspiration to notoriety."

The principal was no less impassioned about matters of social existence, continuing to consider his mission as encompassing a complete education. There was a period of terrorist attacks in Paris, and the CRS began to protect Jewish schools. Policemen were stationed at both entrances of the Enio, on rue Michel-Ange and on rue d'Auteuil. Having nothing better to do, some of the students decided to call out from the windows: "CRS-SS! CRS-SS!" This sent Levinas reeling, mad with rage that the SS might be associated with representatives of the French state.

It would be wrong, however, to infer some sort of staunch conservatism from this. For example, he felt very strongly about the condition of prisoners, having a very personal perspective on the fate that society reserves for its outcasts. He would say, it is necessary to punish with severity and treat with love. He maintained, for instance, that the culprits had to be placed in a pleasant, well-kept room, must have access to books, and may watch television. What mattered, for him, was the privation of freedom; that alone was the penalty. "I was struck by this notion," says Ariel Wizman, "because I thought that an entire philosophy could be articulated from it, that it was the skeleton of a true moral system: penalty for actions and benevolence in intention."

He employed tactfulness whenever others were concerned, girls and boys alike, but he also showed a genuine care concerning relationships between them. Quite a few couples were joined together in the classrooms. It was not without some pleasure, in fact, that Levinas watched over these school-corridor trysts that would at times develop into something serious. He was often asked to be a signing witness at marriage ceremonies, and certainly every time he was invited to a wedding, he made it a point of honor to be of service. Upon hearing that Claude Sultan, a future rabbi, was seeking the hand of a young woman at the Enio in marriage, he invited him to spend a *shabbat* at the school. "We need to know the future spouse of our student," he insisted.

SCOUTS, GUIDES AND THE TALMUD

The director of a Jewish foundation, Rafy Bensimon, the husband of Viviane, whom he did not meet at the Enio, gives the following narrative of his first *shabbat* at the school.

He had arrived from Morocco with a high school diploma in hand, ready to do his year of teacher's training. During the first week, he asked permission from the principal — at the time, he did not know him to be a philosopher — to spend *shabbat* outside the school. Levinas granted him permission without any questions. The young man wanted to go to Orsay, to the home of Léon Ashkénazi (a.k.a. Manitou), quite unaware of the "crime of lèse-majesté," as he put it, that he was about to perpetrate. Upon returning on Monday, he was called up to the fourth floor: Do you have family in Paris? Where did you spend *shabbat*? He reported: "I spent *shabbat* at the school in Orsay." Immediately he saw Levinas turn pale. "What did you do in Orsay?" The young man mumbled: "I am on good terms with the principal in Orsay and I have a few friends there, so I spent *shabbat* in a familiar environment." "I wasn't sure at which point I had gotten myself into deep waters," recalls Bensimon. "He said to me:

'Are you a rationalist or a mystic?' I hardly understood. I said: 'No, no, neither. I was just looking for an agreeable environment, so I went there. I very much like Manitou and I like (here I completely drowned myself) his commentaries on the weekly *Sidra*.' He said to me: 'Very well, you will do me the pleasure of coming to hear my commentaries next week.' So on the following *shabbat*, I went to hear his lesson in Rashi, and afterwards, every week, I had the privilege of taking his courses."

After this calamitous beginning, Bensimon hit another snag: "There was something about me he didn't understand. He expressed a liking for me on several occasions, then one day, he said to me, 'You have to explain something to me. You don't seem like an idiot to me, yet I'm told that you are involved with the Boy Scouts. Please explain how a person like you can be involved with the Scouts.' So I had a long conversation with him about the pedagogical worth and the virtues of the Boy Scouts, which seemed to hardly convince him."

To be sure, the Boy Scouts and Girl Guides were not Emmanuel Levinas's cup of tea. That was the domain of Marguerite Klein, who was the head of the girls' school in Versailles. A pediatrician by profession, she had been married to Chief Rabbi Klein, who was assassinated by the Germans during the war, and, as a widow, she had decided to live out the rest of her days in faithful devotion to her husband and, as an act of piety, took up the task of accomplishing everything that he would have done had he remained alive. She was dedicated to education, particularly that of the young girls of Versailles, and to the Girl Scouts, taking on the presidency of the Jewish Scouts and Guides for seven years. Now, this Scout business would not wash with Levinas. The "Good Deed," the mountain hikes, Baden Powell, the claps on the shoulder and the informal mode of address — it took him a while to have any interest at all in these things. Marguerite Klein had to battle with him every time the vacation period began, to obtain money for young girls who wanted to participate in the hikes. Levinas nevertheless consented in the end, and even ended up sending his daughter Simone on occasion.

Basically, apart from the fact that the Scouts and Guides distracted the students from more important tasks, such as the Talmud, Levinas no doubt saw in it an artificial conception of service that, for him, assumed a completely different reality.

The "Talmud group," which I often heard about, was born during the 1960s. The Jewish schools in Morocco were desperately in need of qualified Jewish studies teachers for the last years of high school, so the Alliance decided to select and train a small circle of teachers in a particular curriculum. The courses took place at Livry Gargan, in an unfinished little house, with Rabbi Epstein. Uniquely dedicated to Talmud and its commentators, the program was continuous, spread over two years. This nucleus, among other things, was supposed to energize the whole school. Gabriel Cohen took part in it:

> At that time, Levinas established a Talmud course on Tuesday nights with Dr. Nerson, in addition to the Saturday lesson in Rashi. It was attended by auditors, some religious people like Dr. Elie Temstett, and the students of the Talmud group. I had the impression, moreover, that this Tuesday night course was partly born because of us. When he saw that we went to Rabbi Epstein, he wanted us to be bound to him instead. What we got, of course, was a completely different view of the Talmud. What it expressed, what it explained, was a different world. I remember thinking that no one could argue with him, that he was a master without peers.

Simon Hazan was also among them, but for him the praises go to the man first, before the talmudist: "With my Talmud education completed, I had to return to Casablanca or continue my studies in Israel. For personal reasons, since my parents were no longer in Morocco, I wanted to continue my studies in Paris, but I had nowhere to go, and not a cent in my pocket. No uncle, no aunt. I was alone. I opened up to Levinas. For my first year on the faculty of mathematics in Paris, he graciously let me have a room at the Enio and, in return, asked me to teach a tenth grade Bible class. I took on the course. I was given room and board, I had my laundry done, and I was even given a small allowance. This was his human side. Besides the great philosophical ideas that he dealt with, he also knew how to handle situations of distress that were close at hand."

MADAME THÉRÈSE

No one ever knew her real name, but the alumni all remember her well. They called her "Mme. Thérèse." She was Levinas's shadow. Nothing could be done without her; the entire administration of the school fell to her. From October 1953 until Levinas's departure from the school, which coincided with her own, she worked at his side, even sharing the same office during the first years. "I didn't have an office of my own, but I never thought about the fact that this meant he didn't have one either," she muses today.

The first years were difficult. The two of them worked alone, attending to every little matter, the problem of the broken showers, the student outings, the girls who had to be watched so that they did not end up with the boys, and vice versa. And this, 24/7. Levinas did not dare go for a walk with his family on Sundays because he had boarders. And for *shabbat,* he went down to dinner with the students. He was completely immersed in the school and flooded it with his presence.

"If he took this on himself," says Thérèse Goldstein, "it was because he wanted to be in the fray, surrounded by Jewish students, hoping to transmit something to them. It wasn't at all because other options were not open to him. He had his situation at the Alliance, he could have remained there. In the office on rue Bruyère, he could have written a lot more, no doubt. There is no question whatsoever that he was utterly committed, and he said as much elsewhere."

When Thérèse Goldstein thinks of him today, she always pictures a ball of energy. This was a period when he smoked a lot of unfiltered Gauloises cigarettes and always spat out tobacco fibers. "He was constantly bubbling. Big bubbles in his brain. Covered in sweat after simply giving a philosophy class. He worked without stopping. Constantly boiling over. The fact is, he had an impressive capacity for work. This was a man who was physically very powerful, who was always running. I don't know if the students were prepared for him. He spoke very quickly, his mind working faster than his mouth could speak. It was permanently overheating, a turbine, this man. He was able to accomplish so many things in one day."

One day, Mme. Thérèse tried to catch him in the street when he had forgotten a document. She ran after him just after he had stepped out. He walked as he always did, with small steps, but at a very rapid pace. Thérèse was young, so she ran. Levinas walked. But she was unable to catch up to him. "He had an extraordinary energy, he was in good health in general and had a great resilience."

When she arrived at the school in 1953, Chouchani had just left Paris, and Levinas began to write. He had already been working on *Totality and Infinity* and did not have much of a social life. The family was very close-knit (they telephoned each other ten times a day, or looked for each other in every corner of the Enio); received few guests, or just the Nersons; took vacations from time to time, in Switzerland or in Normandy, always in places where a piano could be found since that was something "sacred." The rest, the philosophical part of Levinas's life, escaped Mme. Thérèse. On a friendly basis, she would help type out articles or certain chapters from books, but she was busy above all in resolving his administrative worries.

"I saw the evolution he underwent," she recalls, "but I had no idea of the immensity of the thing. Then again, I was young, I didn't have the maturity. And he himself was not aware of it. He was never preoccupied with his public life. Things partly came to him through the friendship and visits of Jean Wahl, but I never had the impression that Levinas was interested in notoriety. He worked, the ideas bubbled forth inside of him, but until the end, he was surprised. He did not understand why his work was so worthy of admiration. He was always very modest, you know."

From 1953 to 1961, he was the only philosophy professor at the Enio, as well as the only Jewish studies teacher. After his oral examination for his thesis in 1961, he began to teach at the University of Poitiers, but he remained principal of the school, at least in title, until 1973. During that year, as the institution entered into a contractual agreement with the state, his status as a civil servant consigned to tertiary education made it impossible for him to continue as principal of a private institution. The administrative responsibilities of the nonresident were thus handed over to Mme. Picard, an English teacher at the time. But in effect Levinas remained the dominant figure at the Enio until his official departure in 1979.

"I didn't know very many philosophers," continues Thérèse Goldstein, "but this was someone who lived out his philosophy in his life from day to day. He was no different in his attitude. He had a humanism, or a humanity that was — I'm not sure how to say it — quite remarkable. He lived the lives of others. He was concerned with those who had a problem, either a personal one or in relation to the other students. He did everything to help people and to get them out of their difficulties. For example, when we had to calculate the salaries of the lower-paid staff, he would say to me: 'Figure it out so that they get the best deal.' That was his formula."

STUDENTS AND DISCIPLES

In 1979, Levinas gave up the directorship of the school. He was replaced with a teacher who came from Morocco, David Serfaty. Levinas nevertheless continued to live in the same place for a while, until his family moved into an apartment at the other end of rue d'Auteuil, closer to the Saint-Cloud gate. José Garzon, who was in charge of the boarding school, went to see him every week to bring him his mail and to note down the passages to be studied that week in the traditional Rashi course, which had to be passed along to the student in charge. The course continued until his very last years, or in any event until the beginning of the illness that eventually took his life. Over the years, Garzon would show up every Tuesday morning at Levinas's apartment. Often he had to wait for the former principal to finish his morning prayers and wrap up his phylacteries. Levinas continued to take interest in the life of the Enio, to pose questions about this or that person. The school thus remained family for him, until the end. No one could say that its significance was limited in the life of the philosopher. Perhaps it even gave him strength. In any case, he never ceased to cultivate connections with the little galaxy of the "old high school," its thousands of alumni, now spread out all over the world. Many of them came to pay him a visit from time to time to say hello or to help out in the traditional Saturday course. Some of them carefully held on to letters in which the master inquired about them, asked for news about their families, gave them advice where they had asked for it, or simply took an interest in what they were up to.

And were there actual disciples among them? A difficult question. Actually, it provoked an awkward reaction when I posed it to the alumni who were reunited in the community center in Paris. Many among them remembered having been somewhat disoriented by his teaching style, both in the philosophy classes and in the Rashi lessons. But the question can be debated.

Gabriel Cohen's reaction: "When one stood before him, he had a monopoly on speaking. He did the talking. If one asked him a question, it would immediately make him uncomfortable, he would actually become destabilized and lose his train of thought. It was strange enough; but this perhaps explains why he never had disciples." He adds, nostalgically, "Despite all the consideration, all the affection we have for him, I think that in a certain way he was oversized for the Enio. He was a 48 for a 42 waist."

Meyer Sisso, a teacher involved with a Jewish community in Aulnay-sous-Bois, has very confused memories about the course: "At the risk of being shocking, I would say that he was not a good teacher. He had a philosophy course that was very rich, but disorganized, muddled. You couldn't always understand what he was saying. He would open up a parenthesis without ever closing it. It was afterwards, in reviewing the notes that you could make sense of it, after giving some order to what he said. We were teachers ourselves, and we came to think of his class as, in effect, a lecture. There was very little exchange with the students." This perspective is challenged by Jean Ellouk, a graduate of the first graduating class who became an engineer, and who wants to be counted among the circle of devotees. He strongly objects: "I was a philosophy student of Levinas. I had a very peculiar relationship with him, very different from the ones I've heard about. I suppose now that it was a challenge at the time, but I let myself talk to him as an equal. Outside the philosophy course, on Saturdays, I would sometimes go on walks with him in the gardens of the Enio, where the reproduction of Michelangelo's sculpture of Moses can be found. We'd walk around and chat. About philosophy, phenomenology, psychology. I was very taken by all this at the time; I believed I could continue along that path. Things turned out otherwise. But in any case, I can say that it was easy to communicate with him, he welcomed discussion, and contradiction. It was not merely a lecture, one could speak freely."

Multiple testimonies, at the risk of seeming contradictory, and perhaps at the risk of a poorly documented posterity. Simon Hazan, who remained an assiduous talmudist, challenges the very question of discipleship as it is typically posed. Hazan continues to read a page of *Gemara* every night before he goes to sleep, and for a number of years, in his own manner, has been keeping up the spirit of the traditional Saturday Rashi course for a small circle at the Enio synagogue. He reflects: "In the Talmud, the question is asked: How do we know about the resurrection of the dead? The rabbis discuss the issue over a dozen pages or so, wielding arguments, citations and allusions. And among the allusions, a reference is made to a passage from the Song of Songs where there is mention of 'one who makes the dead move their lips.' This is given as proof that the dead are resurrected. But in what situation does this happen? When one quotes someone who is dead, when something is said in his name, when what he said is now relevant. Levinas may not have left any disciples behind, but thousands of students are still able to make his lips move."

7 | THE RASHI COURSE

Rashi — as Rabbi Shlomo ben Itzhak (1040–1105) is known acronymously — the illustrious biblical and talmudic scholar from medieval Champagne, composed a commentary on the Torah that became a classic, a reflection on the sources that itself became a source. Tracing his steps footprint by footprint, Emmanuel Levinas, a Lithuanian Jew living in France, would rejuvenate the art of exegesis. The craft, as the poet René Char might have said, would attract diverse personalities, each arriving by a different road, but each one of them concerned with *meaning*.

No account can recreate the living voice embodied by Levinas's readings. But here, in the form of supplementary traces and stenographic summaries, taken from one weekly *sidra*[1] reading or another, are some impressions and memories of a few *shabbatot* on d'Auteil.

THE RITUAL

As soon as the eleventh hour approached, the congregants rushed in to look for their books and take the first seats near the desk of the master.

The fact is that the farther away you were from the first rows, unless you had a trained ear or knew how to lip-read, the more inaudible was Levinas's voice. The best moments, those when a personal trait came through, were always whispered, just barely suggested. So in the back rows one would invariably hear "What?" and "What did he say?" cropping up here and there like murmurs of approbation rebounding off the speaker's words in successive ripples.

The oldest devotees of the course remember how, in the early years, Levinas gave two courses on Saturday. The first one in the morning, on Rashi. A second one, in the afternoon, geared primarily toward the school students and focusing on literature. There was constant reference to Tolstoy, Dostoyevsky, Proust, Agnon — the authors he liked and tried to get others to like by applying the same discipline — unveiling the profound sense of the words, making these texts about particular lives vivid, always reading with imagination, even the most arduous passages and the driest passages. "All the great books," he said, "are sacred books."

TALK ABOUT THEM

The expression is taken from a passage that is recited twice daily, in the morning prayers and the evening prayers, and is found in the weekly *sidra* (Deut. 6): "Hear O Israel, the Lord is our God, the Lord is one. And you will love the Lord your God with all your heart, and all your soul, and all your strength. And these words that I command you today will be upon your heart. And you will teach them to your children. And you will talk about them." Rashi explains: "So that what is essential in your words be hallowed, make them essential and not an accessory."

"But to what extent must one talk about them?" asks the master. At what point does one become *yotzei*, meaning, at what point has one completed one's duty and been released from further obligation? The philosopher recalls how, upon receiving a doctorate *honoris causa* from an Israeli university, and in response to laudatory speeches, he gave an address on the Bible and Hellenism in which he commented on this expression. What it means, perhaps, is that one must "talk about them" until one comes to talk about them in Greek, until one translates the teaching pointed to in Deuteronomy 6 into the language of philosophy, which is to say, essentially, until these teachings have been made accessible to everyone. Addressing the little group, Levinas adds, laughing, "But rest assured, once one has begun to speak Greek, there is still a lot to talk about."

HERE AM I

There was an imperceptible dramaturgy at work behind these classes: the straight reading, the labor of cracking the text, translating word for word, the explanation of a point of etymology, of grammar or logic, or, very simply, the unraveling of the narrative. It was the student who was charged with the task, and those from the school took it seriously, even a little solemnly. Then, with a smile, or a pirouette, the master would suddenly quit the text, forget the students and take off on one of those expositions in which he so excelled. He would build it until the delicious, awaited moment arrived like a gushing. Everyone anticipated this dazzling instant, and when it came, a sense of delight ran through the audience.

This week he commented on a few verses from Genesis where Abraham responds to the divine call with the word *hineni,* "here am I," in the accusative mode. About this word, Rashi comments, "A sign of modesty and availability."

"The affirmation of the self, the sovereignty of the 'me,' is overtaken," explained the philosopher, always happy to find themes that were dear to him. "It is a Here-I-am that is also a Do-with-me-as-you-will." And he added, "Without these saintly figures, the Torah would be nothing more than a page of eloquence!"

Then he closed his book, looked at his watch and asked the regulars, "Do we still have a few minutes?" Everyone responds with an ardent "Yes!" It is the moment, everyone knows, of the talmudic apologue, always selected in thematic relation to the biblical passage just read, or at least to the weekly Torah reading.

This time, it is a text from Tractate Yoma (20b–21a): Why is a voice better heard at night than during the day? Because of the movement of the sun that scratches the sky like a rattle. What sound can be heard from one end of the earth to the other end? The noise of the sun, the noise of the mob in Rome, the noise of a soul soaring into the heavens.

Silence falls on the classroom. The first row, the regulars who would not miss a session for anything in the world, nod their heads in silent appreciation or exchange knowing looks. The lesson is complete with this "noise of a soul that soars."

Go

"And God said to Abram: Go, leave your land, your birthplace, and the house of your father, to the land that I will show you" (Gen. 12).

"Go to yourself" would be the literal translation of this *lekh lekha.* The philosopher cites a similar Russian expression where the "go" has an inward sense. "No one speaks Russian here?" he asks with a slightly vexed tone.

"And you will be a blessing." You will be a source of all benedictions, says Rashi, you will be the measure of all benedictions. "Excellence in these texts," explains the master, "is not an abstract notion. It is attested to by human figures like Abraham."

"Go to the land that I will show you." God avoids designating the land by name, says Rashi, in order to make it more precious in Abraham's eyes. As in the episode of the near-sacrifice of Isaac where God asks Abraham to take his son, his only one, the one whom he loves. His son, but which one? I have two! The only one? But each one is an only son to his mother! The one he loves? But I love both of them!

"And Abram took Sarai his wife, Lot the son of his brother, and all the goods that they had accumulated, and all the souls that they made in Haran."

Rashi's commentary: "Abram converted the men, and Sarai the women. And the text considers this conversion as a begetting. As if they had forged souls, as if they had made them."

We pass over to the talmudic passage following the lesson. On this one occasion, the instructor picks up the "Steinsaltz" — a modern edition of the Talmud that features a Hebrew translation alongside the original Aramaic — from the school library (this time he did not have the little piece of paper folded carefully in four). The passage is from the Tractate Berakhot (34b).

What distinguishes messianic times from present times? Nothing more than Israel's "subjugation to kingdoms," which is to say — the master explains — politics. As for the future world, in the Garden of Eden, the talmudic text continues, "no eye has seen it."

Not even Adam? it is asked. No, say the rabbis of the

Talmud, not even Adam, because the river, the Gikhon, cuts across the earth and sequesters the Garden of Eden.

But what, it is asked further, is meant by the expression, "no eye has seen it"? What is this category of things that the eye does not see?

Well — listen to this sublime, magnificent response, exclaims the philosopher, lifting his arms and moving his lips like a gourmand — it is "the wine contained in the grapes of the first seven days of Creation!"

PROPHECY

The features striking, the neck floating in the collar of his shirt, the principal prepares to sit down at his table to begin the class. But first, before starting, he confides to the little circle of regulars how the last verse of the *haftara*, the section from the prophets that is read at the end of the service after the Torah reading, sparked a certain excitement in him. It is from Amos. "God had spoken, who would not prophesize?" Yes, says the instructor, rather enraptured, who would resist being transformed into a prophet?

Prophecy as a moment of the human condition, as inspiration. Prophecy posed as the fundamental fact of being human. It is I, holding up the universe.

We proceed to the weekly *parsha*. "And Jacob settled in the land of his fathers, in the land of Canaan" (Gen. 37). Rashi comments, "Jacob wanted to achieve some tranquility, some rest; so that is when the troubles with Joseph began." There is no rest for the righteous, insists the master, the righteous may not slumber. To be righteous is to be awake.

But it is the personality of Joseph that evidently inspires him this morning. "I had another dream, and behold, the sun, the moon and the stars bowed down before me." This is to be understood, says the master, in the sense that everything smiles upon him, a kind of grace. His father reproaches him: "What does this mean? Will your mother, your brothers and I bow down at your feet?" And Rashi is surprised at this question: is his mother not dead? Rashi then answers his own question: From here we learn that every dream contains useless aspects.

"Nothing is properly thought through in a dream," explains the teacher, "it is not like a page of Talmud. Judaism cannot be built on dreams."

THE ROCK

"And Jacob left Beersheba for Haran" (Gen. 28). Rashi asks, Why does it not say, "And Jacob went from Beersheba to Haran"? Answer: When a righteous person leaves a place, he leaves a void behind. So long as he is there, he is the glory of the city, its radiance, its majesty. As soon as he leaves, glory, majesty and radiance grow dim.

The philosopher's face becomes animated: "Paris is not its lights, its streets, its traffic; it's Bergson, it's . . ." The audience waits for the next item, the next name, which does not come. It is Bergson.

A second verse: "And he reached the place." Rashi explains: The ground advanced under his steps, it came toward him. "And he fell asleep because the sun had set." Rashi explains: "The sun set quickly, before its proper time, to permit him to sleep." "He took rocks from the place and placed them under his head." Rashi: "The rocks argued among themselves, 'Upon which one of us should the righteous one lay his head?' . . . until God fused them all together into one single rock. And this is why it says later: And he took *the* rock he had placed under his head."

The following verse: "And he slept in this place." Rashi: "This is a term of exclusion. Hitherto, he had not slept. During the fourteen years he spent with Shem and Ever, he had not slept for a single moment, teaches the Torah."

And the master comments: "A strange idea — that a righteous man could shut an eye!"

Followed by the text: "The ground on which you slept, I will give to you and your descendants." Rashi: "God folded the entire land of Israel under him so that it might be easier to conquer."

The master highlights this peculiar manner of playing with time and space. The ground that advances to meet the patriarch, the rocks that gather and fuse into a pillow for him, the earth that folds up to facilitate his journey, the sun that sets early to let him sleep.

He continues, after some frivolousness — "Do you have time?" "Yes!" cries the little rock — with a passage, not from the Talmud, but from Midrash Rabba (65:9).

Abraham, reports the midrash, clamored to God for old age. Why? Because a man and his son show up and we do not know who to honor. This is the reason, it is said: "And Abraham was old and full of days."

Isaac asked for suffering. "Because if a man dies without having suffered, he is dealt with more stringently in the next world." This is the reason that "the eyes of Isaac were dimmed."

Jacob asked for sickness. "Because it is not good to die without warning." This is why it was announced to Joseph, "Behold, your father is ill."

FACES

He is short, stocky, voluble. Originally from Egypt. He always sits behind the central table so that he can only see the speaker from the back. He listens with one ear, or in any event something seems to leave him indifferent, the philosophical digressions or the low voice perhaps. What does interest him, those moments when he leans in with his ears perked, like a ready spy, is when the master is about to make a citation, or better yet, when he is fishing for one. At this moment, our little man leans in, absorbed in concentration, and the phrase suddenly pops out, as if by magic. This is because Mr. Cohen holds everything inside his head. If one cites the beginning of a verse from Psalms, or Prophets, or a liturgical text, he immediately finishes the citation or provides the verse number. This is the role he has chosen to play in the course, and this is what gives him pleasure.

From time to time, the master searches for a quote, or seems to search for one — for the sheer pleasure of hearing him give the reply — and he turns his head gently toward Mr. Cohen, or puts out the question, and right away, as if by a miracle, the words emerge. Afterward, the quote-master becomes disinterested, the problem is no longer his. But at the instant when he is solicited, he is happy, he smiles, at ease.

What do the attendees like about the course, fundamentally? What makes them come back? It is this, this pleasure in experiencing a shared knowing. This communion around a book. This way of keeping it legible, of maintaining a vital connection to it.

This week we read the episode of the exodus from Egypt. The student reads the passage of the "bitter waters" (Exod. 13). God shows Moses a tree. Moses throws the tree into the water, and the water becomes sweet. The philosopher explains the meaning of this teaching. It is sometimes necessary to traverse the harsh forest of apprenticeship, the rough ride that reveals its softer corners only near the end.

Everyone assumes that there is also an allusion here to his manner, at once severe and pleasant, of tackling texts. The brutal woods and the sweetness of the water.

AFFECTION

Large eyes of a faded blue, salt-and-pepper hair, a handsome man, very distinguished, a bit mystical. He is a musician, he used to compose for piano, until he encountered God, who now monopolizes his time. Now he runs to synagogue, puts phylacteries on everyone who crosses his path, and brings the good word to the four corners of Paris.

Unable to leave the synagogue after services and yet equally undecided about joining the classes, he wavers back and forth. Over the years, the regulars, who used to feel sorry for him at the beginning, have come to watch with amusement the little game of successive entrances and exits. The circle of students presently settle into their seats around the old master. The designated student begins to read the first set of verses from Rashi's commentary. It is then that his trailing steps can be heard approaching. He hesitates between two chairs, then decides to remain standing, sits down for a moment, retraces his steps, exits through the synagogue door, returns through the corridor, before disappearing altogether.

He is not really attracted to Levinas, who is too rationalistic for his tastes. What he has is just a touch of affection for him.

THE CLOUD

Among the "fauna" of the course, there was a strange couple. She was blind, always attired in lively colors, her head covered in a white kerchief. During services, she sat in the first rows in the women's section, following a large book in Braille. One could see her lips moving and her fingers scanning the pages to the rhythm of the prayers. After services, she would sit near the master, with her companion at her side. She chose the best seat, made herself comfortable, as if sitting down to a feast. As soon as the class began, she silenced everyone around her, listened with extreme attention, her face leaning toward the speaker, her mouth open as if to better savor the words. She did not hold back from commenting on what was said to her neighbors, now and again slipping in a blessing in Judeo-Arabic or invoking divine protection.

Her companion did not speak. He had a hieratic face, a blotchy complexion, and a large, somewhat wild, salt-and-pepper beard that made his face longer. He was dressed like a Hasid, with a long black frock, a felt hat and long white fringes dangling from the waist. They held hands, riveted one to the other. From time to time, she would turn to her neighbors. He did not say a word.

The instructor would often look at her. At times one even had the impression that he was addressing himself to her, that he singled her out from everyone to be the witness to or the spectator of his demonstration. He would speak to her, and curiously enough, in such moments, as if she vaguely perceived something, her face would rise slightly and nod in agreement.

Sometimes one could almost believe that the class was for her. As in the last verses of this week's text: "Moses went into the midst of the cloud" (Exod. 24), to which Rashi adds: "God made a road for Moses inside of it." A beautiful exegesis, stresses the philosopher. We must grope for a footpath in the fog, but a little bit of fog must always remain.

THE LAW

This week's Torah reading contains the Ten Commandments (Exod. 18). As usually happens at this time of the year when this portion is read, the master likes to recall that tradition enjoins us to place the first five commandments across from the last five, so that the first one and the fifth one are face to face. To "I am the Lord your God" responds, as an echo or an elaboration, "You shall not kill." God's manner of revealing himself is to inscribe himself in the face of the other like a prohibition against incursions. The only way to fear God is to fear for the other.

A double intentionality, comments the philosopher, as when you say that you are "afraid of the dog" to signify that you are "afraid for yourself." A girl in the audience whispers to her neighbor, "That's funny; my dad, who is a complete atheist, only calls on God when it's a matter of protecting me!"

The master turns to the last verses of the reading: "And everyone saw the voices." Rashi: "They saw with their eyes what could only be heard." A musician in the class remarks out loud, triumphantly, "It's like in music, you see the score, and you hear the voices."

"And Moses approached the cloud where the Lord was." This is how it is in Judaism, explains the master. It is necessary to move aside the obscurity in order to discover a spark of the divine.

At the end of the class, he is in conversation with a few of the students who surround him discussing a book that is about to appear in print, a collection of essays in which he pays homage to one of his own masters before the war, in his native Lithuania. "Yes, for him, nothing existed but Europe.

And Europe meant Germany, Goethe, Schiller . . . while France, Bergson were negligible entities."

THE POOR

"If you see the ass of your enemy bent under its burden, take care not to turn away; help him to unload it" (Exod. 22). Everything is brought back to concrete cases, explains the instructor. What does the "Love your enemies" of Christianity mean? Precisely this, to help your enemy's donkey suffering under its burden.

Furthermore: "Do not be partial to the poor in his litigation." Rashi interprets: "Do not give him honor in the litigational process by thinking: he is poor, he deserves to be shown some favor." The philosopher comments in turn: "The proletariat must not be exempted from the human condition."

The talmudic passage chosen this week is taken from the beginning of the Tractate Berakhot. This is the first tractate of the Talmud, often picked up by beginners, and the class is well acquainted with this classic passage.

From what time may one recite the *shema* in the morning ("Hear O Israel," the key liturgical recitation in the mornings and the evenings)? Answer: once daytime proper has begun. But how do we know daytime has begun? Two initial opinions are offered by the sages of the Talmud: either when one can distinguish white from sky blue, or when one can distinguish white from leek green. Alternatively, a third criterion: when one can recognize the face of an acquaintance at a distance of four strides.

Ritual, commandment, liturgy, rejoices the philosopher — look for their signs in the appearance of a face in the light of day.

FOR SAYING

From the weekly Torah portion, the master has chosen the description of the construction of the sanctuary by Betzalel (Exod. 31).

"And God spoke to Moses with these words." The word *lemor* may be translated, as the student has just done, following the traditional translation of the French Rabbinate, as "with these words." But this is only one possibility. Literally, by itself, the word means "for saying." Ah, this *lemor!* When he was in full form, the philosopher could give five or six interpretations of this word — probably the most frequent in the Bible — which he received from his own master. This time, he limits himself to one of them: "God spoke to Moses for him to repeat it."

The student reads on: "See, I have called by name Betzalel, son of Uri, son of Hur, from the tribe of Judah, and I have filled him with a divine inspiration, with wisdom, with intelligence, with knowledge . . ."

Rashi explains each one of these expressions. Wisdom: "This is what one hears from others and understands." Intelligence: "This is what one understands by oneself from things that can be grasped." Knowledge: "Divine inspiration."

Here, says the philosopher, we have three modes of apprehension that need to be interconnected. Pure sensitivity or inspiration cannot exert itself without being put to work by intelligence. Intelligence cannot by applied until it is joined to an apprenticeship. It is the harmony among the three that excites emotion and compels admiration. The veritable work of art must draw from these three components.

And the verses that recount the breaking of the tablets of the law? Whenever he came to this passage, without fail, he would underline the fact that the fragments of the first set of tablets were piously preserved alongside the second set within the area of the tabernacle — an image of a sanctuary transporting stones that were whole together with broken pieces. Accomplishment and rupture. Acquiescence and doubt. Affirmation and fracture.

SOBRIETY

"And the Lord said to Aaron: Do not drink wine, nor strong liquor, neither you nor your sons, when you enter the Tent of Meeting" (Lev. 9).

This divine prescription, an invitation to sobriety addressed to the high priest of Israel, follows upon the episode of the death of Aaron's sons, Nadav and Avihu, who "brought a strange fire before the Lord, which he had not commanded."

Rashi explains what this "strange fire" signifies: "They entered drunk into the Tent of Meeting."

What we have here, comments the philosopher, is a rejection of effusiveness, of religious enthusiasm, of ecstasy. Judaism is a religion for adults, sober adults. The approach to God is never a mystical adhesion. It is an obedience to the Most High. It is not a communion.

EVIL TONGUE

"And the Lord said to Moses and Aaron: if someone has a swelling or a scab on his skin, and his skin has become leprous, he shall be brought before Aaron the priest or to one of his sons" (Lev. 12).

He must be isolated, explains Rashi, in the same manner that he himself provoked isolation through gossip and slander, through bad-mouthing, the "evil tongue."

The philosopher particularly cherishes this relationship

established by the commentator from Champagne between the "evil tongue" and leprosy. As if the "they say" of the gossiper, whispered into someone's else's ear, were suddenly brought into the open, mushrooming on his face, affecting his entire body, and even his clothes and dwelling. As if the cunning insinuation, proffered in secret, away from the public eye, was in itself the onset of leprosy.

It is a reminder, moreover, that in the Jewish tradition, speaking evil, becoming guilty of the "evil tongue," means simultaneously involving the guilt of three individuals: the author of the gossip or slander, the listener, and the one spoken about. All three are held responsible and culpable. The interlocutor could have lent a complaisant ear, if need be, or, in any case, could have cut the chatter short. But the subject of the gossip is also not exempt. He is absent, to be sure, but we can assume that he would not have been indemnified by this gossip had he not opened himself to attack somehow, had he not somehow incited the "evil tongue" in spite of himself. No one leaves this affair entirely innocent.

PROSTITUTION

The instructor concentrates on the end of the weekly Torah portion, where a certain woman is in question, Shlomit bat Divri, whom Rashi identifies as a prostitute.

"It happened that the son of an Israelite woman, whose father was an Egyptian, got into a fight with the children of Israel. A quarrel arose in the camp between this son of the Israelite woman and an Israelite man. And the son of the Israelite woman pronounced the holy name blasphemously. So they brought him before Moses. His mother's name was Shlomit, daughter of Divri, from the tribe of Dan" (Lev. 25).

How do we know that she was a prostitute? Rashi derives this fact from her name, Shlomit, which comes from *shalom*, "hello," and Divri, which comes from *davar*, "word." The medieval French exegete explains: "She chattered endlessly, saying hello to this one and to that one, hello to everyone."

Rashi, comments the philosopher, thus derides chatter, this speaking to everyone without taking responsibility. The redundancy of the word, the free word, or the excessive word — that is the beginning of prostitution.

MOSES

The weekly Torah portion deals with the death of Moses. "Moses went on to address the children of Israel. See, I am one hundred and twenty years old, and I can no longer go out or come in" (Deut. 29).

Rashi: "I can no longer go out from, or come into, the words of the Torah. The traditions and the sources of wisdom became opaque for him."

Moses no longer had access to his own sources, comments the philosopher. And the midrash adds that in a dream he saw himself in the talmudic academy of Rabbi Akiva, where, mysteriously, he could not follow the lesson.

Making a reference to the end of the text — "No one knows the place of his burial" — the midrash, moreover, relates that Moses himself did not know where he was buried. He did not know the last words of his own work. This surprising midrash sets up as a principle the fact that exegesis is always both a fidelity and a treason.

Is this not to some degree what the philosopher attempted every Saturday in his lessons? At once to comment and to subvert? To flow with the tradition of commentary in order to breath a new vigor into the text?

LINEAGE

The lesson was very brief. From the beginning, the attendees could sense that he was not feeling well. He remained sitting in front of his open books while coffee was being served nearby in the school cafeteria.

A young girl read out loud clearly, articulating each word, just as he liked. In other circumstances, he would have complimented her warmly. But now, he seemed absent, enfeebled. The class lasted fifteen minutes, then he asked to be excused.

"These are the descendants of Aaron and of Moses" (Num. 13). Rashi comments: "For what reason are the descendants of Moses not mentioned (and only those of Aaron)? When one teaches the Torah to the sons of one's fellow man, it is as if one had engendered them oneself. The true descendants are students, those whom one has taught."

"You see," says the philosopher, "this is why I stayed, to tell you this. That the true filiation in Judaism is giving instruction."

8 THE TALMUDIC LESSON

Rabbi Daniel Epstein, the Hebrew translator of the *Talmudic Lectures,* describes Levinas's approach to the Talmud as a "phenomenological reading," a kind of "phenomenological midrash" that consists in reading each passage by inscribing it into the more general context of the *sugia,*[1] and in lighting up the hidden horizons of the text, the forgotten, the ignored, the obfuscated.

This, essentially, was his method. No doubt it was as much the product of his phenomenological development — he began to give his talmudic lessons as soon as he completed his magnum opus, *Totality and Infinity* — as of the visits from the formidable Chouchani.

The Talmud rejects the theoretical and the conceptual in order to turn fully to everyday life, to matters of human commerce, family relations, birth and death. "Back to the things themselves!" said the phenomenologists. "Sublime materialism!" Levinas would say one day.[2]

These texts hardly count as writing, properly speaking. At least, they are indifferent to style. They are the traces of a teaching that was originally oral, and the fact that they are dialogical discussions precludes any closure. Each reader enters into the discussion and participates in it with the uniqueness of his personality, with the irreplaceable character of his reading. The contribution of each reader in each era traverses history. Commentaries are juxtaposed on commentaries, weaving together the very life of this work.

What Levinas learned from Chouchani was the refusal to ever see an archaism, or to ever take it lightly; an approach that consisted in his introducing himself to the text and then nourishing himself by drilling, by returning, by turning it over and over; a subversive way of reading that had nothing pious about it, that even justified itself as a conquering freedom. In the introduction to his first collection of talmudic lessons, Levinas writes: "To this freedom, [this approach] would like to invite other seekers. Without it, the sovereign exercise of the intelligence recorded in the pages of the Talmud can change itself, too, into the litany or pious murmur of a consent given beforehand, a reproach that could be made to talmudists whose familiarity with these pages is nevertheless to be envied." And he concludes his introduction: "The four lessons to be read here merely evoke from a distance the great teaching whose modern formulation is missing."[3]

THE COLLOQUIA

It was Edmond Fleg and Léon Algazi who, in 1957, conceived the idea of a colloquium of Jewish intellectuals in France, which would convene every year under the aegis of the World Jewish Congress. From the start, the two men solicited Emmanuel Levinas, who agreed to participate.

In the first year, he took part in the discussions but was not one of the program speakers. For the second colloquium, in September 1959, he gave a lecture on Franz Rosenzweig. It was not until the third conference, in September 1960, that he gave his first "Talmudic lecture," although the exercise did not yet go by that name. The theme of the session, which was presided over by Vladimir Jankélévitch, was "Messianic Times and Historical Times in the Tractate *Sanhedrin*."

After that year of 1960, this would become a ritual. The colloquium would open with a biblical lesson from André Neher and would conclude with the talmudic lesson of Emmanuel Levinas. Subsequently, the philosopher would compile many of his lessons into five separate books, the last of which appeared one year after his death:

> We have perhaps unlearned the skill of reading; we no longer know the difference that distinguishes the Book from documentation: the inspiration that is distilled of all the events and all the "experiences" that were the occasion of its offering itself in Writing where each soul is summoned to exegesis, controlled at once by the rigorous reading of the text and by the uniqueness — unique in all eternity — of its connection to the soul, which is also its discovery, also its portion. It is in this sense that a great master taught us to read the liturgical formula, "Give us our portion in the Torah."[4]

The "great master" to whom Levinas is referring here is Chouchani, who initiated him into the Talmud, who taught him how to read these old tractates.

Another student of Chouchani, Shalom Rosenberg, had his own way of describing this very special apprenticeship: "For us these texts were like letters from a distant lover, which one holds against one's heart, which one embraces in passionate belief, and which one turns over and over a thousand times, like a text printed onto our soul, which gave it shape, with which it had been wrestling since the dawn of time."

Professor Ady Steg, a cardiologist, president of Alliance Israélite Universelle, recalls,

> I would almost say that I knew Levinas quite well before
> the Alliance, through the Jewish intellectual colloquia that
> were organized by the World Jewish Congress after the
> war. These conferences were a real event, because in that
> distress and despondency that gripped the intellectuals
> immediately after the war, the conferences functioned to
> reinvigorate them. This was a kind of defiance or revenge.
> And this presentation of Judaism was altogether new in
> the sense that the Talmudic lesson was a particular genre.
> It was a study starting from the text, a return to the text,
> that is so fundamental to Judaism. Levinas would distrib-
> ute copies of the talmudic passage to be commented on,
> in Hebrew and in French, so that even those who did not
> know Hebrew had the text before their eyes. This was
> important because a lecture by Emmanuel Levinas was not
> a study about a text but a study of the very text itself. The
> biblical lesson of André Neher was more traditional. The
> Bible was referenced. The Bible was familiar to the intel-
> lectual world, to the non-Jewish world as well. But the
> Talmud was something totally ignored, reserved for those
> good Jews with long beards from Poland or Morocco. The
> idea that the Talmud could be studied in French, in pub-
> lic, and in the same manner that it was studied by the Jews
> from Eastern Europe or from Maghreb, was extraordinary.
> And when I attended such a session for the first time, I
> was truly gripped and moved. I found myself in a familiar
> country again, yet in a different language. This was a com-
> pletely different presentation, by someone who was a
> philosopher, but who in no way betrayed the teaching of
> the Talmud as I had known it. It was a colossal event in
> and of itself. Levinas taught — this also struck me — like
> in the talmudic schools; that is to say, without looking for
> apologetics, without looking to be moralistic, but quite
> simply in the tradition of *yesh omrim*.[5] He left to the audi-
> ence the task of drawing their own conclusions. The dis-
> course was constructed, directed and well ordered, but he
> never imposed his interpretation. During these years, his

teaching was revolutionary, and at the same time made a considerable impact.

The conferences took place most often at the Enio, sometimes at the Rashi Center, and much later were held in Parisian auditoriums or at the Sorbonne. Many people attended. In fact, one day, Rabbi Josy Eisenberg, who presided at a session, declared, "I am happy to be president, it's the only way for me to be sure I'll get a seat!"

The talmudic lesson came to resemble a High Mass. It would punctuate reflection, anchoring it in texts. At the same time, it was something of a spectacle, an exercise that had its rules, its mise en scène. The Talmud page was distributed in Hebrew with a French translation. The speaker began by dividing and ordering the text into small segments before commenting on each one. On one occasion, after distributing the texts, he called out into the audience: "Please don't take these home!" The written text must not be separated from the oral commentary. "When the voice of the exegete no longer sounds — and who would dare believe it reverberates long in the ears of its listeners — the texts return to their immobility, becoming once again enigmatic, strange, sometimes even ridiculously archaic."[6]

The speaker was not, for that matter, discontent with the arid character of the distributed text and even took delight in the fact that the French translation maintained this aridity, since this permitted him to "draw a bit of water from this desertlike text." One metaphor, among others, that he liked to use: "Like the hammer that hits the rock and causes sparks to fly." Or — an image that I heard from my father's rabbinic sermons, before discovering from Levinas that it came from Rabbi Chaim of Volozhin — "Like the ember on which one blows and that turns into a flame, or that remains a cinder if the blowing is too brief."

The commentary played between different eras, contexts and places, as if the exegesis was nothing more than the opportunity for one time to make sense in relation to another time.

He was not preoccupied with the viewpoint of historians or philologists, or with the age in which these texts were written. It was enough for him to have found an intelligence, a subtlety, a spirituality. Should the opportunity arise, he did not shy away from drawing brief comparisons with contemporary events, collusions between these ancient, millennial texts and the daily news as heard on television.

TWENTY-THREE LESSONS

At the first colloquium in 1957, as already mentioned, no address was made by Levinas. He made only a few remarks, which were piously recorded by Jean Halperin, the architect and pioneer of these conferences over the decades and one of his closest friends:

> Judaism is not a religion — the word does not exist in Hebrew — it is much more than that, it is a comprehension of Being. The Jew introduced into history the idea of hope and the idea of a future. Plato laid out the plan of an ideal city for us, but there is almost no indication of its realization. Moreover, the Jew has the feeling that his obligations with respect to the other come before his obligations to God, or more precisely that the other is the voice of high places, even of the sacred. Ethics is an optics vis-à-vis God. The only voice of respect vis-à-vis God is that of respect toward one's fellow human being.

And Halperin comments:

> I find all of this absolutely emblematic, because in this first citation there is as a pithy synopsis of his whole view of Judaism and of his manner of taking it seriously, in his

relation to God, in his relation to the other. Everything is already announced in this citation. And in the session that followed, in the same colloquium of 1957, he evoked the voice of Israel that we are waiting for and that will indicate to us how we should live today, where justice is to be found, and the need that we have for an authentic Jewish thinking. This was almost like a declaration of intention of everything to be produced in the forty years to come.

Timidity and audacity. Morals and politics. Messianism and the end of history. Pardon. Temptation. Israel. Does the world need Jews? Judaism and revolution. Youth of Israel. The Jews and a desacralized society. *Shabbat.* The solitude of Israel. War. The occidental paradigm. Muslim community. Religion and politics. Community. The Bible today. Israel, Judaism and Europe. Idolatry. *Zekhor,* memory and history. The seventy nations. Money. The question of the State. Aloofness.

Thus runs the list of the colloquium themes that followed, from 1957 to 1989. Levinas participated in all of them, with two or three exceptions. He gave twenty-three lessons, was involved in the preparatory committees almost every year, and helped out until the end, even when his strength was in decline, in sessions with elaborate subject matters.

Jean Halperin recalls:

> I must say, when we dedicated our thirty-sixth colloquium to Levinas, under the title 'Difficult Justice, in the Footsteps of Emmanuel Levinas,' in which we wanted, not simply to commemorate or honor his presence among us, but to reinstate him in what he brought to us, and in what his thought represented for us of the fundamental, I presented an exposé on Levinas and his lectures over the years. I took up these twenty-three lessons. In each one I experienced the same bedazzlement before his method, the mastery and care with which he responded to the demand at hand. Not only did he reflect for weeks and months on a talmudic page that he had chosen to illustrate the thematic

question of each colloquium, but moreover he himself prepared the translation of the passage to be commented on. And when he was given a transcript of what he had said, which was recorded by a stenographer or a tape-recorder, he was incomparably scrupulous not to rework the thought he had expressed, but only the words he had said. These lessons, in other words, occupied a very great place in his life and in his work. And I venture to say that, on the Jewish side of Levinas's thought, the lessons assumed a central position.

How did he choose his talmudic page? He once confided in Claude Riveline, a professor at the Polytechnic, a member of the preparations committee of the colloquium, that he looked into Maimonides' *Mishne Torah*[7] for the subject closest to the theme of the colloquium and then traced Maimonides' talmudic sources. In this way, he always had an oblique, indirect, distant relation at the beginning that became increasingly substantial as the lesson progressed.

During the colloquium on the question "Is Judaism Necessary for the World?" held in 1966, he chose a passage from the Tractate Sanhedrin.[8] The Mishna speaks of the judges of the Sanhedrin, and in particular of how they are to be seated. "The Sanhedrin formed a semicircle, in such a manner that the members could see one another." On the basis of what biblical verse, asks the Gemara,[9] is this fact established? "We learn from the Song of Songs (3:7): 'Your navel is like a round goblet full of fragrant wine, your belly is a heap of wheat, hedged about with roses.'"

An erotic text as the basis of a tribunal and of justice? This query is the point of departure for the philosopher. It goes on to become a pretext for an exposition on society as an "assembly of faces."

For the colloquium on "The Example of the Occident," he turned to a text in the Tractate Menahot[10] that concerns the furniture of the temple and the "show-bread" that has to be set on the table "continually." The philosopher would linger on what this "always" signifies, this category of things that belongs to "always."

Reading is study, it is effort, it is violence done to words. As in this text from the Tractate Shabbat,[11] commented on in the colloquium on "Temptation" in 1964, where it is said that "a Sadducee saw Raba so absorbed in study that he rubbed his foot until blood spurted out." Levinas's commentary: "Rubbing until blood spurts out is perhaps the manner in which the text must be 'rubbed' in order to arrive at the life that it conceals."

An open dialectic, inseparable from living study. A text that raises problems instead of imposing solutions, but that also contains an entire hidden science, accessible to those who know how to rub.

REVOLUTION AND THE CAFÉ

The topics of the colloquia were often in sync with current events. In 1969, it was "Judaism and Revolution." This permitted Levinas to remark in his introduction how he dreaded the presence of superior scholars of the Talmud in the auditorium. And moreover how, this year, he was afraid of "protesters" against Judaism, adding derisively, "Evidently, these ones are not like the former; they fill many people with dread."

The philosopher chose a passage from the Tractate Bava Metzia.[12] The *mishna* stipulates that an employer may not force his hired workers to begin their day early and end late if this is not in keeping with the customs of the place. The Gemara raises the issue of the time needed by an employee to get to work and then to return home. Basing itself on a

verse from Psalms, it specifies that the time it takes to travel
to work must be reckoned as the employer's time while the
homeward journey is done on the employee's time.

From the same passage, Levinas then recounts a bizarre
dialogue between Rabbi Eliezer ben Rabbi Shimon and a
functionary in charge of arresting thieves: "Come," says Rabbi
Eliezer, "I will teach you how to go about it. Arrive at the
inn at around four o'clock. If you see someone drinking wine
who falls asleep with his cup in his hand, make inquiries
about him. If he is a scholar, it is because he got up early to
study. If he is a day laborer, it is because he left for work at
an early hour. If he is a night worker, he may have been
manufacturing needles. If he is none of these, he is a thief
and you can arrest him."

This gave the philosopher occasion to write an eloquent,
astonishing page on the life of the café. It is "an open house,"
he writes, "on street level, a place of facile society, without
reciprocal responsibility. You enter without necessity. You sit
without fatigue. You drink without thirst. . . . The café is not
a place, it is a nonplace for a nonsociety, for a society without solidarity, without common interests, a game society. The
café, a house of games, is the point through which the game
penetrates into life and dissolves it. A society without yes-
terday and without tomorrow, without responsibility, without
seriousness, a distraction, a dissolution."

Did this pregnant page, this condemnation without appeal,
constitute his response to May 1968? Is it the Latin Quarter
that is being ridiculed here? Was he thinking of the postwar
Sartre and the existentialist band of Saint-Germain-des-Prés?

The fact is that this was not his world, not his place, not
his "thing." He was never seen in, and in fact never sat in,
the terrace of a café. Already at the Enio he looked askew
at anyone who went to waste his time in such places.

Responsibility does not cease with a change in surroundings: "I am not declaring war on the corner café, and I don't want to incite all the café owners of Paris against me. But the café is only a realization of a form of life, it emerges from an ontological category, and this is the category that Rabbi Eliezer ben Rabbi Shimon caught sight of in the primitive inns of his times, an essential category of occidental existence, and perhaps also oriental, but rejected by Jewish existence."

Even as an ontological category, though, it would seem strange. Especially since a number of biblical scenes, like the romantic meetings of some of the patriarchs, had a well for their setting. A well is no doubt more poetic than a seedy café and perhaps less accommodating of idleness and vices than an inn, although . . .

Incidentally, during this same colloquium, Levinas is said to have read a letter from a correspondent whose name he withheld — but everyone came to recognize Maurice Blanchot — specifying only that he held a prominent place in the literary world and that he fully participated in the movement of May 1968. The prestigious author of the letter confessed to having distanced himself from certain small, ultra-left splinter groups due to the hostility they showed toward Israel and was worried about what his friend would have thought.

WAR

In November 1975, two years after the Yom Kippur war, the theme of the colloquium was "Faced with the War." Levinas chose to comment on a text that did not confront the subject directly. It was taken from the Tractate Bava Kama,[13] where the issue of damages caused by fire is dealt with. A particularity of the text: it focuses on a *halakha*, a law, a precept that teaches the comportment required in a tort situation. But the *halakha* very quickly came to be translated into an *agada*, a homiletical passage, what Levinas defines as "the mode in talmudic thought whereby philosophical views are presented, that is to say, the religious thought proper to Israel." And he adds in parentheses, which is so often his way of slipping in the essential: "Philosophy, I believe, is derived from religion. It is summoned by religion that is adrift, and religion is probably always adrift" — an idea often repeated by him, in diverse forms. Philosophy can lead us only to the threshold of mystery, into which it cannot enter.

The Gemara relates: "Rav Assi and Rav Ami were sitting before Rabbi Yitzhak the blacksmith. One of them asked him to expound on *halakha* and the other on *agada*. When he began with a *halakha*, the second one stopped him. When he began with an *agada*, the first one stopped him. So he said to them: I will tell you a parable. This is like a man who had two wives, one young and one old. The young one pulled out his white hairs, the old one pulled out his black hairs, until he was completely bald."

Levinas indulged in a joke about this parable — "I know that baldness is not degrading, it is only a denuding of the scalp," he said with a sense of humor that was reserved for these colloquia but was absent from other contexts — before getting to the heart of the matter, namely, the problem of the conflict between tradition and modernity, between those who learn in order to remain riveted to the law, even when it loses its luster, and those who belong to the cult of innovation, even at the price of being cast adrift. "This division between young and old," stressed Levinas, "this separation between revolutionaries and traditionalists, is condemned. Against the cult of traditionalism and against the cult of modernity. The spirit loses its sovereignty."

In each one of his discourses, he would make sure to inform everyone that he came to the Talmud quite late, and under the strict authority of a master, but that he was not a dilettante, a Sunday talmudist. From time to time, he would explicitly pay homage to Chouchani. At other times, he would mention the reassuring presence of Dr. Nerson.

Sometimes, he would let fly some arrows in the direction of the "young men" (brilliant, always brilliant) of Paris (which for him always signified the latest trend), the "Parisian intellectuals" (a phrase signifying a certain annoyance), the "poster-boys" of the journal *Le Monde* (meaning *doxa*), but always attenuated by a sense of humor.

Other times, he would take aim at the skeptics, the scoffers, those to whom "it is better left unsaid." Whenever this happened, very often Vladimir Rabi would end up shouting up a storm, becoming the official protester as well as the necessary interlocutor in these presentations.

A judge and literary critic, a part-time skier, a brawler, always cordial, Rabi had the gift of suffering from calculated "outbursts" that were designed to shake up the gathering. His favorite target was André Neher who, for him, symbolized the orthodox establishment. He respected Levinas, avoided attacking him head-on, but readily managed some sarcasm and derision. His bouts of anger were awaited and dreaded. During the last years, for that matter, he no longer harbored any prejudices and would denounce pell-mell the Neherolatry plaguing the Jewish community, the Manitoulatry, the Wieselolatry, and even the Levinasolatry.

There were, inevitably, some lively exchanges with Rabi. Levinas enjoyed them well enough. He found this genteel troublemaker stimulating. Whenever something that appeared "obscure" came up in the texts, or whenever he was interested in the text's genesis more than its exegesis, it was Rabi

he would address, with just a touch of affection; it was Rabi
who symbolized the school of thinking. After all, Levinas had
a selection to choose from. He could have put the question
to this or that regular attendant of the colloquia, Albert
Memmi or Robert Mizrahi. But no, it was Rabi, the skepti-
cal or hostile interlocutor, the friendly critic, who had to be
convinced.

The choice of themes for the colloquia was the decision
of the preparatory committee. But often Levinas's opinions
were heard as was the case after the collapse of the Berlin
wall — one of his last appearances on the committee. Claude
Riveline recalls: "With the collapse of communism, the idea
of progress suffered irreparable damages. He came up with
an elegant formula: 'We have a clock that is badly adjusted.
Time has lost its Orient.' He also proposed: 'What time is
it?' These are the kinds of formulations he liked best. In the
end, we opted for 'Disoriented Time.'"

The last colloquium in which Levinas took part — it was
in 1989 — dealt with "Memory and History." He dedicated
half of his speech to Vassili Grossman, the dissident writer,
author of the monumental *Life and Fate*. This book, discovered quite late, at the end of his life, read by him directly in
Russian, made a profound impression on Levinas and became
something that he often invoked.

"It was in these colloquia," says Jean Halperin,

> that he best expressed his Judaism. It was here that he
> made it most comprehensible and vibrant. Various texts
> have appeared in different contexts that attempt to tell
> Levinas that he is a Jewish thinker. But he did not care
> very much for such etiquette, and he did not want to
> remain confined to a confessional thought. He wanted to
> be understood and perceived as a thinker, period. But he
> could not deny that his thinking, taken as a whole, was in
> reality often read as Jewish thinking. Because it was entirely

inspired by this Jewish education, this *ahavat* Israel, this Jewish knowledge that he had always possessed. When you open *Totality and Infinity* or *Otherwise Than Being* or *The Humanism of the Other,* you will find phrases or paragraphs without references and without footnotes, but which, while reading them, you can feel are fundamentally Jewish thoughts that are being presented by Levinas in his philosophical works.

An encounter

It was a Sunday. Rabbi Adin Steinsaltz was in Paris for the recent publication of one of his books. It gave me the idea of introducing him to Emmanuel Levinas. As surprising as it may sound, the two men had never met. They read each other's works, in mutual appreciation, but had never met face to face.

The meeting would occur at my place, around a cup of tea and some cake that I took care to purchase in a glatt *kosher pastry shop on rue des Rosiers. The atmosphere was fairly cool. Steinsaltz drew on a pipe and looked at his interlocutor out of the corner of his eye. Levinas, courteous, attentive, chose his words carefully in a deliciously biblical and assiduous Hebrew. What could two talmudists who met for the first time, on a Sunday afternoon, in a Paris apartment, talk about? What subject would they choose for conversation? One might well have guessed it: the weekly* parsha.

Sharp, provocative, as he is, Steinsaltz took up his favorite exercise, the paradox: "The explorers of the parsha *are the intellectuals!" An assertion made with a certain aplomb and illustrated with reference to the varieties of mood found among "beautiful souls." Unfortunately, the insight did not arouse much enthusiasm from the philosopher. Just an amused smile. A round of watching. Evidently, my two guests were sizing each other up.*

"Won't you have some cake?" I mustered up the courage to ask. And turning toward Steinsaltz, I added, "You know, I

*bought them from a pastry shop not far from your hotel. They
know you there, and made them especially with you in mind."
The response burst out: "I was about to eat them! You should
know, anyway, I'd consider it a greater sin to embarrass you
than to eat nonkosher food." This beautiful reply stayed with me
for a long time, a lesson in good manners from a man of faith
from whom lesser masters might take example. It must be said.*

*Steinsaltz began to speak of himself, his education, his studies
in mathematics, in Hilbert notably. "Hilbert argued that there is
a sharp distinction between applied mathematics and pure
mathematics, that the two worlds have nothing to do with one
another." The response from Levinas: "It is a position that can be
defended. Husserl made the same claim."*

*The conversation turned to Chouchani, the mysterious man
who was Levinas's master, who initiated him into the Talmud
and who himself was also keen on mathematics. Steinsaltz knew
him a little, in his childhood ("I might have guessed," exclaimed
Levinas, "I recognize the company"). He came across him in
Israel, as Chouchani had returned there in the 1950s, where he
had known Steinsaltz's father for a long time. "I have long
believed that that Chouchani had cultivated this mysterious side
from the Shoah. My father explained to me that this had nothing
to do with it. He knew him before the war."*

*With the mention of his master, Levinas became animated. He
began speaking of this strange history of the Talmud: the fact that
until the fourth century, until the appearance of Rav Ashi and
the ordering and redaction of the Talmud, people could store up
the entire Shass — the thirty-six volumes of the Talmud — in
their heads, entirely in their heads. The unique experience of an
ocean of knowledge memorized over the centuries. Finally recorded.
Clarified much later by the interpretations of Rashi. Finally
translated into Hebrew and commented on by the efforts of the
man with the pipe seated before us.*

Steinsaltz: "In the university, one labors to present ancient things as if they are new. In my own commentaries, I attempt to say new things in endeavoring to present them as ancient."

Levinas: "There are many levels at the university. At a certain level, it is as you say."

Steinsaltz was returning from a lecture tour in the United States. "It was exhausting. I presented a paper at thirteen conferences. And it so happened that not one lecture resembled another one!" Levinas: "There, too, I recognize the mark of Chouchani!"

I recall a telephone call from a friend that afternoon, and an expression he used: "I'll let you go. You are between two mountains." A talmudic expression if there ever was one. In the graduations of verve and intelligence among students, the Talmud distinguishes between the baki, *the "expert," the* harif, *the "sharp one," and so on. At the top of the classification is the* oker harim, *the "uprooter of mountains."*

When I returned to the living room, where they were seated, my two guests were immersed in a very Levinasian exchange on grammar, its virtues and its variants. The game of "vous" and "tu" in French. The distance of "you" in English. The ceremonious "he" in German, sometimes also in Hebrew.

Steinsaltz, a bit ironic: "The French have a love for the phrase, a profusion of discourse!" Levinas: "Forgive me for speaking like an assimilated Jew, but the French language has a marvelous ḥeyn *about it, a particular grace."*

Steinsaltz: "I will write an article one day about how the Jews, in each of the countries they inhabited, restored a quintessential element to their national cultures. It is not necessary to look like this or that individual. It is necessary to gather into oneself the whole spirit of the nation." Levinas' face lit up: "Yes, that's it, Descartes and Pascal!"

Throughout this encounter, there was no mention of the appearance of the Talmud in French. The project was not yet in the works. But the two men discussed the problems besetting such a translation — the English "Steinsaltz" had appeared in the United States with notable success.

The Talmud in translation? How could the man to whom we were all so very much in debt for the talmudic renaissance in France be indifferent to the hermeneutic approach of Steinsaltz? "A magnificent work!" he said, before adding, "The difficulty with translating the Talmud is to preserve the opacity in the work, of knowing that clarity can never dissipate the fog."

And the man with the pipe nodded his head, musing perhaps that the day would come when one would judge for oneself.

II. Faces

9 | THE FERRYMAN AND THE METEOR

Faces, proper names, glistening eyes: Emmanuel Levinas's destiny was also decided in the course of meetings, discussions and debates. Among those who surrounded this still-careerless philosopher standing on the margins of the university, two prominent figures, both free-spirited and enigmatic, played a role that was as decisive as it was unequal. The metaphysician Jean Wahl and the talmudist Mordechai Chouchani each in his own way inspired the man and his work, to the extent that he would never hesitate to underscore his debt to them, even if only in a discreet fashion. To enter into the depth of these two relationships is, in a way, to sneak into the workshop where, during the same period, what became the resolutely personal thought of Emmanuel Levinas was being worked out.

In 1947, with the publication of *De l'Existence à l'Existant*, Jean Wahl invited Emmanuel Levinas to deliver a series of lectures at the Collège Philosophique. These were postwar circumstances and Levinas, already principal of the Enio, had de facto given up on a university career. He had to earn a living, being married and father to a young daughter,

Simone, born in 1935. Moreover, Leon Brunschvicg, who caused the sun to rise and to set at the Sorbonne, and whose courses Levinas had attended for a while, had dissuaded him from pursuing the *agrégation*. Maurice de Gandillac, his companion from Davos, also volunteered this advice to the young philosopher: "With your accent, you will never pass the oral *agrégation*," thereby eliminating the competition. Levinas continued to write and to publish articles in philosophical journals. He would frequent the soirées of Gabriel Marcel, the seminars that the author of the *Journal Métaphysique* would hold at his home on Fridays. This Christian philosopher, who had tried his hand on different occasions at theater and at painting, personified, vis-à-vis Sartre, an existentialism concerned with faith. Close to that of Martin Buber, he would develop a philosophy of relation, and especially of interrelation, that could hardly have left Levinas indifferent. Thus, in the salon of the old master of rue de Tournon, the young principal of the Enio found a rather anticonformist milieu, away from the ponderousness of the university and promoting a free approach in philosophy.

Levinas would also attend the courses of Alexandre Kojève at the École Pratique des Hautes Études. The stakes were different there. This Russian thinker, French by adoption after a sojourn in Germany, cast a spell on the whole Parisian smart set. Pioneer of a renewed reading of Hegel, his courses, of which Raymond Queneau became the editor, attracted personalities as diverse as Sartre and Caillois, Bataille and Lacan. His numerous lectures, starting from Marx and Heidegger, on the master-slave dialectic, came to influence generations of students, and his seminar, for many, became an event. By being present, Levinas demonstrated how, in the years after Davos, he intended to keep abreast of what was going on in the philosophical world, continuing to construct his thinking by staying in touch with his contemporaries.

He would participate, finally, in the work of the French Philosophical Society, where he often met Jean Wahl. Between the two men, very different from each other, not belonging to the same generation, a strong friendship developed.

Xavier Tilliette, a Jesuit priest, professor at the Institut Catholique de Paris and the Gregorian University in Rome, who wrote his doctoral thesis on Schelling under Jean Wahl, knew both of them. He draws an ironic and savory portrait of his old master, "with his scarf, his coat down to his feet, his battered hat, his face like a tawny owl. One might have thought: a tramp." At the Collège Philosophique, which Levinas often frequented, one would see Wahl hunched over his mounds of paper, posing a few pithy questions like a wasp planting its sting, not waiting for the reply, muttering his "yes, hmm, yes . . ."

THE POET-METAPHYSICIAN

A personality at once whimsical and philosophical, a historian of philosophy and poetry at different times, Wahl occupied a place of his own in the French university. Within the existentialist movement, but somewhat on the sidelines, with an artistic temperament, he frequented the surrealist exhibits, wrote poems in French and in English. He introduced Kierkegaard to France, lectured on Heidegger, and, after Brunschvicg, would hold the chair of metaphysics and of general philosophy at the Sorbonne.

"The friendship between Wahl and Levinas," says Tilliette, "even with the age difference, since there were seventeen years between them, was that of equals, and I would say that it was all affection." Levinas would go to see Wahl at his home quite often. Tilliette also remembers how at one point there was a question of giving him Hebrew lessons. "Mme. Wahl was insistent that her husband practice some kind of religion. If he did not wish to become Catholic or Protestant, then he should at least be a good Israelite. She wanted him to learn Hebrew. But it didn't go off. Jean Wahl was surly." Having an excellent practical grasp of languages, able to read the tragedies of Aeschylus and Sophocles in the original Greek, writing and speaking fluent English and German, he was nevertheless resistant to the idea of learning the language of the Bible.

Nothing, however, demonstrated the eccentricity, and even the rebelliousness, of the man better than the war of Jean Wahl. It was of epic proportions. He showed himself to be nonchalant and imprudent. To begin with, he refused to wear the yellow star. Forced to retire from his position and banned from the university, he nevertheless continued to teach in his usual manner. He ventured to gather together some young people in a hotel room, on rue des Beaux-Arts, to study texts, including those of Heidegger.

Then, on one fine morning in July 1940, he jumped into the lion's mouth by turning himself in to the Gestapo. They made him wait. He flew into a rage and barged into the office, throwing a pile of books on the table in a provocative move that caused him to be arrested immediately and transferred to Drancy, where he was detained for some weeks.

According to Gandillac, who was his colleague at the Sorbonne, Wahl was released thanks to the intervention of a certain Gillet, former professor of philosophy who in the meantime was part of Marshall Pétain's cabinet. And it was Pierre Boutang, a former student of Wahl and the instigator of this intervention, who put him up in Morocco before helping him to reach America.

On the occasion of his release from Drancy, in the autumn of 1941, Tilliette reports the following story that he heard from Jankélévitch. Wahl managed to be pulled out from the camp, not without difficulty, and he was getting ready to depart for the United States. His friends came around and threw a little party for him. One of them, in his excitement, blurted out: "*Monsieur le professeur,* how happy you must be!" To which he replied with a placid and laconic "Yes, quite." Wahl would return from America after the war, married, with three girls and a boy. It was at that time that he established an institution meant to succeed the prewar circle created by Marie-Madeleine Davy, the historian of medieval philosophy and mysticism, who organized conferences in the Latin Quarter, on rue Cujas, opposite the Sorbonne, where she received young students.

LE COLLÈGE PHILOSOPHIQUE

Wahl found a new name for these meetings, Le Collège Philosophique — and a location across from the church of Saint-Germain-des-Près, a hall for rent. The idea was to establish a lively forum where philosophers, writers and artists could meet. The format was hardly original: a lecturer addressed the public. Jean Wahl presented the speaker, but in his own special way, which had nothing traditional about it, dwelling on details, going from one idea to another, mixing up genres. The sessions took place every week and lasted for two hours. Michel Butor collected contributions at the entrance. During the first years, among those standing in line one could see Gabriel Marcel, Jean-Paul Sartre, Alexandre Koyré, Francis Jeanson, Vladimir Jankélévitch, Jacques Lacan. Sometimes no one showed up, or a very sparse crowd. Other times, as for Sartre's lecture in 1946 on "Existentialism Is a

Humanism," the room was bursting at the seams. Levinas was invited to deliver the four lectures that would come to be published as *Time and the Other*.[1] "The purpose of these lectures," he said upon opening the series, "consists in showing that time is not a fact about a subject who is isolated and alone, but that it is the very relation of the subject to another."[2]

Tilliette, one of the regular session attendees, recalls, "Levinas was a name. No one would have thought that he would write such important books and that he would become one of the glories of French philosophy. There was the book on intuition according to Husserl, written in a style that was very French, very clear, very different from what he would adopt much later, in *Otherwise Than Being*, which became very ornate and convoluted. He was one of the French philosophers who stood quietly in the margins, if you will, due to his nonuniversity status. But, after all, this was also true of Brice Parain or Maurice Blanchot."

One might nevertheless suppose that the lack of a university career might explain the maturation of Levinas in this kind of high solitude where not only thought but language was being sought after, something inevitably new, for reasons that were just as much biographical and philosophical.

As a result, these first lectures did not make a lasting impression on Tilliette:

> He was challenged with a small voice, which made it hard for him to articulate himself, although he did manage to capture the audience. He was generally not a brilliant professor, except at the end, notably in the courses that some of my friends told me about, on death. In these sessions, everyone was hanging on his words. He had certain expressions that hit the nail on the head, yet it was all quite difficult to grasp. His language was certainly interesting, although ultimately it was an artificial language, a bit fantastical, behind which lay Russian, German, and Hebrew.

A somewhat brittle affectation with surprising intonations. His writing style is also quite unique. It was, at the very least, an *artistic writing*, if you will. But I think that, in all his life, this writing that he was able to create — which is not at all like Blanchot's, Blanchot writes differently — is very interesting. It comprises the body of his philosophy.

FROM THESIS TO GOOD-BYE

Wahl animated the College for twenty-odd years, but Levinas was seen there less frequently until the beginning of the 1960s.

After 1947, Judaism came to dominate, with the deepening of the texts, the study of the Talmud in the presence of a master discovered late in life, Chouchani, together with a systematic reading of Hegel. The writing all but stopped. These were the years of the maturation of *Totality and Infinity*, the great book whose foundations must be sought, according to Jacques Roland, precisely in *De l'Existence à l'Existant* and *Time and the Other*.

And even then, Wahl had to go after Levinas to get him to defend his thesis. The text turned out to be something of a revolution at the Sorbonne in 1961, breaking with the other more sociological and Marxist approaches current at the time. But even more, the sentiment was that a *terra incognita* of thought was in the process of being discovered. "We are here to evaluate a thesis about which other theses will be written," said Wahl. "This proved his good judgment," comments Tilliette. "He was not mistaken." The philosopher André Jacob, Levinas's neighbor on rue d'Auteuil, his colleague at Nanterre, who was also present at the defense, recalls another assessment: "This is not a work, it is a masterpiece."

Totality and Infinity is dedicated to Marcelle and Jean Wahl. The book appeared in 1963, hailed notably by a long and complimentary article by Jean Lacroix in *Le Monde*.[3] Lacroix wrote, among other things,

> The impression of strangeness and the feeling of unfamiliarity, literally of admiration that one experiences while reading this work, no doubt emerges from its simultaneously modern and traditional character. An entirely religious current is present throughout as inspiration, but never revealed as such. Cartesian reflection and Kantian reflection are grasped at their core and translated into terms of existence. The brilliance of existence, which is sometimes at risk of being abandoned to a clatter of words, is always borne up, animated by the double passion of the human and the transcendent. This philosophy has a style, if style is the perfect agreement of ground and form.

Lacroix would take up the pen again, ten years later, for the publication of *Otherwise Than Being*, with the same certainty that yet a new language was being encountered.

Wahl was therefore the discoverer, the gadfly, the ferryman. Even while he was taken for someone who became easily besotted with people and who dropped them just as easily — "I don't know if I am on good terms with Gabriel Marcel at this moment" — this unclassifiable philosopher, diametrically opposite from Levinas, had made him his protégé. Gandillac put it very well: "Wahl perhaps left a mark on Levinas, but I don't know whether Levinas left a mark on Wahl." No connection of this sort could ignore reciprocity. To the affection of the old master, the young philosopher would always respond with gratitude, a Levinasian theme and exercise par excellence. For Wahl's funeral in 1974, this man who let himself die, refusing a cataract operation and living out his last years cloistered in his room wearing pajamas and a robe, had asked for the presence of a priest, a pastor and

The Lithuanian passports of Emmanuel Levinas's parents, Dvora Gurvitch and Yekhiel Levinas, discovered in the Kaunas archives.

Near Niemen, rue Kalejimo, the Levinas house, divided into two wings. Raïssa's parents, who owned the premises, lived here.

In Kaunas, Llaisves Aleja, freedom alley, where Yekhiel Levinas's stationery store was located.

In Vilnius, Gaon Vilna's house, the glory of Litvak Judaism.

Coll. S. and G. Hansel.

Maurice Blanchot and Emmanuel Levinas, during the 1920s, during their studies in Strasbourg. On the back of this photograph, someone wrote, *"Doublepatte et Patachon."*

Coll. L. Jakubovitz

Emmanuel Levinas in uniform, interpreter trainee, chief warrant officer.

At the Fallingsbotel camp, Stalag XIB (Levinas with a kepi, in the second row).

Coll. L. Jakubovitz

Emmanuel and Raïssa Levinas after the war with their daughter, Simone.

Their son Michael Levinas, born in 1949, composer and pianist.

The Levinases on holiday in Holland.

In front of the Enio school building, with Jean Heymann, general overseer.

In Morocco in the 1960s, for a meeting in Tioumlinine.

Levinas was often invited to meetings such as this one at Castel Gandolfo with Pope John Paul II and Paul Ricoeur.

At a colloquium at the Rashi Center, next to Bernard-Henri Lévy.

© M. Pierce

© T. Martinot

Levinas gave his first talmudic lecture to the Colloquium of French Jewish Intellectuals in 1960 and gave another almost every year for almost 30 years. He wrote a great deal and accepted invitations to speak in various circles during the 1960s, 1970s and 1980s.

Levinas at Salomon Malka's wedding in 1978.

© D. Mordzinski

Emmanuel and Raïssa Levinas at their home in Paris. From a shared child-hood in Kovno, she was a constant presence throughout his life until her death about a year before his.

a rabbi. There was no rabbi, but it was Emmanuel Levinas who spoke at his graveside.

Twenty years later, as another exercise in fidelity, Mr. and Mme. Levinas, both enfeebled with age, would visit Wahl's daughter, Beatrice, at her home, paying homage to the memory of the late philosopher-poet.

THE TRAMP AND THE PROPHET

From Wahl to Chouchani, from the philosopher to the talmudist, despite the fact that I met neither one of them, I am nevertheless always struck by a kind of physical resemblance between these two ferrymen who transported Emmanuel Levinas and left a mark on his life. The unkempt appearance, the tie askew, the worn-out hat — but what other parallels can be drawn? The two men belonged to two different worlds, which could nevertheless collide with each at more or less the same time.

Levinas never had much to say when we tried to get him to talk about Chouchani. He came to know him in the years following the war, through Dr. Nerson, invited him to stay in his home, rented a room out to him at the Enio below his apartment, and spent many nights, for almost three years, under his tutelage.

Very little is known about this personality. We do not know his name — Chouchani was not his real name. We do not know his origins, his place of birth, where he grew up, where he completed his studies. What we do know, as witnessed by all who encountered him or who crossed his path, is that he possessed an exceptional memory, that he had a vast knowledge, as much about Judaism and Jewish sources as about mathematics, physics, philosophy, languages, arts. He lived out his entire life like a tramp, with no fixed address, wandering from one city to another, passing from New York to Strasbourg, from Strasbourg to Paris, then to Jerusalem, finally ending up in Montevideo, Uruguay, where he died in anonymity, with this epitaph on his tombstone: "His birth and his life are bound up in a secret."

Everywhere he went, he was surrounded by small groups of students to whom he would impart lessons in the Bible or Talmud in exchange for room and board and occasionally for money. And everywhere, in the four corners of the world, he left his disciples — among them, the Nobel Peace Prize laureate Elie Wiesel — with the memory of a man of prodigious erudition and unparalleled teaching. Who was this man who passed through life like a meteor, whose students — spread throughout the world — still portray him as a kind of Jewish Pico de la Mirandola?

Not long ago, I made an attempt in a modest essay to unravel this mystery with which Chouchani, amusing himself, surrounded his existence, his origins and even his name. The Israeli philosopher Shmuel Wygoda reproached me for having focused too much of my book on the enigma of his personality rather than on the content of his teaching, and for having produced more questions with my investigations than answers.[4] This much is true, I confess. My only sadness has been to note that the publication of this work,[5] which I had expected to spark the appearance of other evidence about the man, disappointed my expectations. Nothing appeared. Nothing, in any event, that altered the view of this strange figure who was extraordinary in every sense of the word. I received hundreds of letters from France, Belgium, Uruguay, Israel, Greece and even Japan. All of them did nothing but repeat what I had already heard a thousand times, or further exacerbated the enigma. One person sent me a long missive by e-mail to relate an encounter in Terrasson in 1942 and the extreme lucidity of Chouchani, before the events in Europe, and also a long and passionate conversation about art. Another, a young woman of twenty, indicated to me that on a certain page of Henry Miller's *Plexus,* one could find a depiction of Chouchani's doppelgänger. I looked it up and again found myself on a false trail. Some filmmakers have expressed an interest in this personality. Some experts have offered to carry out handwriting analyses. A number of correspondents advised me to orient my investigations differently, to proceed in another way, to ask my interviewees other questions.

In Israel, Yoram Brunovski had published a long review of my book in *Haaretz,* which produced some results. Avraham Oren, a native of Strasbourg who lives today in Tz'dei Eliahu, had recorded his memories in the kibbutz's bulletin. He wrote:

> Few members of our community remember a temperamental person who arrived here in the middle of one particularly hot summer. The secretary of the kibbutz took care to find him lodging in the difficult conditions of those times (the 1950s). He sat, covered in sweat, in one of the huts, and taught Torah to a small circle of listeners. We managed to persuade him to give courses to a larger public, and so he did on several nights, in the cultural center, on the Book of Malachi. His way of life was bizarre. He was very concerned with his diet, very harsh with his audience, but for those who came ready to rise to his altitude, it was an unforgettable experience. The man possessed a perfect mastery of the Bible, the two Talmuds, the Midrash, the Zohar, the work of Maimonides. . . .
>
> He followed our reading of a tractate of the Talmud, whichever one it might be, and was in step with every page, and by heart, correcting us on this or that commentary by Rashi or the Tossafot. After a short period, the man

disappeared as suddenly as he had arrived. He could have again created other circles of students in other places in the country, in Saad and in Be'erot Yitzhak. Some thought he held some high office in the heart of the national department of education. But here, as elsewhere, he refused to settle down and pursued his wandering across the continents.

Until his death, no one had any real knowledge about who this Chouchani was. I still remember his appearances in Strasbourg, in France, before the Second World War. And after the Shoah, when we were receiving refugees from the camps, he was again among us. . . . He spoke practically all of the languages familiar to the Jews of Europe. His knowledge of literature, the sciences, and in particular mathematics, was phenomenal.[6]

But the content of his teaching? His vision of Judaism? His approach to texts?

TRACES OF AN ENIGMA

The sole trace of Chouchani's teaching is found in Levinas's books, in the talmudic lessons, in the Rashi courses. It is in these texts that his spirit lingers.

What did Levinas get from Chouchani? Something that he often expressed in paradoxical terms: the Bible is particular to Israel, the Talmud is what constitutes the Jewish contribution to the universal.

What did Levinas owe to Chouchani? He once confided to François Poirié, "Certainly, the history of the Holocaust has played a much bigger role in my Judaism than the encounter with this man. But the encounter with this man gave me back a trust in the books."[7]

Emmanuel Levinas never left Jean Wahl for Mordechai Chouchani. He met with both of them, and during the same period. But just as certainly, study with this man who came from elsewhere, those nights of discovery and insomnia, gave a different orientation to his life and his work. Albeit not in the way one might suppose, or not exactly that way. One might have wished to confuse this moment into collusion with a return to Judaism. The story goes that Chouchani brought Levinas back to the sources, diverted him from his work, caused him to retreat from everyday life. That is not exactly true.

Levinas was always interested in his Judaism. "As in my own substance," he said. And he never gave it up. No doubt something like a distancing can be observed between 1923, the date of his arrival in Strasbourg, and 1933, a decisive date for him. It is the only period in which he managed a few Jewish readings, busy as he was learning French, before beginning his apprenticeship in philosophy. But, even including the years of his stay in Strasbourg, he would return every summer to Lithuania where he reestablished contact with his roots, his family, and the traditional library of his parents. Therefore, he found himself at a certain distance during this period, but nothing more than a distance. He never experienced either "true ruptures" or "true recoveries."[8] This time-continuum suffered only two shocks, two jolts, two blasts of the alarm clock: 1933 with Hitler's rise to power, and 1945 with his encounter with Chouchani.

According to Jacques Rolland, moreover, the effect of these two events on the life and work of Emmanuel Levinas was not equal:

> I am convinced — because I wrote it while he was alive and he did not contradict me, even though he knew very well how to do so on other points — that 1933 was decisive for him. It was the horror. The very rise of Hitler to power, the significance that this had for the Jew, to be not only prey to Christian anti-Semitism as in previous centuries, but also to be ineluctably welded to his Judaism,

and the betrayal of Heidegger. . . . Therefore, if we want
to talk about a return, it is something that took place in
1933. By contrast, what was at stake in 1945–1946 was not
a return. It was the assignment of a task, to himself and
others, the task of a spiritual and intellectual reconstruction of French Judaism. And I believe that it was at this
moment that he became aware of the necessity to turn to
the Talmud. The biblical education that he had enjoyed
in his youth and adolescence did not measure up to the
enormity of the task. But I would add that, for him, the
manifesto that constitutes the twenty-page introduction to
the *Four Talmudic Lectures* is extremely clear about this.
There is no difference between the magnitude of the problems posed by the Talmud and the magnitude of the problems posed by philosophy. And the intellectual rigor in
each field is exactly the same.

Wahl and Chouchani. The poet and the prophet. The academic and the traveling acrobat. Two sides, no doubt, of
Levinas. Two temptations perhaps. In any event, two men
who very much counted in his life, one because he was at
the origin of his university career, and the other because he
modified his perspective on the Hebrew sources of his childhood and opened new paths for him. Between the figure of
the de-Judaized Jew and the deep-rooted Jew, between the
philosopher and the talmudist, Emmanuel Levinas was invited
to blaze his own path, one that would perhaps fuse this double inspiration.

10 | THE BAD GENIUS

"He was born, he worked, he died." This is how Heidegger once began a course on Aristotle. Perhaps the philosopher from Freiburg wanted this sentence to be applied to his own life. And, to some extent, a number of his admirers in France did in fact grant him this wish. They praised his work, praised it to the ends of the earth, in complete indifference to the "vicissitudes" of biography. What of the compromise with Nazism? The membership in the Nazi party? The episode as rector? Accidents, no doubt. Deviations. Moments of folly. Besides, Heidegger was the rector of the University of Freiburg only from 1933 to 1934. He resigned thereafter. The fate that Heidegger's philosophy enjoyed in France was built upon this thesis, yet the debate over the political involvement of the author of *Being and Time* was never closed — it was revived from year to year. The history of Heidegger's reception in France is chaotic. It embodied the best and the worst, as shown by Dominique Janicaud in a large two-volume work of more than a thousand pages where the question is examined.[1] It was also marked by passions and misunderstandings, beginning after the war with his being discredited, the suspension from his professional functions in Germany, the visits from French intellectuals in the immediate aftermath of the war, his friendships with Jean Beaufret and René Char, the travels to France (Paris, Cerisy, Aix-en-Provence, Le Thor) — right up until the Farias controversy at the end of the 1980s, which would cause a commotion in Landerneau's philosophical circle and even beyond that. Victor Farias, a young Chilean academic, and a student of Heidegger who would later teach at the Freie Universität in Berlin, conducted an investigation that produced some very incriminating information.[2] Martin Heidegger's commitment to Nazism had not been a circumstantial adherence, and his resignation was not followed by protest. His attachment to National Socialism began long before.

BEFORE AND AFTER

Despite the major role he had played in introducing phenomenology to France, Emmanuel Levinas never bore the Heideggerian stamp. When, in the 1950s, Cerisy-la-Salle brought the German philosopher into one of his prestigious decades, Levinas was absent. He no longer helped, nor was he invited to the seminars of Thor in 1968–1969. He was never counted among the devoted, always taking pains to avoid them.

Jacques Rolland, a disciple and friend, recalls how he once heard Levinas say on the subject of Martin Heidegger: "If I had encountered him after the war, I wouldn't have shaken his hand." Jean-Luc Marion heard this from him: "What do you want? Nihilism? Here you are. The greatest philosopher of the century is Heidegger. And Heidegger was a card-carrying Nazi. These are the times in which we live." Paul Ricoeur describes it as a "permanently polemical rapport."[3] A mixture of admiration and repulsion, fascination and horror, extreme closeness and utter divorce, Emmanuel Levinas often pointed out this paradoxical relationship so as to emphasize that Heidegger was all the less to be forgiven precisely because he was Heidegger. He nevertheless knew whatever there was to know — all of it, right away, very quickly. When Victor Farias's book appeared, Levinas was asked for his opinion. He replied: "After Farias, certain details have become clearer, but there is essentially nothing novel there."[4] And, in an interview in *Nouvel Observateur*, he stressed that he had known or guessed of Heidegger's pro-Nazi involvement, "perhaps even before 1933."[5]

In the 1980s, the Italian philosopher Georgio Agamben once came on a Saturday morning to assist with the Bible lesson, which was attended by Jacques Rolland. At the end of the class, a discussion ensued between the two men in which Levinas asked his visitor: "But after all, Mr. Agamben, you were at the Thor seminar at the end of the 1960s. How was he there?" Agamben replied, "I can't tell you what I saw, I saw a gentle man." And Levinas: "Well, I knew him in 1928–1929. I knew a hard man. I have to believe you because you say it is so, but I cannot convince myself that this man could have been gentle." And Agamben added later on, for the benefit of Rolland, "It should be said that defeat was already in the past by then!"

For Levinas, as for Heidegger, there had been a "before" and an "after," but for Levinas it was an altogether abysmal defeat that was at stake, not that of one country or one regime, but one that universally addressed all human beings, and each one individually. Even more so than Hannah Arendt's relationship with Heidegger, where romantic interest played a part, Levinas, in his entire trajectory, from enthusiastic student of Davos to the painful realizations won in the anguish of captivity, was the Jew who had walked down the very path of Heidegger, to end up questioning him about an omission more essential than that of Being. That the relationship was not nurtured by meetings, correspondences, or even open polemics, changed nothing. The opinion of the philosopher of ethics, understood in light of its conceptual debt, could only condemn the philosophical genius at work.

ANGER

On this subject, an attitude of vehemence in Levinas was rarely detected. Except once. William J. Richardson, today a professor of philosophy in Boston, recalls Levinas's manner during an international colloquium that took place at the University of Loyola on May 20–23, 1993. Richardson had organized the event at the prompting of Adriaan Peperzak.[6] He begins by recounting his first meeting with Emmanuel Levinas, which took place in 1963. Richardson was about to publish a book with Martinus Nijhoff entitled *Heidegger: Through Phenomenology to Thought,*[7] a revised version of the thesis he had defended at Louvain in Belgium. As a result, he was invited by the same university to present his candidacy for the title of *maître-agrégé,* the equivalent of a doctorate in France or of a *Habilitation* in Germany. To do this, it was necessary for him to defend the work publicly before an international jury. The candidate himself could make suggestions, and upon approval, invitations would be sent to the appropriate universities. Emmanuel Levinas's name was among the first on his list.

During their first meeting at Levinas's home, the French philosopher very courteously asked Richardson to leave the book with him, telling him that he would read it and let him know his response.

The second encounter was equally cordial. Levinas agreed to be a member of the jury, but cautioned that, being no friend of Heidegger, he reserved the right to speak freely. Richardson could only respond, "This is the very reason we invited you."

The defense took place, with the requisite solemnity. When it was Levinas's turn, he once again appeared — according to Richardson's own account — very amiable. Everyone waited for a brutal attack. But the only real criticism was about the "very scholarly," overly "pedagogical" character of the text in question. But the philosopher added, in the form of a question, that he wondered why a believing Christian could "spend so much time studying Heidegger!"

At the close of the oral defense, a reception was given at the home of the president of the university. Richardson, still according to his story, went from one person to another shaking hands, when, suddenly, someone appeared behind him and gave him a vigorous tap on his shoulder. Turning around, Richardson saw that it was Levinas and extended his hand to once again express his gratitude for his presence and his remarks. Ignoring the extended hand, Levinas looked him straight in the eye and whispered, "I was just talking about your book with some old friends, making them laugh. I thought you might be interested to know why we were laughing. You recall where you write in your book that '1943 was a very prolific year'?" "Yes, I know the place," replied Richardson. "Well, in 1943, my parents were in one concentration camp and I in another. It was certainly a prolific year!" And with that, Levinas turned on his heel and disappeared.

Richardson, staggering, confronted an angry man, very different from the courteous academic who had respectfully listened to his exposé before the jury only one hour earlier.

"If he had wanted to take such a shot, why didn't he do it during the oral defense? There would have been a real confrontation in an academic arena! Instead, he waited until the meeting was over!" Richardson, who at the time felt prey to an "unseemly" attitude, asked himself, "Where is the place in Levinas's thought for such a scandal? What status does it give him?"

Interviewed today about this former anecdote, he revisits it on practically the same terms. "The time gone by has not changed my opinion of Levinas. He was an admirable man and an important thinker. This anecdote is only indicative, in my opinion, of a shortcoming in his thinking, which does not take into account a characteristic element of human phenomena, namely the unconscious. The meeting where this text was presented merely served to give occasion for this shortcoming to be revealed."

A strange appreciation! Whose unconscious is in question? That of Levinas? His own?

It is nevertheless easy to imagine how reading a book of seven hundred pages on the evolution of Heidegger's thought without the least reference to his political involvement, other than a lighthearted remark on his "prolific activity," could have been painful for Levinas. The fact that Richardson prefers to understand the incident in general terms, in terms of psychoanalysis and Levinas's stance on the subject, only repeats, no doubt "unconsciously," as he likes to say, the insensitivity for which he was reproached.

This was therefore one of the rare violent "outbursts" of Levinas. This man, who was criticized for his overcautiousness, could at times prove himself to be quite brusque. The episode, at any rate, reveals a pain that was still alive and was never really assuaged.

THE KNOT OF CONTRADICTIONS

The introducer of Heidegger to France never abandoned his admiration for the author of *Being and Time*. He never allowed the criticisms of the man to reflect on this book that, in his eyes, was a monument. At the same time, what he reproached his former professor from Freiburg for above all, perhaps, was the failure to render impossible, inoperative, inadequate any connection between his philosophy and his attachment to National Socialism. It is the intricate connection between the man and the work, in fact, that he never forgave.

According to Jacques Rolland, "what is certain is that Levinas always believed that he had the good fortune, and partly the bad luck, of encountering two geniuses in his life: Heidegger and Chouchani. He said two geniuses. He never went back on that point, even if it made him uncomfortable." Moreover, in 1932, on the occasion of the publication of his first important article on Heidegger, "Martin Heidegger and Ontology," in *La Revue Philosophique* — reprinted later in *Uncovering Existence* — Levinas announced a future work on Heidegger. Once 1933 went by, it became clear to him that this book was no longer possible.

By 1935, in a short essay entitled "On Evasion" (which first appeared in *Recherches Philosophiques* under the direction of Alexander Koyré, Albert Spaïer, Jean Wahl and Gaston Bachelard), even though Heidegger's name is absent, the conflict, a silent one, was already apparent, as Rolland suggests, who published the text with notes and a letter written by Levinas.

In 1947, when Levinas published his first personal effort, employing notions that were proper to him, in *De l'Existence à l'Existant,* he thus specified that his reflections were inspired in part by Heidegger's philosophy, but not without adding that they were dictated by "a profound need to leave the climate of that philosophy."[8]

Then, in the foreword to *Uncovering Existence*, a collection of writings on Husserl and Heidegger, he emphasized that these studies were not intended to plead the case, after the years of 1939–1945, "for a philosophy that does not always guarantee wisdom."[9]

In the years following the war, even though Heideggerianism triumphed in certain milieus in France, Levinas did not give up on this double perspective, to which he held on until the end. Just as he, knowing what he knew, was heard expressing his debt to the one who had educated an entire generation about "the sonority of the verb 'to be,'" he also spoke, in a departure from that, of the necessity for him to precisely "exit from Being."

In an interview in *L'Arche*, a monthly publication of French Judaism, he could thus declare, "It is always with shame that I admit to my admiration for the philosopher. We know what Heidegger was in 1933, even if he had been that only for a short period, and even if his followers, many of whom are very respected, forget this. For me, it is unforgettable. One may be anything — except Hitlerian, even if one is so by accident." Was this the case with Heidegger? "I cannot tell you if it was accidental," replies Levinas, "To what extent did he not take part in that which, in a particular German culture and milieu, is profoundly alien and hostile to us?"[10]

This contradiction between the thinker and the militant therefore proved to be painful for Levinas, who felt enthusiasm for the first, disgust for the second, and nonetheless always wanted to remain standing over this chasm without justifying it.

THE FUTURE OF DEATH

In 1961, Levinas published a text in *Information Juive,* later reprinted in *Difficult Freedom,* entitled "Heidegger, Gagarin and Us," in which he seized upon the exploits of the Soviet cosmonaut, first man sent into space, in order to develop a reflection on technology. This was the pretext for some examinations of the genius of place, of rootedness in the world, of sacred forests and other images behind which the hermit of Todtnauberg stands in the shadows.

"Technology wrenches us out of the Heideggerian world and the superstitions surrounding Place. From this point on, an opportunity appears to us: to perceive men outside the situation in which they are placed, and to let the human face shine in all its nudity. Socrates preferred the town, in which one meets people, to the countryside and trees. Judaism is the brother to the Socratic message."[11]

He has been criticized for oversimplifying Heideggerian thinking concerning technology. Yet it is hard to imagine a more severe response and a better alliance against the neo-pre-Socratic thinker who saw the beginnings of a certain decadence in Plato's master.

It is in the same year that the major work, *Totality and Infinity,* appeared that the divorce with Heidegger was finalized. "In fact," writes Dominique Janicaud, "until the end of his life, Levinas never stopped wavering between subtle homage and devastating criticism." And he adds, regarding the book, "In this exposition, the frank repudiation of Heidegger played an absolutely central role in the shift."[12]

In June 1979, Richard Kearney and Joseph O'Leary organize a colloquium in Paris on "Heidegger and the Question of God." There they brought together the followers of the

German philosopher, Jean Beaufret, François Fediér, François Vezin — but also Levinas, Ricoeur, Marion, Dupuy, Breton, Greisch. The confrontation took place at the Irish College of Paris. The tension was lively. The organizers had arranged the meeting under the title of the "double affiliation" of Hebraism and Hellenism.

Ricoeur set the tone: "What often surprised me about Heidegger was how, it seems, he systematically evaded confrontation with the entirety of Hebrew thought. It occurred to him to take the Gospels and Christian theology as points of departure for his thinking; however, by continually avoiding the Hebraic corpus, which is the absolute stranger in relation to Greek discourse, he avoids ethical thinking with its dimensions of the relationship to the other and of justice, of which Levinas has said so much."

In the wake of these ideas, Levinas situated his discussion by asking if, in terms of the question "Why is there Being rather than nothing?" it is not necessary to substitute another "against nature, against the very naturalness of nature: Is Being just? Bad conscience. The question most suppressed, but older than that which seeks the meaning of Being."[13]

In fact, Ricoeur was responding here to the silence of Heidegger, who had refused to answer him many years earlier, in Cerisy, when the philosopher and the Protestant exegete had boldly raised the question of a biblical God as defined within the horizon of Being, particularly in the Book of Exodus, where this God exclaims, "I am what I am." An interpretation that Levinas could understand all too well.

But beyond the encounter between the God of the Bible and Being there remains, still more alive, that encounter with the Good, "beyond Being." Bernhard Casper had organized a colloquium in Pays-Bas, and Levinas, as usual, made the detour through Liège, and then Maastricht, so as not to pass though

Germany. Jean Greisch went with Levinas and found himself in the same compartment with him and his wife. "I can still hear," he recounts, "as if it were happening today, Levinas telling me how surprised he was that thinkers could be amazed by the fact that there is something rather than nothing, and that this is the radical point of departure of metaphysics. Then he added that, to his mind, the fact that in a world as cruel as ours, something like the miracle of kindness could appear was infinitely more worthy of amazement."

The final trace of this contradictory relationship was seen in March 1987 at the International College of Philosophy where Miguel Abensour had asked Emmanuel Levinas to speak about Heidegger. At first, the philosopher mentioned his youthful admiration, "irresistible still today," saluted once again "a philosophical intelligence among the greatest and fewest," and then immediately followed the praise, as he always did, with the comment on "the irreversible abomination attached to National Socialism in which the brilliant man could have, in one way or another, it does not matter how, taken part."

For his talk, Levinas read a text entitled, "Death for. . . ." Citing a passage of verse from 2 Samuel 1:23 about the death of Saul and Jonathan, "Cherished and amiable throughout their lives, they were not separated by death, lighter than angels, stronger than lions," he developed a commentary according to which, contrary to the Heideggerian analysis, death is not the final point, that it does not dissolve everything, that we do not always die alone, that one can die for the other, and that, in a certain way, one always dies for the other.

There is, in humanity, this possibility of surpassing the animal movement of life. And of concluding on this "future of death in the present of love."[14]

11 | THE DOUBLE AND THE OPPOSITE

In 1964, an essay by Jacques Derrida appeared in *La Revue de Métaphysique et de Morale* — later reprinted in *Writing and Difference* — entitled, "Violence and Metaphysics: An Essay on the Thought of Emmanuel Levinas."[1] Astute, dense, and rigorous, it was the first study of *Totality and Infinity,* as well as the first great critical examination of the philosopher's major work. In well-developed strokes, Derrida went through all of the work's articulations of thought with a fine-toothed comb, full of praise for its originality, its audacity, its style. At the same time, dissecting the concept of alterity, he pointed out a basic weakness. For him, the idea of the irreducible, absolute alterity of the Other was problematic. The Other is not what he is, the neighbor, the stranger, if he is not an alter ego, if he is not also an I. The critique was technical — Derrida used Husserl against his own disciple — but it touched the heart of the project, and moreover it led Levinas to modify certain aspects of his thinking on the nature of subjectivity. Was this critique the catalyst for the eventual evolution in Levinas's thought from *Totality and Infinity* to *Otherwise Than Being*? There is no proof of this in written form, and the two men themselves never clearly indicated it, but one detects a possible influence by Derrida's essay when studying the two works. At any rate, the essay was decisive. It situated Levinas as an authority within the philosophical debate, and gave his first great work a standing that it would be assigned again and again.

THE MEETING

For a long time, I wanted to meet with Jacques Derrida. He was very busy, always between trips. On one occasion he gave the excuse that interviews caused him anxiety and that he had a phobia of tape-recorders — a bit like Levinas. On another occasion, he said yes on the condition that I first write to him about the subject, and on his books, before agreeing to discuss it. How could I tell him that I felt incapable? That his work, so vast and multidimensional, intimidated me? Then, there were a few exchanges between us at Levinas's graveside amid the emotions stirred upon hearing his text, recited under the open sky, titled "Adieu." And there were new readings as well. The discovery of a more literary Derrida, one who was suddenly closer. Writing that is decentered, disconnected and diffuse, where one is carried away by music, by long phrases, wild punctuation and a syncopated rhythm, where one is cast under a spell without always understanding what is being said. Writing as in a trance, like one of those dances where one spins around, faster and faster, closing one's eyes, discovering one's breath anew with each turn. A fracturing of language, this deconstruction, that is perhaps nothing more than a way of rediscovering the power of words. This manner of calling the reader to witness, grabbing him by the throat, hypnotizing him.

There are more personal evocations later on — for example, his writing about circumcision, which is haunting, obsessive, and which Geoffrey Bennington calls his "malaise of belonging."[2] Or the story about the chickens and the roosters, slaughtered by a rabbi the day before Yom Kippur, that continued to run around headless. These memories from childhood that, when one shares identical ones — I often dream about them, about being a kid — and when they are reawakened through the grace of writing, arouse something like gratitude.

Still other things made me turn to him: the importance of expressing acknowledgment and the celebration of proper names; a thinking that was always on the extreme edge, always hyperbolic; the affinity for certain Levinasian themes, increasingly affirmed over the years — but which cannot be fully superimposed — such as trace, death, hospitality and forgiveness. And then, the idea of an "unfaithful fidelity," at once so close and so far from Levinas.

Derrida's resistance to meeting slowly faded. The obscurantism, the narcissism of which he is so often accused in France — indeed, one has to go to the United States to discover that this author, who is regarded as the most hermetic, is actually the most widely translated and most celebrated among French philosophers — did not totally disappear. But, henceforth, I did learn to read him.

We agreed to meet at the bar of the Lutétia Hotel. He came from L'École des Hautes Études en Sciences Sociales, where he gave a course on Wednesdays, dressed in a maroon suit, strands of his white hair falling on it, his complexion somewhat pale, but gradually lighting up with a warm smile as he recalled certain anecdotes. It is primarily these anecdotes that remain from that conversation.

TRACES AND EXCHANGES

Philosophical exchanges, actually, hardly ever took place between Derrida and Levinas. Instead, it is better to speak of "a great affection between them." "You know," said Derrida, "I notice that, between philosophers, one does not talk. We do not talk about philosophy. This was the case with Althusser, with Lacan, even with Ricoeur, to whom I was an assistant." Only an affection. And meetings, a good number of them. Fifteen or so, each time at Levinas's home. "We also wrote each other a lot, when there were publications. And then, as is often the case in Paris when there are many, we stop. But all the books are dedicated, and dedications are often occasions for saying something." Other meetings took place during joint participation at colloquiums. Like the time in Strasbourg when Levinas, speaking about God, said something that made the whole auditorium laugh: "Now, when one says God, it is necessary to say: pass me the word, would you!"

His voice grows sad, without any affectation. "We saw each other at the funeral, yes? It's how long now, four years already?" The grief is obvious, evoking a man whose thinking, he says, has accompanied him his entire adult life.

Derrida has many memories, but first and foremost he wants to hold on to those that emerge out of everyday life and that illustrate Levinas's way of being. A dry sense of humor, a liking for people, a striking character. Indeed, one day, at his home on rue d'Auteuil, Levinas complained of being burdened with all kinds of papers, which were crammed into an office because he could not bring himself to get rid of them. "What do you do with your papers? I don't know what to do with them. I have a mind to burn them one day, but I haven't yet resigned myself to throwing them in the garbage." Another day, Derrida tells Levinas that his son has written to him, telling him that he had decided to sign his name with a pseudonym rather than using his father's name. This decision bothered Derrida, but Levinas said, "But on the contrary, I find that to be quite noble on his part, quite a mark of respect!" "I was moved by that," says Derrida. There were also phone calls sometimes, just to talk, or to get some advice. Like the time Levinas was invited to participate in a conference at Johns Hopkins University in Baltimore and he called to find out how things worked there, what he could expect, and most importantly, whether he could bring Michael's piano.

Their relationship basically began in 1964 with the appearance of the article "Violence and Metaphysics." The text was published in two parts. Derrida went to see Levinas. Derrida recounts, "He said to me: 'You anaesthetized me in the first paper, then operated on me in the second.' That's it. We never spoke about it again. Except one time, when he said to me in passing, with a smile, and invoking the essay: 'Basically, you reproach me for taking the Greek *logos* in the same way one takes a bus, in order to get off.'" And Derrida adds, "A few years later, when another essay appeared in a collection of essays in his honor, he didn't say a word. Perhaps because it was in a very different style, more fictional. Maybe he didn't have the time to read it."

This reminds me, in fact, of a conference on psychoanalysis and Judaism in Montpellier attended by Levinas, well on in years by that time. It was during a lunch break, the atmosphere was relaxed, and we were talking about the collection that would be dedicated to him, *Textes pour Emmanuel Levinas*,[3] and in particular the essay by Derrida. I said, naively and a bit out of habit, that I did not understand any of it. He added, a bit politely, definitely out of politeness: "Me neither," which he then quickly took back, mumbling, "To tell you the truth, I just received the collection, and I haven't had the time to look into it."

GAPS AND CRACKS

Affection, then, between the two men? Without a doubt. Even more, respect and attachment. Jacques Rolland, nearest among the near, speaks of "a very great admiration." What brought them together? Husserl, of course. Levinas very much liked *Speech and Phenomena.* Indeed, he read all of Derrida's writings on Husserl. There was this strong kinship. And what about Heidegger? Derrida is silent.

I then risk the question about Judaism as inspiration and the man with the white hair confesses that, for his part, he does not possess a real Jewish culture. "But I don't know," he adds, "are we conscious of that which makes us write?" I quote a line from the Hazon Ish, a Polish rabbi who lived during the eighteenth century: "Judaism perhaps wholly consists in knowing the true significance of words." He becomes tense: "Yes, but we could say that about all cultures, about all of civilization!" I: "Here it is probably pushed to the limit. That's what the Hazon Ish is saying." He, exacerbated: "So it is better here than in the others?" I: "No, but it's pushed to the extreme." He: "So it's excess that is Jewish!" And we laugh, the two of us.

More seriously, what separated Derrida from Levinas, what posed a problem for him, as he mentions in some of his writings, was the relationship to the opposite sex, those passages concerning the feminine in *Totality and Infinity,* as well as his position on Israel, very Zionist, which he maintained rather uncritically. And finally, his general attitude toward France, which Derrida deemed too patriotic, but which he nonetheless found understandable since Levinas was grateful to France for welcoming and protecting him during the war. "I permit myself certain discrepancies," says Derrida, referring here to his own attitude toward the war. One asks how, in an era when he was forced to quit school because of racist laws, he became extremely attuned to racist abuse, and at the same time rebellious against any attitude of seclusion in a community. How, in the face of rejection, did he rebel and refuse to attend the school on rue Maupas — was it Maimonides School? — to which they wanted to make him return? Once again, "unfaithful fidelity" — rather analogous to the "fidelity without faith" described by Levinas. Didn't Derrida write somewhere: "There is always more than one father and more than one mother"?

At that point what naturally cropped up in the course of the conversation was the issue of circumcision, so present in his work. Derrida explained that, from the time he was young, he dreamed of writing a book on the subject. He collected texts, conducted research and reflected for a long time on it. His intention was to use a form of autobiographical writing that traversed this umbilicus, a kind of "circonfession." But then, he came to realize that he would never write this book — although traces of it can be found in *Glas* and at the end of *The Postcard*. I risked saying that, basically, "you are both philosophers of the gap, of the wound," borrowing this expression from Michael, who used it to describe his father. Yes, he acknowledged.

THE BEAUFRET AFFAIR

To be sure, the relationship between the two philosophers was also nourished in various ways by the history of French philosophy in the second half of the twentieth century. In

1967, François Fédier wanted to publish a collection of essays in honor of Jean Beaufret. He solicited Jacques Derrida, Roger Laporte, Michel Deguy, René Char, Maurice Blanchot. It once happened over lunch that Laporte warned Derrida about an anti-Semitic remark made by Beaufret. It was in reference to the nomination of a professor at Clermont-Ferrand and Beaufret asserted that, if it were up to him, he would not vote for a Jew. The professor in question was Levinas. Immediately, Derrida decided that it would be impossible for him to participate in the tribute to Beaufret. He withdrew the essay he had submitted to Fédier. Fédier, flabbergasted, retaliated by saying that this was really a cabal at work, a "new conspiracy" against Beaufret. In the meantime, Maurice Blanchot made contact with Derrida, and the two, shocked, met at Levinas's house. The philosopher greeted them very calmly, taking the news lightly, shrugging his shoulders. For him, none of this was important. He did not want to dramatize the situation. Indeed, he felt the texts should be published. "I was very surprised," says Derrida, "because Beaufret was an anti-Semite, and had attacked Levinas quite strongly."

After Beaufret's death, it was discovered that he had supported Robert Faurisson, a historian in Lyon and leader of the Holocaust denial movement in France. A sycophant of Heidegger, moreover, his constant advocate and apologist, his interlocutor — to whom the *Letter on Humanism* is addressed — this later historical revisionism shows itself to be a symptom. How could a young undergraduate, majoring in philosophy and German, a cayman of L'École Normale after the war, a mentor of many generations of students, crown his life with such stupidity, incomprehensible to both his friends and students? Perhaps the answer is found in the Greek and pagan exaltation that dominated Beaufret's youth, which had him submit unconditionally to Heidegger in whom he found the perfect expression of a rebirth of an anti-Judeo-Christian occident, the political expression of which he found in the emergence of the "New Right," also pagan, at the end of the 1980s. More important than such hypotheses, though, is the fact that the symptom is still there, once again in the form of silence: if Beaufret's most important work is his *Dialogues avec Martin Heidegger*, one finds no mention of the Jewish question.

The book paying homage to Beaufret appeared finally under the title, *The Endurance of Thought, in Honor of Jean Beaufret*.[4] Maurice Blanchot's essay was included and dedicated to Levinas, with this statement: "For Emmanuel Levinas, with whom, for forty years, I have been bound by a friendship that is closer to me than my own self: in a rapport of indivisibility with Judaism."

THE BOUTANG EPISODE

It was altogether different with the Boutang episode. On March 19, 1976, the university board of directors at the Sorbonne nominated the philosopher Pierre Boutang for the chair of metaphysics, as the successor to Emmanuel Levinas. About one hundred left-wing thinkers, including Jacques Derrida, published a petition denouncing this nomination, pointing to Boutang's past when he was a young follower of Maurras. "I signed and collected signatures for this petition," Derrida says, "and I went to see Levinas to tell him that I was not soliciting his signature so as not to make it awkward for him. He said to me, 'You are right, I will not sign it.' Derrida was nevertheless surprised: "God knows he wrote such abhorrent things, that Boutang!"

This case, no doubt, was more complex. The young Pierre Boutang, born in 1916, was a leading university figure before the war. Jean Wahl compared him to Hölderlin, Georges Pompidou spoke of him as a man of overflowing genius in his *Mémoires*, and Maurice Clavel recalls how his "Cothurne" saved him from fascist temptations. Moreover, unlike the experiments of Maurice Blanchot and Claude Roy, Boutang was purported to be a strict royalist, and it is under this affiliation that he wrote for l'Action Française in the summer of 1939 at the age of twenty-three. An officer in the army during the collapse of the French forces, spurning Vichy and the lot of the occupation, he quickly left for North Africa where he worked in General Giraud's cabinet before joining the Liberation forces.

It was upon his return to France after the war that Pierre Boutang's destiny was forged. Asserting an unconditional support for Charles Maurras, Boutang vehemently denounced the charge of collaboration filed — in his eyes, unjustly — against this master of his youth. The Gaullists, of whom Boutang was an adversary while in Algeria, demanded his expulsion from the university. From 1947 to 1954, Boutang shared the same fate as the reprobates of l'Action Française who, once Maurras died, cast him out in turn. It was thus during this time period that Boutang wrote his most polemical and most reprehensible works, works that he himself would eventually come to condemn in self-criticism.

Boutang asserts that, in founding La Nation Française in 1954, he wanted to break with all the old demons of the right, which were, above all, anti-Semitism and the shadows of Vichy. Under his guidance, this journal, wherein the likes of Gabriel Marcel, Roger Nimier, Antoine Blondin, Philippe Ariès and the painter Mathieu rubbed shoulders, went on to fulfill a crucial role in a number of ways: in 1958, by pushing for General de Gaulle's return to power; in 1962, by advocating the decolonization of Algeria; and in 1967, by supporting Israel and recognizing the fundamental rights of Zionism.

But alongside this meandering political trajectory was Boutang the philosopher, poet and novelist, translator of Blake, author of *Ontology of the Secret,* which earned him the friendship of Georges Steiner, the Cambridge critic who put this work on the same shelf as Plato and Plotinus. When, finally, Boutang succeeded Levinas at the Sorbonne, it was also for the purpose of teaching Rashi, whom he began to study in the 1960s.

Heidegger was unpardonable. But Boutang, for Levinas, was pardonable. He forgave him completely because he had helped Jean Wahl during the war, and also because he was able to make a twofold return, both a biblical one and a political one, for his youthful mistakes in the very core of his thought. According to University of Jerusalem professor Michael Bar-Zvi, a former student of Boutang in 1968 in Turgot, who attributes his own discovery of Judaism and his *Aliya* to Boutang, Levinas once confided in him: "There you have a teacher!"

DIFFERENCES AND PROXIMITIES

These, then, are some of the scenes remembered by Derrida that punctuated their years of friendship, and to which their work bears witness. And not just in the later works when Levinas's presence asserted itself more and more. This presence was there for a long time. It is worth noting that Levinas was a member of the jury at Derrida's dissertation defense. And Derrida claims affiliation with three names: Heidegger, Blanchot, Levinas. But it is also true that this presence was most perceptible in the later books and, of course, in the "Adieu" text.

Levinas himself wrote little on Derrida. There is one essay, which was initially published in 1973 in the review *L'Arc* under the title "Altogether Otherwise," and then later reprinted in a collection of essays entitled *Proper Names*. It is an ambivalent essay in which Levinas speaks of a "new ripple" (borrowing Victor Hugo's term for the poetry of Beaudelaire) in response to Derrida's "new, so new" text of 1964. With a very difficult passage bearing the heading "Tomorrow Is Today," in which Levinas compares him to a barber he encountered as a soldier during the collapse between Paris and Alençon. The latter invited the "lads" to his shop, proclaiming to everyone present: "All shaves are free today!" A harsh critique, the article nevertheless concludes with an amicable salute: "The ridiculous ambition of 'improving' a true philosopher is assuredly not my intent. Our crossing of paths is already very good, and it is probably the very modality of the philosophical encounter. In emphasizing the primordial importance of the questions raised by Derrida, I have desired to express the pleasure of a contact at the heart of a chiasmus."[5]

He did not keep up with all of Derrida's work. Each philosopher had his "thing," as he used to say about himself. He most certainly regarded Derrida to be a prolific writer; too much so, perhaps. But that did not deter his "respect and admiration" for him, according to Jacques Rolland, who claims to have repeatedly witnessed these sentiments. This did not exclude certain reproaches. Rolland has a little story. "What do you want?" Levinas said one day to him, "Derrida? He's like an abstract painter. One always wonders whether he has the ability to do something true."

What separated them? Without a doubt, it was the aesthetic side of one of them and the religious side of the other. Faith in spite of everything for one, and eternal suspicion for the other. But they both embraced the same violence, despite everything said by Levinas's detractors about the "saccharine" aspect of his thought. This is what François-David Sebbah,[6] a disciple of both men, called the "uninhabitable" character of their work.

And then, there was the point of convergence, the nexus, with Derrida's famous 1964 essay. This "trumpet call" (Adriaan Peperzak) had a decisive influence on many, albeit not all. Not only on the work's reception, but also on its very evolution.

Although Levinas never confessed, either in public or in private, to being influenced by Derrida's criticisms, the mark is evident, at least in form. There were two Levinases: the one who wrote *Totality and Infinity* in 1961, and the other who wrote *Otherwise Than Being* in 1973. The two books belong to a single continuum, and yet the themes are abandoned or at least less apparent: femininity, maternity, eros, sameness, totality . . . while in the second work we find the neighbor, substitution, persecution, enigma.

"There is continuity in the project," says Jacques Rolland, "but there is a hiatus in the writing, in the formulation, and ultimately in the outcome. And I am convinced that what constitutes the bridge, or the leap between the two, is Derrida's 1964 essay."

One expert on the work is Stephane Moses, a professor of German literature who teaches at the University of Jerusalem. He argues, "The only one who understood everything, very quickly, very early on, is Derrida." He himself posed the question to Levinas one day: "What happened between these two books? What took place in your life?" And he received this answer, on which he continues to reflect: "What happened is that I became good!"

To be sure, *Otherwise Than Being* cannot be reduced to this dialogue with Derrida. The work was born from his own vision. It stretches its roots down into the depths of

Levinas's life, experience and thought. He himself admitted, upon being asked, that he had yet to know how he came to write it.

What happened between these two men, between these two corpuses, was an implicit dialogue coupled with a mutual friendship. This dialogue ended with Levinas's death and the "Adieu" essay, the eulogy in which Derrida gives thanks to "someone whose thought, friendship, trust, and 'goodness' . . . will have been for me, as for so many others, a living source, so living, so constant, that I am unable to think about what is happening to him or happening to me today, namely, this interruption or a certain nonresponse within a response that will never come to an end for me for as long as I live."[7]

So to speak

This God who comes to mind, to the idea, at the end of language, who is there only if called upon, who appears and disappears, who is present and absent, and who rises up only if one truly wants to meet him, is a God who is revealed in the Book, who speaks to us through the Bible, who asks us for our fidelity, who remains the God of Abraham, of Isaac and of Jacob, but who is henceforth without promise. Like a powerless benevolence.

It is the One of Maimonides, for whom knowledge is impossible, and for whom one can only follow the trace.

It is the One of the Song of Songs, with the sublime image of a knock at the door, without knowing who knocked, or even whether it was really heard.

It is the One of the Gaon of Vilna: "Not a single person knows what God is about, not even if he exists."

And it is the One, of course, whom he considered his own.

We spoke one day about the names of God as they are found in the Jewish tradition. He devoted a lesson to this theme, detailing each of them (Elohim, HaShem, El Shaddai . . .) with the proper signification attached to each one. There was one that he did not know, namely Kavyakhol, which I told him my father used sometimes — it was before I learned from Chaim Brézis, a mathematician and lover of biblical exegesis, that the word is found in rabbinic literature.

Literally, it means: "Making necessary allowances." Or more simply, "So to speak."

So to speak. Like an otherwise said. Or an otherwise than being. He liked the expression very much. He repeated Kavyakhol, Kavyakhol, like a candy melting in his mouth.

12 | THE NEAR AND THE FAR

To retrace Levinas's journey is also to reconstruct the views of others, the juxtaposition of itineraries, and the successive meetings that left their mark on the course of his life and that enriched his work. The encounter with Paul Ricoeur, a believer and a philosopher living out this inner dialogue at the heart of his thinking and always avoiding the confusion, much like Levinas, is first among those intellectual and human moments that need to be recalled. Ricoeur is not to be found among those "proper names" to whom Levinas paid tribute in his collection of essays recognizing the men and women who surrounded him in every sense of the word. To be sure, Ricoeur arrived much later in Levinas's life.

Born in 1913 in Valencia, Paul Ricoeur was orphaned at a very young age, having lost his mother in the first months of his life, and then his father during the war of 1914. A war orphan, Ricoeur found his home in books, and later in writing and in teaching. He, too, was an initiate of the "Fridays" of Gabriel Marcel, to whom he was quite close; was nourished on Husserl's teachings in the early 1930s; and was an associate of the review *Esprit* founded by Emmanuel Mounier.

A welcoming and always vigilant spirit, he went through a pacifist period between the two wars and fell prey to Munich's sirens. Mobilized in 1939 and then, like Levinas, taken prisoner to a Pomeranian camp, he succumbed to Pétainist temptations during the early years, making sense of it only after the war. "The truth is that, until 1941, I was seduced, along with others — the propaganda was tremendous — by certain aspects of Pétainism. I probably took my feelings of having participated in the Republic's failure and turned them against the Republic itself."[1]

Their itineraries overlap, albeit several years apart from one another, in Strasbourg, where Ricoeur went to teach after the war. There he even struck up a friendship with one of Levinas's old classmates, Rémy Rontchevsky, a Marxist philosopher who was connected to the review *Esprit*, and had among his students a young scholar by the name of Alex Derczanski, who had a keen interest in Judaism and Yiddish. It was also during this period that the Protestant philosopher frequented an interfaith "biblical symposium," where he made the acquaintance of André Néher. Levinas at this time was just starting his Saturday morning Bible class at the Enio.

At the beginning of the 1960s, Ricoeur took up the position of philosophy professor at the Sorbonne at the same time that he was teaching in the College of Protestant Theology in Paris. And when the University of Nanterre, annexed by the Sorbonne, opened its doors, he was asked to preside over the nascent department of philosophy. In 1967, as dean of this department scouting for a teaching team, he called upon his friend and companion in captivity, Mikel Dufrenne, from Poitiers, and solicited two other candidates. One was Sylvain Zac, a philosophy professor at a Parisian high school who had defended his dissertation on Spinoza but was prevented from completing his *agrégation* before the war due to certain laws against foreigners. The other was Emmanuel Levinas, who was also teaching at Poitiers where he had received an appointment two years after defending his thesis.

ABOUT THE BIBLE

Châtenay-Malabry, a Parisian suburb. A building at the far end of the park, under a sign reading "White Walls," houses what used to be a community. Despite the sun sweeping across a bay window, the atmosphere has a certain rustic feel to it and there are traces of a communal society that once existed here. Mounier, founder of the bygone community, lived right below the apartment where Ricoeur lives today. On the mailbox one can still read the name of Jean-Marie Domenach, longtime director of *Esprit*.

"People are disappearing around me," my interviewee says. Before our conversation begins, a telephone call brings news of the death of a Jesuit priest in Krakow, who was a friend of Cardinal Wojtyla — Pope John Paul II, about whom there is a lot to say in our interview.

"Don't expect details, dates, names of places. . . . As they say, we have more memories than the young, but we have less memory."

Protestant philosopher, biblical exegete, Paul Ricoeur was the companion, colleague and friend of Emmanuel Levinas. Their first meeting was an indirect one. Ricoeur had heard about Levinas when he was still in Strasbourg, when the young Levinas published his first work on Husserl. Jean Hering, professor of New Testament studies in the faculty of theology at Strasbourg and author of a "phenomenology of religions," spoke highly of it.

Some years later, Ricoeur was present at the first lecture

on "Time and the Other" at Jean Wahl's school on Saint-Germain-des-Prés. "I heard Sartre's famous lecture on existentialism and humanism. The world was outside, while here, it was more intimate." He recalls, though, this statement by Wahl: "You have genius, you must write!" and the speaker's embarrassed smile.

"I helped out with this kind of birth, there at Saint-Germain-des-Prés, under Jean Wahl's patronage. It is Wahl, actually, who introduced me to Levinas, before the appearance of *Totality and Infinity* and the bedazzlement over his book."

The personal relationship developed later, much later, in fact. Initially it was an academic affair. "I was very proud to have lured him to Nanterre," says Ricoeur, "because he had not completed his *agrégation,* he was not really a graduate. I was not one either, for that matter. But there was a prejudice to overcome, and I succeeded in doing so with what little power I had."

It was from then on that their personal relationship began — "this kind of closeness and distance that was befitting of him" — the discussions, the encounters, the visits. Ricoeur often went to the school via rue d'Auteuil, and was readily received at the Levinas home.

> I got to know Mme. Levinas, and to witness the depth of their intimacy and attachment. Levinas did not travel to any conference without Mme. Levinas. It's why I understood the extent of his pain when she died. I truly valued and understood all those admirable pages in *Totality and Infinity* on domestic grandeur, and that beautiful page on the caress. Before Derrida, there was no one besides him who spoke about it in this way. This side of Levinas was not always visible. But I could see perfectly, during this period, this note of intimacy, in its great proximity.

From 1967 to 1973, the two men met regularly at Nanterre. At one point, Ricoeur had the task of establishing a center for the philosophy of religion. He had in mind to recruit Levinas for Judaism, Henri Duméry for Catholicism, and himself for Protestantism. Unfortunately, the project was derailed by the events of May 1968. François Dosse, his biographer, would describe this as a great disappointment for Ricoeur.[2]

In a certain way, and much like Jean Wahl before him, therefore, the Protestant exegete and philosopher assumed the role of intermediary between the world of the university and Levinas, who easily would have been held back from this world.

In 1973, François Wahl asked Ricoeur to intercede with Levinas in order to get him to bring his Nijhoff publications over to Seuil. In 1978, he repeated his request. But the transfer did not take place. Levinas remained faithful to his Dutch editor for his philosophical works, just as he remained faithful to Minuit for his so-called "confessional" works. In these loyalties, too, there was a kind of modesty at stake.

Around the Pope

Later on, the two men regularly crossed paths in Rome at the "Castelli colloquia," and then at Castel Gandolfo's colloquia. Every year, at the beginning of January, the two colleagues met up at these Roman conferences. They enjoyed the cordial confrontation, the open discussions presided over by the rather eccentric aristocrat Enrico Castelli.

Castel Gandolfo was something else, however. Originally, it was the idea of Pope John Paul II to gather thinkers around him in order to reflect on the future of the world.

"I had to go four times, I believe," recounts Ricoeur. "The pope attended the discussions twice a day, remaining completely silent. He would invite us to share a meal, and I recall one of these occasions. We were invited, Levinas and I. Levinas said, 'You sit at the Pope's right, and I'll sit on his left.' I said: 'No, the other way around.' We had a little skirmish over prerogatives, and each one of us understood what it meant."

A Jewish philosopher and a Protestant philosopher sitting with the pope! "It's one of those enigmas for me, John Paul II's personality," says Ricoeur. "He is surprisingly aware of relations outside of the Church, and considerably severe with regard to Catholics. This is why he is often perceived as being repressive, when in fact he is a man who probably has the greatest understanding of the planet's fullness. He is the great voice when all is said and done. Look at the trip he made to Israel, a flawless trip, with all the right gestures, done at the right moments, like at the Wailing Wall. . . . For me, it remains an enigma. Not being a Catholic myself, I enjoy this generosity. And I think that, more than I, Levinas deserved it and appreciated the symbolism."

But the pope's high esteem for Levinas was not, Ricoeur insists, without philosophical reason. "As it happens, John Paul II was originally not a product of scholasticism. He was a student of Roman Ingarden, a Pole nurtured on Husserl. There was a Husserlian lineage, therefore, that was eventually cut off to some extent. But there was this profound affinity, and, in any event, a deep respect and very great admiration."

The last colloquium at Castel Gandolfo in which Ricoeur participated took place in the fall of 1994. Levinas was not there. Pope John Paul II took his guest aside to confide in him, "Would you please give my regards to Levinas and tell him of my respect and admiration." Immediately upon returning to Paris, Ricoeur telephoned Levinas and went to visit him.

"He was filled with the pain of his wife's death. He said

to me with irony, 'In the end, a Protestant is needed for a Catholic to speak to a Jew.' This is the kind of humor we had between us, always with a wink of the eye. We knew perfectly what was not said in everything that we did say." And he adds, "You could see every element of the complicit competition between us. This is why there were attempts, on several occasions, to pit us against each other, but we never let ourselves be locked into such opposition."

THE GOOD, THE NAME, AND THE FAITHFULNESS

Following Levinas's death, Ricoeur wrote a piece in *Réforme* in which he commented on the strange coincidence of dates. "The day that was Christmas for me would be the date of Levinas's death."[3]

One month later, during a soirée organized by the Sorbonne in honor of Levinas, Ricoeur devoted the essential part of his speech to hyperbole — that philosophical method that is always at play in the work, and which proceeds by emphasis, exaggeration and excess:

> I now believe that this is the Russian side of Levinas. When he says 'I am guiltier than others,' in my opinion, this is not Jewish but Dostoyevsky, it is *The Brothers Karamazov*. You know that he could recite Pushkin by heart, that he was nurtured on the great Russian authors. To my mind, this influence has not been sufficiently attended to. That was part of my little debate with him over the use of hyperbole. Say more in order to say less — that is Levinasian hyperbole, but it is a Dostoyevskian hyperbole.

Ricoeur nevertheless confesses that there is a kind of extreme attitude at stake here that he never quite understood.

"When he says, 'I am the hostage of the Other,' it is vital to see that Levinas was hostage to no one. One did not get one's claws into him. When he says, 'I am here, do I not take another's place?' — if you were familiar with the man, you would know that he quietly stayed in his place. I must say that, for my part, I cannot comprehend this. I have difficulty reconciling the great philosopher, the person who was so delighted to be selected by Paris IV and then by the Sorbonne, with this type of viciousness of writing. I have never been able to bring these two together."

Certainly, the itinerary, the wartime captivity, the Bible, phenomenology, an affiliation with and a common attraction to exegesis, a concern for observing one's religious tradition, together with a kind of cheerfulness in everyday life and a sharp sense of humor, all of this brought Ricoeur and Levinas together. Yet each one followed his own path. Carried along by a culture of action and a taste for political engagement, anchored in the left, Ricoeur responded to all the entreaties of the times. This was not the case for Levinas, who was more reserved and, some would say, more cautious. But even the philosophical approaches and orientations were not altogether devoid of divergences. The Levinasian priority accorded to the Other is not immediately accepted by the Protestant philosopher. He explains,

> I am more and more apprehensive about this supposedly head-to-head opposition between us that some have tried to establish. For Levinas, one begins with the Other, I am told, whereas for you, you are still attached to the subject, or to reciprocity. But one begins where one can! These are the angles of attack, and everything depends on how one continues from there, and how one encounters the Other, and where one encounters her. So I encounter the Other in reciprocity. I always asked myself where I am in Levinas's text. Am I the one who says "I" — or the one who is spoken of as the "Other"? And Levinas, where is he? Does he say "I"? Or is he already "the third"? A certain interrogation is needed there for me, therefore. Which place does one occupy?

In the end, this relationship with Levinas, and the recapitulation of it, remains disjointed for Ricoeur. Regarding the student from Strasbourg whom he knew at first only through his reputation among university colleagues whom he visited in Paris, and then, decades later, after the eclipse of years of maturation, the sudden appearance of *Totality and Infinity* and the proliferation of other books, Ricoeur, without forgetting the impact of these philosophies, is unable to integrate the different faces.

"It is our encounter, in fact, that is disjointed. If I may say so: a staccato encounter. But it is so." What brought them together? In what space did they meet?

> It is twofold. There is Husserl, that is to say, a philosophical radicalness that was both for him and for me unjustifiably covered up by Heidegger. And then, on the other hand, Judaism, which is for me the family, the "elder brothers." My perception of Christianity is really built on the Hebrew Bible. Thus, I have two points of connection that are admittedly disconnected, and I ignore how they function together: Husserl and the Torah. And I don't know how this works for Levinas, either. There are no quotations from the Bible — except one or two maybe — in *Totality and Infinity*. It's Plato. It's Descartes. And when he reads in Plato that the idea of the Good is beyond Being, he is thinking of the unpronounceable Name, and he makes a kind of short-circuit that is never named as such. That the Unsayable and the Good of Plato are superimposed at a point that itself cannot be named, is something that I sense to be very deeply buried, something profoundly dissimulated and always said indirectly. But after all, I have a similar problem for my own part. My relationships, as a philosopher, to Judaism and to Christianity, at once separate and at the same time indivisible, are of the same nature. There was a fidelity in his philosophy to his Judaism, as I have to my Christianity.

For all that, Levinas disliked the fact that he was categorized as a religious philosopher. That he was stuck with a label. That he was placed in a niche. "Me, too," Ricoeur agrees,

I don't like it when I'm called a Protestant philosopher. One is a philosopher or one is not. I would 'protest' against that. I would say that I have a philosophical reading of Christianity. I have the Christianity of a philosopher. I dare say that Levinas has the Judaism of a philosopher. For his sake, I would put that on record as an honor. Not a Jewish philosopher, but a philosopher who has the Judaism of a philosopher. He belongs to the great Jewish family, but he comes with the approach of a Husserlian and an antagonism against Heidegger. He comes, bearing the philosophical totality, to inhabit the great Jewish space. But in my opinion, he is a philosopher who stands wholly apart. In *Totality and Infinity*, he speaks philosophy. These are two philosophical categories, totality and infinity. And Being and essence, these are not words of the Torah. I, too, would challenge this manner of categorizing us, and hence of marginalizing us.

But is it not also the legacy of their respective traditions that permitted the two of them, as philosophers, and consequently their communities of origin, to cause a stronger echo?

François Dosse, Ricoeur's biographer, says about them: "It is the inquiry into ethics that placed them at the heart of French intellectual life during the 1980s. There is between them, as products of the same generation, a truly shared affiliation of being deeply rooted in phenomenology, as well as a distance, resulting from divergent paths, with regard to the teaching of Husserl. They have the same urgent need to respect the specificity of the philosophical form, while at the same time pursuing parallel research into the texts belonging to their religious traditions." And he adds that, with Levinas as with Ricoeur, "if one makes this distance too radical, one bypasses the multiple reverberating effects on two sides of the frontier."[4]

EUROPE

"The approach of a Husserlian with an antagonism against Heidegger," says Ricoeur. We return again, in the course of this conversation, to his contradictory relationship with the author of *Being and Time*. A relationship that, according to Ricoeur, is constitutive of Levinas's work:

> Did you notice that the last published series of lectures is the one on death, where Levinas is still confronting Heidegger? He never stopped explaining himself in terms of Heidegger. Because he was the closest stranger. This was an ontology without ethics. And the problem, for Levinas, was to exit ontology and to make ethics the first philosophy. To do that, it was always necessary, as I have said, to continually deconstruct the hegemonic pretenses of Heideggerian ontology. Levinas never completed the rupture. Heidegger's moral character was not equal to his work, whereas Karl Jaspers was entirely equal to his work. Jaspers could not have been mistaken about Hitler. In the final analysis, Heidegger's is a philosophy that could not produce an ethics. There is a kind of empty place for the hero. Not having developed the ethical and political dimension of his own thinking, as Jaspers did, this is a deserted space, an ethical-moral space. It is therefore a kind of fundamental a-moralism. He was thus the perfect prey for Hitlerism. This is the flaw that had to be recognized and Levinas perceived it perfectly.

With a prejudice against Germany matched only by Jankélévitch, and with roots that Ricoeur deems to be so "Russian," we arrive at the question of Europe, at the numerous texts that Levinas devoted to this subject at the end of his life.

Paradoxically, this man who, after the war, refused to revisit the country of his captivity, was a fierce defender of Europe. He even gave a speech about Europe to the European parliament, and another one on peace. He advocated a European sentiment based on culture rather than simply on the power of the marketplace, but a sentiment informed by real history, including its abysses. It is this definition that he discussed one day in a magazine that had sought his opinion: "What is Europe? It is the Bible and the Greeks." In a short text wherein he developed this formula, Levinas concludes by evoking the ending of Vassili Grossman's *Life and Fate* and the "little kindnesses" that pass from one person to another, which, for him, attested to a new and an old consciousness in the essence of Europe.[5]

"I think," says Ricoeur, "that he held on to a sharp sense of having come from Lithuania, and of having crossed through Germany, this Germany into which he refused to set foot again. Nevertheless, he had to be sensitive to its reconstruction. It is this that distinguished him from Jankélévitch, who broke ties with everything that was German. Levinas was not embarrassed to talk about Husserl and Heidegger. They are two very different ruptures. For Jankélévitch, it was radical and insurmountable, whereas Levinas fully immersed himself in European literature. In a certain sense, yes, he was a great European."

The meeting ends, bringing me back to my earlier conversation with Derrida. Ricoeur, Derrida, Levinas: today, probably the three best-known names of French philosophy in Europe, the United States, and beyond, all three often associated with the canon.

Ricoeur puts it into context. After the war, the most influential movements were Marxism, existentialism and humanism.

Today, these three movements have disappeared. Which one has a claim upon posterity? Who will go down to purgatory and who will be sainted? We recall the case of Sartre, his return after twenty years of being forgotten. Ricoeur responds by praising his many talents — the novel, the essay, theater, philosophy. "To have written *Les séquestrés d'Altona, Les mots* and *Situations,* that is something unique. In this respect, no one could compete with him."

He adds that what perhaps unites the three names mentioned is the fact that they were all teachers first. The week before our interview, Ricoeur had given a talk at the Sorbonne on the notions of narration, memory and history. There were eight hundred people in the lecture hall as well as people in the street. "Yes, perhaps that is it," concludes Ricoeur. "Levinas liked to teach. Derrida adores teaching. And me too."

13 | THE ARCHIVIST AND THE PRECURSORS

Louvain, a winsome city in Flemish Belgium, medieval in character, a bit magical, its downtown laced in cobblestones, is home to a university that was, and remains, an important center for theological and metaphysical studies. From the year 1972, when Levinas received an honorary doctorate from the university, he regularly returned there. The university originally was both Flemish and Walloon. But a student revolt broke out in 1968 which ended in a separation of identities. The Flemish university stayed in the same location, and an entirely new campus was created northward of it bearing the name Louvain-la-Neuve. Curiously enough, both of them maintained their links to Levinas, continuing to furnish him with a veritable cult following. One devotee of the cult is Roger Burggraeve, author of a truly Benedictine labor,[1] namely a complete bibliography of Levinas's works, commentaries and articles about him, which is continually updated, and which to date, on this eve of the year 2000, already contains 222 pages and some two thousand entries.

Lively, passionate, his face perpetually in motion, Burggraeve welcomes me into his office at the university, and relates the story of how he met Emmanuel Levinas and of their long friendship. A Silesian priest, he was sent to Rome from 1963 to 1966. It was the time of Vatican II and the Church seemed to be in a good deal of turmoil. Albert Dondeyne had just published *Foi et pensée contemporaine,* which would have an impact on the evolution of Catholicism, and found himself being consulted by various bishops and council fathers. It was Dondeyne who suggested to Burggraeve, who was then appointed to the theology faculty at Louvain after his stay in Rome, that he concentrate on Levinas's writings. "Did you pick up *Totality and Infinity?* Very good. That's the path to follow!" Thereafter, our man was gripped by an "intellectual obsession" that would never let go. "In his approach to the Other, to the heteronomy of the Other as someone who speaks, I recognized a new approach. And through Levinas, I — a Catholic — rediscovered the Bible."

He remembers how, in college, at the age of seventeen, the year before he completed his studies in the humanities, he had a very talented professor of Greek who taught Sophocles and whose classes "opened his eyes." Unfortunately, this old master was also a teacher of Christian religion, which proved to be a disaster. Why was he incapable of doing with the Bible what he did with Antigone?

It was with Levinas, Burggraeve confesses, that he discovered how one can enter into a universe where the Bible does not stand in opposition to philosophy. And that a text does not have value because it is sacred; that it is sacred because it lays bare a universality.

In 1972, Burggraeve completed his dissertation on Levinas's work. That same year, the French philosopher was invited to Louvain to be made a doctor *honoris causa* of the university. At the end of the ceremony, in keeping with tradition, the entire academic cortege went through the city in a long procession. "In the street," recounts Burggraeve, "Levinas approached me. He stopped, left the procession and came up to me. Our conversation ended with an invitation to go see him in Paris."

Thus began a series of visits, which unfolded in the same manner on each occasion. At rue Michel-Ange, in the sitting room with the white doilies on the table, and the small glasses of Cointreau, which came from a cupboard as soon the chairs were drawn close together. "It was always like that, the cup of coffee and the little glass of Cointreau. Levinas said, with a touch of humor that was always perceptible when he was relaxed: 'According to the Hassidic rabbis, a true question comes from Slivovitz, an alcohol made from prunes, or it comes from the spirit of God. And even then a little Slivovitz can help out!'"

Thanks to Dondeyne, Hermann de Dijn, Adriaan Peperzak, and Burggraeve, Levinas was adopted by the University of Louvain. He gave numerous lectures there, on four or five separate occasions. He once said, "I feel at home here."

MONEY AND THE PRINCE

But the most surprising visit took place in 1986, this time in Brussels, at the invitation of a group of investment banks. The story is worth recounting. On the occasion of its twenty-fifth anniversary, this Belgian group of banks wished to organize a series of special events. Professor Robert Vandeputte, former minister of finance and honorary president of the Bank of Belgium, who also happened to be a keen philosophy student and a reader of Levinas, proposed that the anniversary be marked by their hosting distinguished lectures, and specifically by inviting the author of *Totality and Infinity* to Brussels to speak on "the philosophy of money."

Vandeputte and Burggraeve traveled to Paris to request the presence of the philosopher, who was initially surprised by their approach, but then let himself be convinced. He had many difficulties in writing the text, however, and still more difficulties in making the trip. His wife was unwell and had to remain in Paris. But in the end, on December 10, 1986, at the Palace of Congress, he obliged the investment bank group with a long-awaited lecture that he delivered before a distinguished audience of politicians, economists, and academics, as well as the prime minister.

In the preamble, the president of the group hailed him as "one of the greatest contemporary philosophers" and declared: "Your participation, Professor, in this symposium attests to the fact that the role of investment banks is not limited to collecting funds in order to convert them into credit, but that it must be situated in a much larger framework, touching on all aspects of life."[2]

Levinas very quickly circumvented "the social and economic reality of money" in order to reflect upon "the dimensions that money delineates or hollows out, or reveals in the moral conscience of European humanity." Money and exchange, interest and dis-interest, sociality and justice: the philosopher returned to themes near and dear to his thinking. For that matter, he had to postpone releasing this text and did not authorize its publication until after a good many alterations.

Burggraeve remembers that Levinas refused to take a single penny for this conference. He also remembers an official visit to the royal palace. Received by King Baudouin, the philosopher persisted in calling him "Monsieur le Prince," and blushed with emotion when the monarch began by asking him about his wife.

For Burggraeve, whose students jokingly like to call "Burginas," Levinas was first of all a philosopher of sensitivity. He was perceived as a harsh philosopher because of his insistence on ethics, on responsibility, but at the heart of his work there is the sensitivity of the subject, which is an opening onto the Other. Human beings are sensitive. At each of his talks, Levinas began by looking for his wife. "Where is she? Ah, there she is!" Once he made eye contact with her, he could talk. He also knew how to be very attentive. In 1976, he went to Louvain for two conferences, one on "truth and veracity," the other on "skepticism and reason." "I was sick at the time," recalls Burggraeve. "I had problems with my back and I ended up being hospitalized in a clinic. Levinas came to visit me after the second conference, accompanied by Samuel Hessling, who knew him well. They stayed for ten minutes. His demeanor was not exuberant, but rather, as always, reserved, but genuine. Then they stepped out, and, after Hessling left, Levinas returned and took my hand and said to me, 'God watch over you!'"

STAGES IN NOTORIETY

Louvain may be considered a center of Levinasism. Indeed, it is there, probably before France — one can account for this by glancing through Burggraeve's bibliography — that Levinas's renown began to grow. But other places and other individuals helped to cultivate it and spread it further. One individual who holds a special place in this circle is Adriaan Peperzak, a native of Holland and today a professor at Loyola University of Chicago. At the beginning of the 1960s, having completed his dissertation on Hegel at the Sorbonne, Peperzak assisted in organizing a conference at Louvain on *Totality and Infinity*, which had just been published. The young man had read the book over a week, without understanding it very well, but, certain that he was dealing with a great book, he became fixated on it and went hunting in the National Library in Paris to look for other texts.

Coming across articles in philosophy journals and in Jewish periodicals, Peperzak ended up publishing an inventory of Levinas's work in a journal, which he sent to Levinas, who gave a very kindly response. So Peperzak decided to go further and proposed an anthology of Dutch translations.

> It is a book for which I selected ten little pieces that are Jewish, religious, and some philosophical texts. I brought them together and commented on them. It was the beginning of a relationship that developed into a friendship. But a friendship in which he was the master, and I the one who received. Over time, that changed a bit. We went to the Castelli colloquia together, we got to know each other fairly well, and I became the young colleague of the great philosopher. In that respect, I can tell you that, from a personal point of view, he was a very important man in my life. What I knew was a man who practiced philosophy in an existential manner, not an absolutist one. An orthodox Jew, he was a model for me, but in a way that I would come to translate for myself.

The book was published in Holland under the title, *Philosophy of the Human Face,* and against all expectations enjoyed great success. Seven successive editions. And a circulation that went beyond philosophical circles — into circles of social activism, for example. "I don't know to what this success should be attributed. I suspect that it is the moral dimension that had an impact, or at least the manner in which morality was rehabilitated. Holland is certainly a country bent on morality, on being moralistic even, and everyone likes to get all worked up. This book was a revelation of a feasible, contemporary way to speak about morality."

The meetings came one after the other: the Castelli colloquia in Naples where the lawyer Marotta organized seminars at the Instituto Filosofico, or again on the Dutch frontier at the initiative of the German Bernhard Casper. It is there that Peperzak was asked one day to speak on the theme, "What do Christians have to learn from Levinas?"

"I did my best," Peperzak recounts. "I focused my exposition on the Levinasian critique of the mystical, attempting to show that mysticism was something altogether different from magic. That the mystical union presupposed charity, that whenever charity is missing, mysticism is led astray. Levinas was there. When I was finished, he whispered to me: 'It's true. Not far off at all. But aren't you being a bit heterodox?' I responded that perhaps it was worth the trouble. That gives you an idea of the level of friendship, of convergence, of affinities. But also of differences. We were very respectful." Another time, in Rome, Peperzak began his talk by affirming how much he owed to Hegel, Saint John of the Cross and Levinas. Whereupon Levinas, blushing with confusion, raised his arms, "Ah, you humble me!"

Eventually, Peperzak ended up in America. Levinas's name was hardly known there at the time. Alphonso Lingis had translated *Totalité et infini* and *Autrement qu'être*, but the resulting reverberations were weak. It was only during the 1970s that things slowly began to turn around.

"It would be very difficult to prove this, but it seems to me that Levinas became a celebrity in America from the moment that Derrida proclaimed that it was necessary to read him. When I arrived here, I got the impression that there was no one but him, but Derrida. I called him the pope of continental philosophy in America. From the time he wrote his long essay, which was perceived both as a critique and a recommendation, Levinas became a name."

"There was a tendency, moreover," he adds, "notably with Bernasconi, to associate the two names, to set them up as opposite poles of the same movement, which is not the case exactly."

Peperzak himself made no small contribution to introducing Levinas's work to American universities. From 1975 on, he gave courses at Yale and Boston, participated in conferences here and there, and twice invited Levinas to Loyola. It was at this university, incidentally, in Chicago, that Levinas came to meet Hannah Arendt. "I think it was the first time they saw each other, but I got the impression that they were not on the same wavelength. They spoke of Judaism and of Israel. Not of Heidegger, that was too delicate."

THE CHRISTIAN CIRCLE

Peperzak is a former Franciscan, and today a teacher at Loyola, a Jesuit institution. Interest in Levinas reaches diverse branches of Catholicism. What did Levinas bring to Christian thought? An inspiration, a reference point, more than a path to follow. Might he be able to explain this line by Burggraeve: "I have become a better Christian thanks to Levinas"? Peperzak smiles:

> That can make sense. But I can also say that if I have become worse, it would definitely be because of Levinas. In any case, I learned more from him about Christian theology than during the five years of my studies. It is probably a bit unjust to theology, but I did in fact learn from Levinas a possibility of rethinking the presuppositions of theology. Therefore, I do not know if I have become more of a believer. Perhaps indirectly, because Levinas was not only a master who taught thinking but also a model for how to live life. This was not as a moralist, and I do not like solemnity. Solemnity is not something I ever found in Levinas. There was humor, there was irony. What I probably did learn was the seriousness of the philosophical

enterprise. I recognize myself very clearly in what he was saying in his final years, that philosophy is the wisdom of love, and not only the love of wisdom. Perhaps, too, in the designation of the dangers of magic, the dangers of idolatry. . . . And then, also, it is important to point out that, when I was a student, there were not many opportunities to look at the Bible through the Talmud, for example, or through modern Jewish theology. He was the one who opened our eyes to all of that. For me, he was a voice, the voice of Israel, which compels us to take up again, to reexamine, to readjust our attitude to the history of Israel.

This influence on the Christian milieu, for Peperzak, is all the more noteworthy because it reached the highest level of the Church, notably due to Pope John Paul II.

"The pope read him, and I suspect that he probably took him to be the best Jewish thinker. I cannot prove this, and undoubtedly he met with other Jews. But knowing a bit of what the pope wrote, there is no doubt to my mind that Levinas was, for him, the model of a great Jewish thinker." Beyond this encounter at the summit, Peperzak continues to explain that it is, at any rate, a fact that in Holland, Belgium, the United States, Italy and in South America, Levinas's work found many readers among Christian philosophers and theologians, who perhaps even constituted the majority of his readers. While his work is founded on a long and stable Jewish tradition — even in its most strictly philosophical aspects — it was able to make an impression on many Christians due to its familiar timbre, its orientation and its demands.

Still, we cannot help but wonder at this curious phenomenon: a philosopher, a Jew, Levinas enjoyed a parallel readership within the circle of Christianity, and specifically a Western one. Besides a mark of universality that this suggests, perhaps it is also necessary to see it as the crystallization of a link that simultaneously joins and separates the children of an unfriendly yet common history. To grasp all that is at stake, all of the complexities, it is necessary to return to the Paris of the 1960s where everything began.

Bernard Dupuy, a Dominican priest, was for many years responsible for relations with Judaism after the Conference of the Bishops of France. Dupuy came to know Levinas not in Louvain but through Jacques Colette, a Dominican who at the time was teaching courses on Husserl and phenomenology at the Center for the Studies of Saulchoir and who accorded an important place to Levinas's interpretation. *Totality and Infinity* had just been published. "We were still in the existentialist period," recounts Dupuy. "We were hanging on to Sartre, and Jean Wahl was there. It was so important to have a voice like Levinas's around. It was most welcomed in our efforts to educate ourselves. It was a Jewish voice, first of all, the voice of a believer. Even if he did not express this in his commentaries on Husserl, it was there, transparent. That's how he was read, as I think many Jewish readers came to read him, too."

Dupuy, appointed to teach biblical hermeneutics and criticism, began studying Buber, Rosenzweig and Levinas. He discovered a paper presented by Levinas at the second colloquium of Jewish intellectuals on the thought of the author of *The Star of Redemption*. There he found the key phrase, "Judaism is a category of being." It was not one religion among others, something superimposed onto life, but a category. He was struck by the word. "It's important to point out how much this resonates in the ears of Christians," says Dupuy,

> apart from any notion of dialogue, or, it goes without saying, of confrontation or polemics. After that, Christians

resorted to the same locution. Why? Because during this period they were attempting a somewhat similar critique of religion, one proceeding from a need to get away from the social science of religions. Still, it can be a very delicate theme because the Jew will say in general: We are not a religion like the Christians are. Religion is thus placed in the opposing camp, just as the other takes the exact same approach. The problem for Christians, for that matter, is not in relation to Judaism. It is in relation to politics, nature, the notion of homeland, the notion of rootedness, and in relation to all the neo-pagans in Christianity such as Barrès and others who are flourishing once again. . . . It is not all that surprising that the idea of the biblical source was revitalized in the Judeo-Christian rapport of the times. Buber's review *Der Jude*, for example, deliberately gave a platform to Christian authors in this enterprise. It only lasted three years. They didn't have enough time to do very much. But it was nevertheless in the air.

Coming from Corbeil, where he taught in a faculty of theology close to the city, Dupuy was appointed director of the Istina Center in Paris. He enrolled at the Yavné school on rue Claude-Bernard, where he took classes in modern Hebrew and assisted in the Jewish intellectual colloquia where he met Levinas. With the latter's consent, he also attended the *shabbat* classes in Rashi at the Enio every week for four years. There again, meetings took place. Levinas often invited him to his home, one time along with Gershom Scholem.

SCHOLEM'S VIEW

"I recall that situation very well because I paid a price for it. It was for a *shabbat,* and the previous day he said to me: 'I'm inviting Scholem to lunch, if you'd like to come.' . . . I was very honored, as you can imagine! Because of Scholem. In fact, I drove him around in Paris. I was his host. He had his habits. He stayed at the same hotel. I drove him around every day in my not-so-comfortable two-horsepower vehicle. One time, he wanted to go to the municipal archives of Nanterre to examine some documents. I wasn't very smart; I went to pick him up at four o'clock in the evening, and we got stuck in a traffic jam. He began to groan, 'It's impossible, we will never arrive there! What would you have me do?!' In the end, the documents he wanted were not there and we returned empty handed, again in the same heavy traffic. He cursed. 'I have never seen such an ugly city,' he said, 'yet I know Tel Aviv . . .'"

For all that, Dupuy could not take up the invitation to lunch. He had to attend a conference on the Shoah. "I agreed to go," he continues, "it was set, I couldn't cancel, I was annoyed. I explained this to Levinas. He responded, 'The Shoah? That's not a subject for discussion.' I was completely cornered. I would have to pay the price for missing the lunch, but what could I do? Even so, he insisted." I venture to suggest that he insisted thus so as not to remain alone with Scholem. But Dupuy exclaims, "Ah, but I will surprise you! The one who had the most respect for the other was Levinas for Scholem. Scholem hardly knew who Levinas really was!"

We talk about the Israeli scholar, his unpleasant personality, his taste for provocation, his acerbic criticisms, his impressive and somewhat forgotten work, his poignant analyses — of Zionism, notably. Dupuy notes, "Scholem didn't have a high opinion of Zionism. He was a Zionist, but he was unhappy with how the Zionist movement was led by people who had never seen a Jewish book." Had Levinas said otherwise?

At his home one day on Abrabanel Street in Jerusalem, the professor of Jewish mysticism had a word to say about Levinas which I have quoted elsewhere: "He's more *litvak* than he thinks."[3] A word spoken with a mixture of tenderness and cruelty, without quite knowing which of the two sentiments was the dominant one. Dupuy acquiesces:

> Yes, it is true. I myself began to realize a long time ago that he was truly *litvak*, particularly in his relationship to the Hassidim. It was quite strong. He was in one tradition, with the Vilna Gaon, Chaim of Volozhin. . . . And for him, tradition was a matter of firm ideas, clear ideas. He had long begun to talk about the *Nefesh HaChayim*.[4] That played a role. He did not read the texts all that much, he had a living tradition. And in my opinion, *Nefesh HaChayim* is the Jewish distrust of Dostoyevsky. It's before Dostoyevsky, I believe, and much older, but it's a Jewish distrust of the Russian mentality. And yet Levinas was Russian. He spoke Russian with his wife. He was proud of Russian culture, and he felt he belonged to certain aspects of that world. But this kind of Russian fervor, which is very similar to the one found among the Hassidim — I don't know if it is heretical to say this — was off-putting to him.

Levinas, in some ways split and contradictory, was able to affirm that Dostoyevsky introduced him to philosophy, yet without endorsing the emotional climate of the author of *The Possessed*.

In any event, Scholem himself was not very far off from this rather reserved attitude with its distrustful eye toward Hassidic piety. A question posed by Dupuy — Is it the figure of the *tzaddik*, the "righteous man" of the Hassidim, that influenced the *staretz*, the "saint" of Russian monasticism, or the other way around? — had the power to irritate him to the highest degree. But for Levinas, this went further. He was wary of any manner of enthusiasm or fervor in religion, in faith, in liturgical expression. "If you had set him down in a Hassidic community for five minutes," says Dupuy, "you would see him tremble with fury. It was unbelievable. I knew that *mitnagdim*, 'rationalists,' existed, but I never saw it to such a degree as that. It was not only an intellectual refusal;

it was literally heresy for him, something that did not conform to Judaism. It was truly radical."

Did not this rejection, this distrust, wane somewhat by the end of his life? Dupuy, who knows his Jewish sources better than anyone — his library is impressive on the subject — denies it. "That may have developed as it does for someone who gets on in years and grows gentler toward everyone. Within the domain of ideas, however, it did not budge one inch. You won't find a single text of Levinas's, even from the end of his career, where he changed his mind about this. Levinas's greatness is the decisiveness, the sharpness, of his thought. His strength — and this is why he is such a point of reference and why he lives on — is that his work is born out of rigor and clarity. It is this philosophical clarity that is striking because, despite everything, he remained a philosopher."

A Vow

Paris, Louvain, Chicago: in this journey tracing Levinas's footsteps, there were, to be sure, other stops, with the exception of one country whose borders he vowed, after the war, never to cross again — Germany. Now, Bernard Casper, to whom he dedicated a book from the last period, *Á l'heure des nations*, with the words, "To a professor, theologian and philosopher, to a friend with a large heart and a high mind," is German. Casper, also a priest, a specialist in Rosenzweig, a charming man of seventy — with blue eyes and silver hair — founded, first in Augsburg and later in Freiberg, a study circle of French phenomenology devoted essentially to Ricoeur and to Levinas. In response to an invitation to return to Germany, Levinas explained, "You know what a religious vow is? It is the possibility for me to be at peace with my psyche." "Of course, I respected this vow," Casper today confides.

Consequently, their meetings took place at the Swiss border or the Dutch border. In Basel, in Wahlwiller, sometimes in Paris, Strasburg, or Aix-la-Chapelle. That is how the famous debate on Judaism and Christianity with the bishop of Achen, Klaus Hemmerle, came about in May 1986 at a convent in Holland. In this debate, Levinas explicated the basis of his thought by way of a kind of confession in which Rosenzweig's name was mentioned as part of the story of his own development. He first recounted his Lithuanian childhood, his initial encounters with the history of Christianity, the Inquisition, the Crusades, as well as his reading of the Gospels and the inconsistencies he found there. And he continued:

> The worst of it was that these horrifying things, the Inquisition and the Crusades, were linked to the sign of Christ, to the Cross. That seemed incomprehensible, and demanded an explanation. Add to that the fact that, strictly speaking, the world did not find itself changed through the Christian sacrifice. That was also essential. Being Christian, Europe could do nothing to redress matters. Whether because Christians had acted the way they did precisely as Christians, or because no one within Christianity had dissuaded human beings from committing certain acts. This is the first thing I have to say. And it remains deeply rooted for me; reading the Gospels was always compromised in my eyes — in our eyes — by history.[5]

He then evoked the Shoah, the discovery of the world's indifference, but also the refuge that the holy orders had offered his wife and daughter. He spoke of *The Star of Redemption* and of the possibility introduced by Rosenzweig, still before the war, of thinking of truth as given under two forms, the Jewish and the Christian, "without compromise or betrayal." And he concluded with a story, one that Hannah Arendt had related on French radio some years before her death, about how, as a child in her native Koenigsberg, she once confided in a rabbi in charge of her religious education, "You know, I have lost my faith!" To which the rabbi replied, "But who is asking you to have any?" Levinas concluded, "The response was characteristic. What matters is not faith, it is action. Action certainly signifies moral behavior, but it also signifies ritual. For that matter, are believing and doing really different things? What signifies belief? What is faith made of? Words? Ideas? Convictions? What do we believe with? With the entire body? With every bone (Ps. 35:10)? What the rabbi meant was, 'Doing what is right *is* the very act of believing.' And that is my conclusion."

Originally from Treves, Karl Marx's birthplace, Casper studied in Freiburg and then in Rome. "My family," he says, "participated a little, but only a little, in the resistance. We're Catholics, and my father saw how the Nazis killed the director of the Catholic Action in Berlin. That created a certain neighborliness toward Jewish thought." In this environment, he first came across Martin Buber's *I and Thou,* which was rather in vogue among the young Germans in the 1950s. An assiduous examination of the work left him with the impression that Buber was drawn by literary proclivities more than by philosophical ones, whereas Rosenzweig showed himself to be more substantial, his work actually implementing new concepts, a new method and vision. What does Levinas owe to Rosenzweig? In one sense everything, in another sense nothing, Casper puts it nicely. "For him, it was a new way of thinking, but only a point of departure. He said to me one day that there were many things in *The Star of Redemption,* that it was too full, too rich."

"Among philosophers in Europe, Rosenzweig is now well known. He is a source of this whole movement that goes by the title of dialogical thinking." Casper then goes to his library to pull down a book he holds dear, the second edition of Rosenzweig's *Hegel and the State*. It is dated 1937. Inside, there is a short inscription by Mme. Scheinman-Rosenzweig dated "1939, Palestine," indicating that it was the only work she was able to salvage, all the other copies having been burned under Nazi orders. A strange paradox! This man, who was quite removed from Zionism, did not live to see his wife and children leave for Palestine. His son, Rafael Rosenzweig, lived out the rest of his life there, and he even accompanied a German group of Judeo-Christian friends that traveled to Israel in 1982. Levinas and Casper were present.

Here again, it was this kind of encounter that sustained the relationship between the two men. There were also the Castelli colloquia where Casper once delivered a paper on "Heidegger and Levinas." And Levinas, decidedly incurable concerning Heidegger, lifted his arms to the sky: "How can you compare an elephant to a fly?" "What could I do?" says Casper, "He only knew the Heidegger of *Being and Time*, but this book, for him, was on par with Plato's *Parmenides*, Kant's *Critique of Pure Reason*, and Hegel's *Phenomenology of Spirit*."

There had also been another trip to Israel, to Be'er-Sheva in 1978, for a conference on Martin Buber. The audience was small, and Levinas became a little disconsolate when he was asked to speak in French, as he was so proud of his Hebrew. Afterwards, the group went to visit a Bedouin settlement in the suburbs of Be'er-Sheva, and when the guide, before letting the participants disembark, explained that the Bedouins were required to burn their tents if they wanted to be eligible to receive stone houses from the government, Levinas remained on the bus. "It's colonialism!" he cursed.

So Bernhard Casper never saw Levinas in Germany.

Nevertheless, it was in German that he filmed and recorded an interview with him, at his home on rue Michel-Ange, for a Baden-Baden television station. It was broadcast twice. Since the beginning of the 1980s, a good part of his work has been translated into German. The reception among Christians, once again, is particularly noteworthy. "It's that we need other approaches for interpreting the Scriptures," Casper confides. "Through his thinking, Levinas can open up paths to the truth of faith. Also, in another respect, for Christianity in the twentieth century, the shame of the Holocaust is very great, and we are looking for a way to bring us into a neighborhood with Jews, within a religious framework."

14 | THE ARISTOCRAT AND THE CARDINAL

The Castelli colloquia, in a certain way, represented the Christian counterpart to the Jewish intellectual colloquia. Beginning in 1969, Levinas regularly attended them, participating in a dozen or so conferences until his last one in 1986. Organized by the International Center for Humanistic Studies and by the Institute for Philosophical Studies of Rome, they took place every second year, at the beginning in January, at the University of Rome. The conferences were the brainchild of Enrico Castelli, a philosopher who was close to Pope Paul VI and the author of *L'Existentialisme théologique*. This Italian aristocrat, a native of Turin, possessed a small personal fortune and an interest in two subjects: hermeneutics and the philosophy of religion. Eccentric, self-taught, nonconformist, with a flair for provocation — once during 1942–1943, after an address by Mussolini, he said, "*Duce*, you should know that the Jews were in Rome before us!," an anecdote recounted by Ricoeur who heard it from Castelli himself — he was not lacking in connections, or in the means to secure the necessary funds for his projects.

Thus, every other winter, Castelli invited philosophers, theologians and exegetes to spend four or five days together and participate each day in six hours of conferences, punctuated by meal breaks. Levinas faithfully attended these reunions, usually going with his wife, who was flattered to be there, displaying a gentle reserve. All of the participants stayed at the same hotel, the Semix, which is near the Mirafiori villa, the site of the faculty of philosophy where the colloquia took place and where they had their meals together. Xavier Tilliette recalls, "He was very observant. There were things he didn't eat. We had to go out of our way somewhat to make sure he was comfortable. But he wasn't very demanding. The day of *shabbat* was complicated. I remember how he once asked me to take down an address for him because he was not allowed to write. But he did that with extreme discretion. For me, since I'm a rather old-fashioned Catholic who learned the significance of the letter of the law from Blondel, I found this neither shocking nor ridiculous." Another time, Stanislas Breton asked him to explain the distinction in Judaism between pure and impure foods and then himself proceeded to give a most complex interpretation. Levinas interrupted, with a smile, "It's to make us understand that God is incomprehensible!" Marco Olivetti, who succeeded Enrico Castelli after the latter's unexpected death on March 10, 1977, remembers how care was taken to ensure that Levinas would not have to travel or to give talks on Friday nights or Saturdays, as he was *osservante*. But it also happened on one occasion that a more aggressive Italian challenged the philosopher to justify his reluctance to convert. Breton notes, "It had to be explained to him that he could eventually put Jesus into the Bible, but not the Bible into Jesus."

The colloquia took place in French, the language Castelli himself used. It was a period in which the French participation dominated and included, in addition to Ricoeur, Levinas and Xavier Tilliette, academics such as Claude Geffré and Jean Greisch. Castelli presided, with a blend of good-naturedness and largesse. His introductions were always a bit obscure and heretical, with a pronounced taste for paradox. "Demythologization" was the theme — initiated by Bultmann, the theologian disciple of Heidegger and deconstructor of the Gospels — that fascinated him above all. "What are religions today? What do they have to say? What is still vital in them?" Characteristic of his research was the approach to sacred texts using phenomenological methods, and the way he based his theory of history and culture on aspects of Revelation and Wisdom, as well as on existential experience, all infused with a special interest in the dialogue between Christianity and other faiths.

Naturally talented as a "discoverer" and organizer, Castelli went to great lengths to get participants from all over the world to come to these meetings. Contact with Levinas was made right from the inception. In August 1965, as noted in his journals,[1] Castelli had lunch with Levinas, Jankélévitch and Bruaire at the home of Jeanne Delhomme. In October 1965, another lunch took place, again at Delhomme's, with Levinas, Dufrenne and Bruaire.

In the same journal, the entry dated November 29, 1967, reads, "We should invite, for January 1969: Skydgood, Guelna, Ricoeur, Heidegger, Kerenyi, Scholem, Levinas." In the actual invitations, the colloquium, destined to become famous, was designated as the "analysis of theological language: the name of God." Heidegger would not be there. But Levinas was present, delivering a lecture, no less famous than the colloquium, on "the name of God according to some talmudic lectures." As far as we know, this was the first of these talmudic lectures at the Castelli colloquia; subsequently, there was one every second year. "The State of Caesar and the State of David," "The Truth of Revelation and the Truth of Testimony," "Hermeneutics and the Beyond."

His last lecture would take place in 1985. Castelli had passed away by then, having been replaced by his disciple and close friend Olivetti. On the theme of *"Ebraismo, Ellenismo, Christianismo,"* Levinas gave a masterful lesson on the kenosis in Judaism, coupled with a long reference to, and analysis of, the *Nefesh HaChaim* of Rabbi Chaim of Volozhin. Here Levinas was confronting his heritage and returning to a text that was essential to him, to the idea of the humility of God in the Jewish tradition; a crucial notion in Paul's epistles, that of God relinquishing his power in order to let humanity live.

For Olivetti, these colloquia had a special virtue: those who came once persisted in coming and became regulars, so that the discussions effectively continued from one colloquium to the next. And in these intellectual duels, Levinas was "a figure of great importance." When he began participating, he was still an unknown — little known even in France, a little better known in Holland. "But it was Castelli who introduced him to Italy, that's undeniable." This may explain why the Italian reception was distinctive, more faith-oriented, perhaps more Christian and Catholic, than philosophical. At any rate, concludes Olivetti, who today heads the department of philosophy of religion at the University of Rome and continues with the work of the colloquia, Levinas opened these meetings with a Jewish dimension. A Stephane Moses or a Paul Mendès-Flore could then pick up from there.

A PHENOMENOLOGICAL CARDINAL

This was the expression Levinas used to evoke Pope John Paul II during a conference organized by the Association of

Catholic Writers on "The Philosophical Thought of John Paul II" on February 23, 1980, in Paris. He spoke of a "phenomenological cardinal." The colloquium took place in the senate, and the invitation made to the Jewish philosopher was in response to an old dialogue that had already borne fruit at Castel Gandolfo. Levinas decided to proceed by means of a succession of notes with this preamble: "I will not here address problems that concern the messages of His Holiness John Paul II. Rather, I take the liberty of making some remarks on the philosophical thought of his Eminence Cardinal Wojtyla."[2]

He first underscored the "extreme fidelity" to the norms of philosophical discourse, "the persistence of analysis in a language that maintains rigor, a natural light, and that — if it can be put this way — is suspicious of theological illumination." Adding, not without humor, "I confess that, respecting the same norms myself, I nevertheless take the liberty, in my modest attempts, to appeal, more often than to the cardinal, to verses and to his hermeneutic."

Husserl was also at the heart of this dialogue. In his philosophical training, Karol Wojtyla defended his dissertation in 1959 on Max Scheler under the supervision of Roman Ingarden. He taught Husserl and Scheler at the University of Lublin. Before assuming the pontificate in 1978, he participated in phenomenological conferences, one of which is worth remembering because it was the first time he met Levinas, albeit indirectly. It happened through Anna-Teresa Tyminiecka.

Originally from Poland, Anna-Teresa Tyminiecka completed her studies in Freiburg, and today lives in Massachusetts, where she founded the World Institute for Advanced Phenomenological Research and Learning. She knew Levinas in Freiburg in Switzerland where he once taught the Talmud

in the faculty of theology. In planning her institute's first
European conference, she wanted Levinas to chair it. She
went to see him with her proposal, and the conference took
place in Freiburg in April 1975. Two years later, a second
conference by the institute took place in Paris at 4 rue de
Chevreuse. Tyminiecka invited Cardinal Wojtyla, whom she
knew. The future pope, then archbishop of Krakow, was to
give an opening address, but for personal reasons he was
unable to attend the session. As Levinas was co-presiding, it
fell upon him to read the address that the cardinal had dictated and sent to him. This Levinas did conscientiously, and
it remained something he always remembered with a mixture of pride and mischievousness.

Some years later, during an international colloquium in
Paris in June 1983 on the occasion of Paul Ricoeur's seven-
tieth birthday, Tyminiecka revisited this episode and the relationship between the philosopher and the pontiff: "During
a number of discussions that I had with Levinas in the course
of my visits to Paris, his interest in Karol Wojtyla was apparent to me. I understood that behind this interest was a respect
not only for his religious vision and his authority, but for the
fact that from the beginning of his pontificate, his conception of the human being as an opening onto the divine
resonated very well with Levinas's moral vision of the 'face-
to-face.'" And she added, "This appreciation proved to be
mutual. Cardinal Wojtyla heard much about Levinas from
me throughout the five years we saw each other before he
became pope. He had read a number of Levinas's writings.
Consequently, Levinas was among the first philosophers
invited to the papal philosophical meetings at Castel Gandolfo,
which took place every second year in August."[3]

Before the Gandolfo meetings, there was a breakfast one
Saturday morning in Paris. It was Pope John Paul II's first

visit to France since his ascension to the pontificate. On May 31, 1980, before receiving representatives of the non-Catholic Christian denominations and going to the Elysée, where President Giscard d'Estaing was waiting, the sovereign pontiff brought together some fifteen intellectuals. He himself had drawn up the list. "This meeting," reports *Le Monde,* "was not an official part of the pope's visit, which leaves us with the assumption that the episcopate was not involved in this decision."[4] At the breakfast were Germaine Tillon, Pierre Chaunu, Christian Cabanis, Jean Duchesne, Jean Fourastié, André Frossard, Geneviève Antonioz-De Gaulle, René Girard, Jerôme Lejeune, Jean-Luc and Corinne Marion, Joseph Rigaud, Agnès Kalinowska and Emmanuel Levinas. The latter missed his *shabbat* course on Rashi that day, a rare occurrence, in order to go by foot from the Enio to the nuncio.

During this same visit to Paris, recounts Bernard Dupuy, a meeting was arranged with a delegation from the Jewish community of France headed by Chief Rabbi Kaplan. When the chief rabbi had finished introducing the members of his delegation, John Paul II's first words were, "You have the good fortune here in France to have someone like Emmanuel Levinas. How is it that he is not here?" Alain de Rothschild, president of the Central Consistory, Émile Touati, president of the Paris Consistory, and the chief rabbi were left dumbfounded.

THE LINK

Levinas did not go alone to the nuncio breakfast. Agnès Kalinowska, who was one of his former students and a goddaughter of the pope, accompanied him. Even more than Anna-Teresa Tyminiecka, Kalinowska served as a link between Levinas and John Paul II. She was at the origin of their acquaintance and played a key role in the ensuing relationship between the philosopher and the pontiff.

It took some time to find her; I had difficulty tracing her whereabouts. In her presence, one could not but respect her desire to leave the relationship in the shadows, a relationship that I sensed to be rich and intense, and that meant a lot to her. She received me one beautiful summer day at her rustic home in the south of France. Above the fireplace, a crucifix. She is a young woman of forty-something, with a round face, clear eyes, salt-and-pepper hair, warm, welcoming.

Agnès Kalinowska is also originally from Poland. Her father, the philosopher Jerzy Kalinowska, was dean of the faculty of philosophy at Lublin. During the 1970s, he asked "Father Wojtyla" — as he was called then — to give courses on ethics, which the latter did regularly until his election to the Holy See of Saint Peter. Kalinowska recalls with amusement how a certain student working on his dissertation in the same faculty saw his thesis supervisor, the new Pope John Paul II, leave for Rome on the following day. Karol Wojtyla was delighted that he had been asked to give these courses and delivered them conscientiously, troubled only that he had never enjoyed a full classical philosophical training. During the war while a student, he had worked in a factory. He was regularly seen with a book in one hand and an eye on the boiler room for which he was responsible. Upon being elected pope, one of his former co-workers from the factory let slip a remark on television: "We knew he was good at nothing!"

Wojtyla was a boarder in Lublin. He rented a room, but spent a lot of time at the home of the Kalinowska family, to whom he was close. He became a friend of the family and was interested in the progress of Agnès's studies, and, later on, her life in Paris. A philosophy student herself, she there completed the highest levels of studies in the humanities, namely *hypokhâgne, khâgne,* and the École Normale Supérieure. In 1975, she enrolled in Levinas's seminar at the Sorbonne, upon the advice of her father. In these last two years of the philosopher's teaching activity at the Sorbonne, the seminar was on the work of Michel Henry. Agnès was responsible for giving a presentation on *L'Essence de la manifestation.* "I was not prepared for such a difficult exercise on such an arduous text," she confides, "but I rose to the challenge." The professor's comment, which she still wonders today whether it was meant as praise: "An excellent presentation from the undergrad!"

Levinas showed himself to be "attentive and welcoming" on his part. A correspondence developed during the summer of 1975, followed by initial meetings in the autumn, and then more regular meetings afterwards.

"We met at the Sorbonne. We had coffee at a nearby café." They chatted about everything, with two subjects particularly dominating: the Slavic, Russian and Polish world, and the exegesis of biblical texts.

Certain phrases running through the conversations come back to her: "One must not idolize God." Or, "One must not sell off the human too cheaply; from the human, we very quickly get to God. Besides, this is the incarnation." Another time, in reference to a Dominican father who confessed to having difficulties with this same incarnation, Levinas was surprised, explaining *mutatis mutandis:* "In the Bible, God created language. As you know of course! But language speaks of chamber pots." Still another time, during a stroll through the Sorbonne: "I'll show you a path you don't know." Lastly, this phrase, possibly born during one of these conversations and later to be found under his pen: "Philosophy is not the love of wisdom but the wisdom of love."

In 1977, Cardinal Wojtyla made a visit to Paris. Returning by car with his goddaughter from Paris to Orsay, he confided in her his admiration for Levinas's work. "There are two great philosophers in the religious sphere: Levinas and Ricoeur." Agnès was surprised and comforted by this, since it was, in fact, the sentiment she herself had about Levinas.

One year later, Wojtyla became Pope John Paul II. And at the time of the Paris visit in 1980 and the famous breakfast, it was Levinas himself, perhaps intimidated or perhaps wishing to include the person who had forged these links, or perhaps for both reasons, who — invited by the sovereign pontiff — in turn invited Agnès Kalinowska to accompany him. "It was pure kindness on his part and it was very educational for me," she recounts. She remembers that, in this learned assembly of chosen personalities, everyone was a bit impressed, no one dared to put himself or herself ahead, and that Levinas very quickly found himself in the hot seat.

"The Saint-Father has a habit of not talking much. He enjoys having other people speak. He very much likes to listen. So, he addressed me. I was probably the only person he knew in the assembly. Right away, I passed the baby to Levinas. Girard joined in, and they spoke about the notion of sacrifice. But I very much had the impression that the conversation between John Paul II and Levinas took up a good part of the breakfast."

Afterward, confides Kalinowska, "things evolved without so much input from me. Levinas let the connection develop. He told me his impressions as a friend. He was pleased about the relationship, and seemed happy on the philosophical level as well. He was a positive person, essentially positive, open, who always saw the good side of things."

After her marriage, the former student from the Sorbonne was appointed to teach at the University of Metz. She focused on exegesis of the Gospels, leaving aside Hebrew Bible studies. The exchanges were less frequent, their connection waned. She lost her interlocutor, but she is happy to have benefited from knowing Levinas during those several years. She still wonders, with a nostalgic smile, whether on rue Michel-Ange one can still see an abstract drawing in black and white entitled "Weakness." It is a gift she purchased at a gallery for him. She is proud he hung it on his living room wall.

A PRAYER WITHOUT WORDS

The meetings with the pope continued. Levinas was invited on several occasions to Castel Gandolfo, the summer residence of the pope located in the outskirts of Rome.

The idea behind these meetings, conceived in the early 1980s, was to bring together researchers and philosophers from the two sides of Europe, separated at that time by the Iron Curtain, to an Institute of Human Sciences based in Vienna. Originally, the institute sought to encourage visits from Polish intellectuals in particular, who would pass through the Austrian capital, the traditional place of exchange between the Soviet world and the Western world. This is why Professor Michalski, who would become the director of the Vienna center, or Lezlëk Kolakowski, the historian of Marxism, were often seen there. The circle then grew. Among the French members of the institute's scientific committee were Paul Ricoeur, Emmanuel Leroy-Ladurie and Emmanuel Levinas. Every second year in the month of August, John Paul II, who had shown his support for and was involved in the project, held seminars in which the participants were invited to submit their reflections on themes chosen beforehand. The first seminar took place in 1983 on the theme "The Image of Man from the Perspective of the Modern Sciences." As Ricoeur recounts, John Paul II would say how delighted he was to take his meals between a Protestant philosopher and a Jewish philosopher.

Only once did Levinas decline the invitation, namely during the Auschwitz-Carmelite affair, when a group of Carmelites decided to affix crosses on the site of the former concentration camp and to make it a place of Christian prayer. The philosopher spoke out against this project, and published an essay in *Le Figaro* entitled "The Mystery of Israel," a dense and moving text in which, here and there, some personal memories can be perceived:

> ʹThe murder — amid suffering and atrocity — of six million Jews in different National Socialist camps of extermination, as well as places on the other side of the barbed wire, cannot, in its monstrous enormity, lodge itself in human consciousness as an image, nor can we find in the French language a noun that designates its full measure. It is an extreme event disproportionate to the content of consciousness. It does not know how, by way of memory, to innocently take shelter in a "state of mind." Everything takes place as if those beings vanished with the smoke, and henceforth, only thought of by us, tore apart subjective interiority and died outside anew, or as if their presence cried out to us for mercy — "the voice of the blood that cries out to God" according to a verse from Genesis (4:19). Is not Judaism in its entirety, since Auschwitz, the constant ascent of this cry, despite the Liberation, despite the State of Israel, despite the messianic promises?

Asking that these places be left to this "prayer without words," of which, he says, we cannot be certain that it is not pleasing to "this from-then-on silent God," he adds, "We need to reflect before substituting other forms of charity for this mercy and this misery."

Levinas closes the article by addressing his Christian friends: "I had the privilege and honor of meeting and associating in friendship, in France and in all the European countries, with a number of Catholics: religious and lay, simple congregants and members of the hierarchy — up to quite a high level — who seemed to me to be entirely faithful to Christian hope and confident in the charity that is opened up through the belief that 'all is accomplished.' I knew what religious impression the history of Israel made upon them. I believe that their charity can never consent to what the passion of Auschwitz, even in noble thought, tore away from the mystery of Israel. It is for them that these lines are written."[5]

Were these last words a direct appeal on Levinas's part? Adriaan Peperzak, in Chicago, confirms it: "I know that Levinas wrote to the pope about the Carmelite affair. I don't know if he received a personal response. But I am certain that it made an impact."

Glimmers

Rue Michel-Ange. He greets me at the door, agitated. He fusses with a copy of Le Monde *in his hands. It is folded back, showing page 2, which features an interview with a French sociologist on the spirit of the times. "I didn't read it," he hastens to say, "but the general tone is clear."*

Obviously he had not read it; it is completely harmless. His wife speaks of Russia and of Jirinowski. The conversation gets muddled. The philosopher confuses Jirinowski with the French sociologist, and I cannot follow what he says.

He nonetheless continues to be attentive. He asks me questions about my daily life, about what I have been reading.

At one point he brings up his Talmud teacher, a weird and enigmatic person. His wife jokes about the fact that at that time there were already numerous legends about him. Some would say, "I'm sure he's not a believer." Others, "No, no, I assure you I once saw him praying." Insinuations that had the knack of thoroughly aggravating Dr. Nerson, a friend of the family and the most devoted disciple of the talmudist.

"Are you talking about Dr. Nerson?" the philosopher asks. His face suddenly lights up: "He was a radiant being!"

We also talk about the writer and friend of the philosopher, Maurice Blanchot. "I must speak to him about this article in Le Monde.*" He keeps returning to this inconsequential article, holding on to it, as if there were nothing more important.*

I learn that Blanchot is not well, that the two men still call each other regularly.

The wife of the philosopher recounts how, during the war, Blanchot let her have his studio in Paris for her to hide in, and how he went to live with his brother. "I didn't stay there for long, only a fortnight or so, I didn't want to put him in jeopardy." And she stoops down to me, as if to confide, "You know, he didn't want to be seen!"

We also talk about the relations between the Vatican and Israel and of John Paul II (official recognition by the Holy See of the State of Israel and the establishment of diplomatic relations were about to be announced). "I've never researched this," says the philosopher, "but we have always had a most cordial relationship."

He recalls that the pope recently invited him again to Castel Gandolfo but that he could not attend "because of this Carmelite business." "It's a big thing," he says, regarding this recent rapport between the Vatican and Israel, "the entire relationship is changing. And this plan by the pope to visit Israel, it is enormous." His face lights up again.

We return once more to the mysterious talmudist. To his false trail. To his fake papers. To the forged birth certificate that makes him out to be a Moroccan national. "Yes," the philosopher's wife remembers, "Chouchani liked to pass for an Arab. During the war, it was like that!"

The philosopher adds, "As far as I am concerned, he was a European, someone from Galicia or from Poland."

Accompanying me to the door, his agitation returns. "The last drop of anti-Semitism has not yet been drunk, don't you think?"

15 | Ritual and the World

Husband, father, grandfather, the private Levinas can perhaps only be described by his family, although one finds passages in his work in which habitation, abode, fecundity, paternity and filiality occupy a place in reflection and constitute the movement of thinking. Indeed, like so many other words from everyday usage, which, originating in an unusual register and then reinvested and reappropriated within his language, enter into philosophical discourse with him. The Other is not only the stranger, the neighbor, the nigh one; he is also the familiar, the brother. He could just as well be the son or the daughter, in a relationship where the I "breaks free from itself . . . without, thereby ceasing to be an I."[1]

What is astonishing, in fact, in the accounts of both Simone and Michael, is how easily each of them alternates between anecdotes about his life and anecdotes about his work, as if these were inextricably mingled and one of them could not be mentioned without the other one being automatically evoked.

A Loving and Awkward Father

Simone, a physician, former director of the Hôpitaux de Paris clinic, is the eldest of Levinas's two children. Born just before the war, the first years of her childhood were spent in difficult circumstances, about which she has only vague memories. What she knows is that at the beginning of the war she was sent to the home of Suzanne Poirier, a colleague of Levinas's from Strasbourg — who appears in the famous photograph called "The Five" perched atop a car alongside a pensive Maurice Blanchot, who is holding a walking stick between his fingers. Suzanne Poirier had married a pharmacist from Rouen, and the two of them lived in the country. With the onset of the persecutions, they thought it would be a good idea to take the little girl, who was five at the time, into their protection. But after two weeks or so, they had to bring her back, the family deciding that the subterfuge was too dangerous.

Blanchot then took over, suggesting that the mother and daughter stay in his apartment in the heart of Paris's fifth district. They stayed there for almost a month, after which Blanchot found a convent in the Loiret, on the outskirts of Orléans, that would shelter them. Simone was sent there, but her mother, along with her grandmother, remained in Paris at the home of friends. Raïssa would come to leave the capital only after her mother was deported, in circumstances that were never elucidated and that left them with bitter feelings.

The grandmother was summoned to the police station. The family that hid the two women insisted that she show up even after she refused. Were these good people in the end afraid of trouble — on account of these two women who spoke only a little French and conversed in Russian between themselves? It is likely, Simone thinks today. Her mother, in any event, always had great difficulty forgiving them. The grandmother reported to the police station, never to return. She had just enough time to scribble down some words on a postcard mailed from the train station before being deported, this same winter of 1943. Raïssa Levinas ended up joining her daughter in the Loiret, where they would remain until the end of the war.

"I am so grateful to Blanchot," Simone says today. "He put us up in that apartment in the fifth district, and he found the convent, the château, where we were received as refugees." Simone has no precise memories of the Monastery of Saint Vincent de Paul. Raïssa Levinas, like her husband, always spoke of it with emotion and gratitude. "What we didn't know at the time," says Simone, "which we learned after the war, is that this convent served as a large parachute landing base for resistance fighters coming from England. We weren't the only ones hiding there. There was a whole resistance network."

From her father, captive in Germany, little news was received. A handful of infrequent letters.

To say nothing of the paternal grandparents, in Lithuania, of whom nothing was known. Only after the war was it learned how they were arrested on their doorstep. The whole family was annihilated, the grandfather, the grandmother, and the two uncles, Boris and Aminadav. Levinas never spoke about it. Not in his writings, not in conversations with friends, not even with his family. It was an open wound in his core, a deep wound. "He never spoke about the exterminations. The Shoah was something of such enormity that it could not be put into words. It was implicit in all that he said, in all that he did."

Generally speaking, Simone adds, her father rarely revisited the past. This does not mean that he was unaffected by it or unaware of it. It was simply not a subject matter for conversation or for meditation. For all that, however, his admiration, his loyalty and his devotion to France were never marred by the war. "My mother often said," Simone recounts, "that had he remained in Paris, he would undoubtedly have been deported. He had so much confidence in the virtues of France. He believed in the French police. They were incapable of doing harm, as far as he was concerned. He would have handed himself over to the police without any difficulties, without the least precaution. He had great respect for institutions in general. School, for example, was placed above everything. When I was appointed to an internship, it was a big day for him. He was radiant."

His character? His everyday manner? Irascible and loving at the same time. He could easily lose his temper, administering resounding smacks when Simone obstinately persisted in not understanding something in mathematics, which was sacred for him, worthy of interest and respect. And, at the same time, he was cheerful, readily laughing and joking. He knew how to have fun with a good word, scene or story. Like during dinner at a restaurant with Jean Wahl. The waiter suggested a tartlet for dessert. And Wahl, quite flabbergasted and suddenly serious, raised his eyes to ask anxiously, "A tartlet of what?" That made him burst out in laughter. The fact that an eminent philosopher could show such interest in the ingredients of a tartlet struck him as the epitome of comedy. This episode was a source of endless amusement for him and his friend, Dr. Nerson.

He could also be awkward. This was, at any rate, the reputation he had in certain settings. When Simone wanted to marry Georges Hansel, the parents of her future husband — those who had raised him — made inquiries about the new in-laws, discovering reports that Levinas regularly made faux pas of all kinds.

"It's true," says Simone, "except that he did it on purpose. They were usually deliberate blunders."

When I recounted to Simone the episode at William Richardson's oral exam in Louvain, although she had not heard the story before, she was not surprised by her father's behavior. "It's perfectly typical. He meant to do him no harm, or to damage his career. But whatever he had to say, he said without mincing words."

THE FAMILY LEGACY

A tireless worker, going to bed late and getting up early — that is how his daughter remembers him. Levinas slept six hours each night, running down the stairs at full speed at the crack of dawn, growing into a mountain of anguish whenever he had to postpone a piece of work. "During the 1950s," Simone recalls, "he would participate once a year in the conference at Jean Wahl's Collège. He worked on his paper nonstop, erasing, tearing up and revising right up to the last minute. It was forever 'not ready.' And I have this horrible memory of him being in such despair one time — he had finished his essay but felt that it was no good — that he rushed outside, flying onto rue Erlanger. Mom ran after him, and I ran behind her. She was afraid of I don't know what, that he would do something stupid or that he would fall under a car, all simply because of dissatisfaction in writing!"

Emmanuel had a pet name for Raïssa, "Raïnka." They were loving with each other, close, accomplices. After all, they had known each other since childhood. She was always there in the background, but as long as she was alive, it seemed that she managed everything, from the home to everything else.

Even when it came to organizing the high school, she was everywhere, appearing on one floor, then on another, busy with the treasury, following each of Levinas's motions.

Jokingly, but perhaps not totally so, the children of Simone and Georges say that she was the true intellectual of the couple. She read a lot. She was always seen either with a book, or at the piano.

Simone remembers Mr. Chouchani, of course, this enigmatic figure who marked her childhood. She herself made his bed, in the room below the apartment on rue d'Auteuil. She talks about him with an excited and admiring smile, as of a great-uncle who was somewhat crazy and by whom her father was very much taken in, evoking with precision his demeanor, his angry outbursts and his jokes. No, it is not true that the two men were antipodes of each other. Something bound them, profoundly, in spite of their belonging to two different worlds. Chouchani was something of a vagabond, impulsive, elusive. His great bursts of laughter were heard from one end of the apartment to the other. What they could not connect on stemmed from the fact that Chouchani did not correspond to anyone, he was truly *sui generis*. Simone also remembers the large meetings Sunday evenings at the house, one time because the strange character had gone far away — somewhere in Uruguay, it was said. Some of the disciples were there — Théo Dreyfus, Bernard Picard, Dany Bloch, and others who dropped in — gathered together for a weekly Talmud class. Dr. Nerson officiated. Her father participated. And there was an attempt to protract the spirit of Chouchani.

Levinas would confide in Georges Hansel, his son-in-law, who also participated in these meetings: "From Chouchani, I learned the method." Perhaps, Hansel adds, he also shared with Chouchani a loathing for banalities. "In his readings, in his encounters, he always looked for the point. And sometimes he idealized the rest because of that. But what brought them even closer together was in fact the method: to take the Talmud in all its facets, not as a doctrine but as many open possibilities."

But the family legacy, Levinas's heritage among his family, stems, before anything else, from a certain presence. For David, the Hansel grandson, there are childhood memories of a great demand for ethical rigor in everyday life, manifesting itself in the most commonplace, the most minute of events, such as when, at a vacation home in Brittany, Levinas grumbled extensively because, upon returning from a long walk, David had rushed straight for the refrigerator and drained the contents of a bottle of apple juice without caring to find out if anyone else wanted some. Today, he recounts with a smile how his own children fight at the dinner table to avoid taking the last piece of food from the plate, and when one of them does so, everyone exclaims, "Ah, he doesn't practice Grandpa's philosophy!" Then there was the trip to Freiburg in Switzerland for a conference. In the morning, as they often did in such settings, they went shopping — something Levinas would never do, for anything in the world, on rue d'Auteuil. The grandson accompanied the grandfather to a store to buy a pair of shoes. The shoes, unfortunately, did not suit him. How to leave a store where one tried on shoes but could not buy them? For him, the problem took on extraordinary proportions.

"These are details, but they keep coming back. They're things that leave an impression on a child." This was certainly the case where the transmission of a daily ethics occurred, but what about Judaism? The friendship with Nerson and the encounter with Chouchani — these two things being connected, as is known — played a significant role in Levinas's "return" to studying it. Nevertheless, he was always deeply Jewish, since childhood, without interruption — even if, as Simone remembers, immediately after the war the family did not keep kosher at home. "He once brought home some ham. It was really good!" But by faith and discipline, by his attachment to ritual, and also by environment, Levinas in his daily life was certainly a practicing Jew.

Practicing, not religious. David, the grandson, very much insists on this distinction. "It is perhaps the first teaching that my grandfather passed on to us. For him, there was no dichotomy of religious/nonreligious, believing/nonbelieving. These categories are not the ones in which Judaism is lived out. For my father, my mother, my brothers and sisters, this remains the foundation of everything. It is perhaps unconventional, and it's not always easy to explain to others. I am not saying that the idea of God is something foreign. But belief is not a primary issue. The first is the responsibility for others, the Ought, obligation, the commandment. These are themes that were developed by my grandfather and that very much branded us."

And how do the works fit within the legacy? The oldest of Simone's four children, David, specializing in the sciences, a physician, is involved in research at CNRS and divides his time among Paris, Jerusalem and the United States. For the last six years, living in Jerusalem, he and his wife Joëlle, a professor of philosophy — she was the organizer of the first international colloquium on Levinas in Israel — have been getting together with a lawyer friend every Saturday afternoon to study the grandfather's writings. The group began with *Ethics and Infinity*, moved on to *Totality and Infinity*, then to *Time and the Other*. As the lawyer is Israeli and does not know French, the readings are in Hebrew or English translation.

It's basically in this context that I read these texts, which are extremely difficult as everyone knows. One of my interests in my grandfather's philosophy will seem surprising, because it is mediated through other texts, in particular those of a great kabbalist and hassid, Rabbi Yehuda Halevi Ashlag. He was one of the three principal kabbalists of the twentieth century together with Rav Kook and Rav Shmuel Eliashiv. And he developed a complete rereading of the whole tradition of Rabbi Isaac Luria. When a philosophy is extracted from this kabbalistic interpretation, one finds items that are incredibly convergent with certain aspects of my grandfather's philosophy. I should stress, of course, that there is no question of reducing one to the other. But in terms of the role attributed to the *mitzvot,* the commandments, and to the concern for the Other as the essence of Judaism, a unique convergence is found.

FREEDOM AND OBLIGATION

"It is forgotten," David continues, "that the first essay written on Judaism, or one of the first in any case, dates from 1937." It is a fairly short essay, read on the radio broadcast "Écoute Israël" on France-Culture on the subject of ritual — ritual as faith. The commandment as care for the Other. Freedom as obligation. And religious practice as teacher of spontaneity of living. Everything is already said quite early:

> Ritual everywhere mediates between us and reality. It suspends the action that we detect in the lonely life of objects. Food is not only something to consume, it is *kosher* or *treif.* Before translating his religious feelings into words, the Jew looks for words in his prayer book; they don't come naturally; they don't seem to be equally efficacious. The seventh day does not unfold like the others; it remains impermeable to the week's cares. Before carrying out the basic act of eating, the Jew pauses to say a blessing. Before entering the house, he stops to kiss the *mezuzah.* Everything occurs as if he had not entered the world on the same

footing in which it offers itself to him; as if, in a world where techniques open up pathways without resistance, ritual constantly marks a time for stopping, as if to momentarily interrupt the current that constantly binds us to things. That is because at bottom, to the practicing Jew, the world never appears as a natural thing. Others feel immediately at home in the world, immediately at ease. The environment in which they live is so habitual that they do not notice it. Their reactions are instinctive. Things are always well known to them; they are familiar, they belong to the everyday, they are profane. For the Jew, on the contrary, nothing is entirely familiar, entirely profane. The existence of things is something that is infinitely surprising for him. It strikes him as a miracle. He experiences continual wonderment at the simple yet extraordinary fact that the world is there.[2]

An astonishing text. It stands as a sharp refutation of anyone who would argue that Levinas's "return" to Judaism and to Jewish practice — to the extent that it is even possible to assign a date to this return and even to speak of it — took place after the war.

David often returns to these early thoughts from 1937 where he finds his grandfather as well as himself. His own efforts at reading his works are summed up in this statement by Benny Lévy, Sartre's old secretary, who lives in Jerusalem today: "The author of *Totality and Infinity* needs to be read like the *Mishnah!*" David agrees: "Yes, in fact, you need to read it in a group, in a *beit hamidrash*. That would be a way to develop a study of Levinas's texts — within a setting that is not academic, on the one hand, but that also corresponds to the Jewish academy in some respects." This does not mean that it is necessary to put Levinas in a *yeshiva*, however, to place him in a certain category, to raise him to classical status. He himself abhorred all categorization. At once a philosopher, a Jew, a religious man, a layman, did he not escape from all those labels that, for him, sustained the system? "Modern Judaism can be lived out without necessarily grounding it in a self-styled synthesis between two modes of life that are a priori contradictory," David says. "He didn't like synthesis. There is a phrase my father told me about, which he heard from my grandfather. Regarding a fashionable philosopher in Paris, he said, 'Yes, she is all about synthesis,' or again, 'She only goes as far as synthesis.' His opposition to the mystical was known. In mystical thought, there is often this search for synthesis. Justice on the one hand, compassion on the other; a midpoint emerges and a synthesis is forged. For him, it wasn't about that."

Evoking his childhood memories, his visits, his trips, his vacations, David returns again and again to two key images. The first, as with Simone, his grandfather's astonishing capacity for work, the permanent tension in which he lived, the rising at dawn and the nights of work — "when he wrote, he was constantly awake, he couldn't rest for more than fifteen minutes" — hyperactivity. And this incessant outpour of books, articles, conferences, courses, seminars. As for the second image, it concerns Raïssa and her presence: "My grandfather and my grandmother could not be separated. When my grandmother died, my grandfather was not at the burial. The doctor recommended that he not be there. At the end of the funeral, there was a prayer organized at the Enio. My grandfather went to that, and I sat beside him. He was already quite ill. When the *hashkava* was recited, he turned to me and his expression was of deep distress. Yes, it is true, he sometimes called her 'Raïnka.' There was infinite tenderness in this name."

16 | MONTAIGNE AND BOÉTIE

Levinas enjoyed meeting others, liked to achieve a full understanding of the works of others, exhibited gratitude toward other writers, including those whom, after having grown up on them, he had outgrown. Testifying to this constant rapport are the various texts dedicated to his contemporaries, to those who had crossed his path, to those who simply remained unnamed and who were alluded to under the sign of friendship. Among his friendships, the one he had cultivated with Dr. Henri Nerson had something altogether special about it. There was no need for him to talk about it. It was obvious to everyone.

FROM NEIGHBORLINESS TO DEDICATION

The two men were as different as could be. The one, expansive, talkative, short tempered. The other, calm, quiet, reserved. They were often seen together, particularly in the school halls. Always standing, never sitting, sober, austere, unassuming — that is how Dr. Nerson appeared beside Levinas. For the students of the Enio, he was part of the institution, essentially its adjunct director. In actuality, he had his own professional life. Originally from Strasburg, he was a medical doctor, a gynecologist. The two had met at the end of the 1940s, being neighbors on rue d'Auteuil. Mme. Levinas, after a difficult pregnancy, lost a daughter in 1946, between Simone and Michael — a subject never discussed, with no more than the mysterious dedication in *De l'existence à l'existant*, published the following year, in the form of three letters, "PAE," evoking a painful wound. Dr. Nerson, approached somewhat at random, proved to be extremely helpful and a source of much comfort to his neighbors. As an orthodox Jew, moreover, he regularly attended *shabbat* services and frequently attended the weekday *minyan* — the quorum required for communal daily prayers — that assembled in the school, conveniently close to his home.

Their intellectual affinities quickly kicked into place, and, before long, emerged into the light of day under the auspices of the legendary Chouchani. When *Difficile Liberté* was published in 1958, the work carried the dedication: "To Dr. Henri Nerson, to a friend, in memory of an education that inspires this friendship." The education in question was not that of the doctor, however, but that of the genius talmudist and vagabond whom Dr. Nerson had introduced to Levinas. The friendship was thus sealed under the influence of a common master. A strong, profound, intimate friendship — former students compare it to Montaigne and La Boétie — albeit never demonstrative. The two men did not call each other by their first names. They did not address one another as "tu." They were never effusive. Yet the proximity between them was plain.

Dr. Nerson's daughter, Evelyne Méron, a tall, blonde woman, elegant and warm, for whom Chouchani is an inexhaustible topic, remembers the introduction to the shared master:

> I believe it's my father who introduced Mr. Chouchani to Levinas. It was right after the war, when I was still quite small. Chouchani and Levinas, these two men gifted with rare intelligence, would certainly be most interested in meeting one other. One day my father said to me, without the least bit of bitterness, that Chouchani must suffer greatly from the solitude in which he's trapped by the extraordinary altitude of his mind, and that Levinas, and no one else, would be able to understand something of Chouchani's teachings. Need I explain that my father himself was rather intelligent, more than average? But with Levinas, and even more so with Chouchani, it was entirely special. As long as Chouchani was living in France, he stayed in the large apartment that the school provided for the Levinas family — which was tolerated by Mme. Levinas, whereas my mother would never have taken him in! So my father often went to the Levinas home to see the teacher. They even held lessons there. Later on, after Chouchani left for Uruguay, my father and Levinas loved to talk about him, among other subjects. Hence, my father had more than one opportunity to serve as a guidepost for Levinas, keeping him on the path of ethics at a time when ethics was not in fashion, when the first students of Levinas at Poitiers turned up their noses at such sentimental preoccupations. My father reminded Levinas that identifying with moral philosophy was a good thing.

Evelyn Méron remembers above all how Chouchani was a controversial figure, at the center of arguments and disagreements. Once, her father — for whom this was the absolute point of reference — related to her a compliment given by the mysterious fellow: "I was bothered that the compliment came indirectly, but flattered." According to her, the fact that they learned from the same master furnished them with a rather similar cast of mind: the same rationalism, the same desire to place themselves "beyond pathos," the same conviction in "loving the Torah more than God," as well as the same spiritual openness toward anything in the world that was not banal. At the same time, there were two important differences between them that allowed them to complement one another, to need one another: Levinas easily navigated his way through the most ethereal of abstractions, while Nerson had a stronger understanding of, and appreciation for, the firm ground of religious practice and moral conduct. Levinas was brilliant, prolix, loved to laugh, while Nerson mostly listened, spoke little, and was gifted with a very disarming, dry sense of humor.

United by their shared interests, it was not long before the gynecologist and the philosopher found each other quite indispensable. Dr. Nerson regularly attended the Rashi courses, sticking his oar into the water from time to time. And Levinas needed this presence. He sought his approval. On Saturday afternoons the two men met for a discussion or a lecture offered to students. During the week, Nerson showed up again for a weekly course on the Talmud. At other times he could be seen in the school lounge bent over the crossword puzzles in *Le Monde*, those of Max Favalelli, of whom he was fond and about whom he and Levinas liked to bicker.

CONVIVIALITY

The two families spent a lot of time together. There were the holidays, Pesach and Succoth, which they spent together, and on two or three occasions they even vacationed together at the same resort. "All this time spent together," recalls Evelyne, "allowed my father to exercise a considerable influence. Little

Michael [Emmanuel and Raïssa's son] regarded my father with a quasi-reverential respect. For example, he made a tremendous effort to stop sucking his thumb on his fourth birthday, after my father had made him ashamed of this habit so unfit for a little man. Michael's parents, not terribly impressed, considered such a great display of willpower from a small child to be excessive, and even traumatic." She adds, "In any event, from day to day, Levinas told my father about everything that was on his mind, including his philosophical ideas as they took shape. In fact, he tried out his ideas on my father; he waited for his initial comments. I think that my father's endorsement was essential to him. There were, however, differences. My father found rather excessive the great Levinasian principle: 'the Other has nothing but rights and I have nothing but obligations.' He appreciated a philosophy only where it could be applied."

The children were all raised together, and in the same manner. Francine Lévy, a friend of Evelyn's, a professor of French — like her — at the University of Bar-Ilan, who herself attended the Enio for a few years, remembers this little consolidated clan. "At the Nersons, life revolved around Evelyne. She was not an absolute genius. Not like Michael, anyway. But she could hold her own quite well. She was — as rumor had it — very, very bright. And destined, naturally, for a dazzling academic career. And very wise. An exemplary little girl, in the category of 'Parisian Jewish Intellectual.' She was petite, moreover, and with red hair, which would have been magnificent had her hairstyle not been so austere. Her ear forever straining not to miss a word, she sagaciously followed her father and his friend as they strolled under the great chestnut trees in the school's garden, engaged in learned conversation. All around them, the students laughed, joked, carried on with each other and flirted. Evelyn was above all of that. She was busy storing up knowledge like a bee her honey."[1]

CHAVA

Evelyn has not changed. In her pretty Jerusalem apartment, surrounded by her big cats, she exudes confidence. Levinas was a kind of paternal presence, half-uncle, half-teacher for her. "Excessively elitist, he divided the world into the geniuses . . . and the others. Of people who were more or less intelligent there was no question in his language. He admitted to being incapable of understanding how a young woman, like one of my cousins, could take her fine diplomas in mathematics down from the wall, and then immigrate to Israel, join a kibbutz, and work as . . . a nursery school teacher! Demanding with his son, who was obliged from a young age to spend long hours each day at the piano, a harsh critic of strangers, readily sarcastic, he even indulged in little cruelties with those who were close to him. With me, for example."

Two memories remain with her in particular. "When I was six or seven years old, I was invited to the Levinas home with my parents for the eve of Pesach, a private meal that took place at the apartment, not at the school. I had such a sumptuous memory of the same Passover meal the preceding year that, when the dessert arrived, I was a bit disappointed with the harsh reality, so I said in a small voice, with a slight flaw in pronunciation, 'There aren't too many fings today.' Greatly offended, Mr. Levinas repeated this phrase to me each year during Passover, at the same time: 'Well, Evelyne? There aren't too many fings today, are there?' When I was sixteen or seventeen, I would have gladly thrown him out the window. . . . Around the age of twenty-three, I acquiesced and

found it touching. The second misunderstanding, less spec-
tacular, shocked me quite a bit. I was sixteen years old, I was
in the eleventh grade, and I received as a gift from the
Levinases a beautiful edition of Voltaire's *Contes*, which I had
studied superficially in class and had dreamed of reading.
Delighted, I thanked them with the greatest sincerity: 'This
is precisely the book that I wanted!' which he took for a
rehearsed politeness. Afterward, he would repeat to me on
various occasions, 'So, Evelyne. This is precisely the book you
wanted?' meaning, 'You're a well-trained little girl, Evelyne.'"

THE SIGNPOST

Evelyne also recalls how he did not like psychoanalysis, that
he preferred repression to release — undoubtedly due to
the combined influence of Nerson and Chouchani. That he
knew how to listen, to watch, and to take a passionate interest in everything. That his stories contained a wealth of teachings. That he did not let himself succumb to fashion. And
that, in everyday life, he was a difficult man to get along with,
seeming to exist only in his head, poorly tolerating the con-
straints of the real world.

"The philosopher is a signpost," he said one day in jest,
"he shows where to go without going there himself." A maxim
that raised the eyebrows of her morally minded father.

Another time, during a conversation about God, he turned
to her, in disbelief, to ask her to explain the exact meaning
of the Latin phrase *Credo quia absurdum est.* Did this famous
line by Tertullian, a church father, really mean, "I believe
because it is absurd"? Was it not instead, "I believe that it is
absurd"? Evelyne had to assure him that, indeed, the Latin
quia signified "because," something decidedly bizarre in the
philosopher's eyes.

Evelyne Méron's childhood remains tied to the Levinas family. And all the images of the past bring her back to the philosopher:

> Despite the cutting little remarks he made to me, unaware of their sharpness, he was so kind to me during my childhood that I was forced to love him with all my heart. He was the only person to call me by my Hebrew name, Chava, making its syllables into a private name, something tender, only for the two of us. He had me talk about the imaginary creature that I had created as my sister, "Pernelle," an ineffective defense against the solitude that came from being the only daughter of elderly parents. Levinas lent her a momentary reality. One day, he played a game of croquet against me in his sitting room. I was hopelessly losing, and ever a poor sport, I cried bitterly. He stopped the game, made me drink a nice cup of tea, fussed over me, talked to me about other things, and lastly proposed that we finish the game. "One never knows when one's luck will change. . . ." I accepted, and strangely enough, I won. I regained my smile, and faith in life. Years later, when I thought about it again, it suddenly dawned on me that Levinas had let me win. I found this thoughtfulness to be admirable. Much later on, I believe he and his wife saved my life. I was staying in Paris, already a mother of four children, and I was sick, but quite unaware of having serious peritonitis. The Levinases literally harassed me to change doctors. I ended up giving in, tired of fighting. During these same difficult days, Monsieur Levinas, quite ill at ease, and worried about being indiscreet, offered me money, in case this was the problem that prevented me from consulting a better doctor. I didn't need the money, but I was infinitely touched by this offer. When this exceptional man took on my father as a tireless listener of his experiences, of his thinking, as the moral touchstone of his nascent philosophy, I listened. I listened at ten years of age, at fifteen and at twenty. They were good times. I very much loved Levinas. It's definitely worse without him around.

On her table in Jerusalem, Evelyne keeps a photograph of her mother, a younger cousin of Gide — "I have entirely rediscovered Gide these last few years," she confides — and two of her father. In one of them we see a Parisian, the face emaciated, the eyes very blue and very soft behind thick glasses, as he is remembered by all the Enio alumni. In the other, we see something entirely different: he has a long beard and a large black hat on his head. Between the two photographs, the trace of a life of companionship and friendship that were part of the life and work of the philosopher.

When Dr. Nerson emigrated to Israel at the end of his life, the two men continued to write and to visit each other. After Dr. Nerson's death, Levinas praised his memory in a Jewish magazine: "His Judaism, rigorously faithful, was perfectly open."[2] And in an interview with François Poirié, he described him a "a man who was extraordinary, due to the height of his thinking and his moral elevation."[3]

17 GOGOL'S NOSE

"Paternity is a relation with a stranger who, while being Other . . . *is* me, a relation of the I with a self which is yet not me."[1] The last pages of *Totality and Infinity* focus on this human and paradoxical adventure where wonder is concealed within banality itself: being a father. The sudden appearance of a being to whom one will transmit all the knowledge that is one's own, from whom one will learn to be, and who, at the same time, provides opportunities for a fresh start, disclosing a multiplicity of possibilities. "Fecundity continues history without producing old age. Infinite time does not bring an eternal life to an aging subject; it is *better* across the discontinuity of generations, punctuated by the inexhaustible youths of the child."[2] These pages make all the more sense when we realize that they were written at arm's length from a son taking his first steps in life.

No one I know, no one with whom I have met from among his colleagues, his disciples, speaks as well of Emmanuel Levinas as his son, Michael.

A musician, taught to play the piano by his mother from earliest childhood, the path of his vocation reads like a blueprint. The Paris Conservatory, the competitions, encounters with great masters — Olivier Messiaen, Stockhausen, Xénakis, Vlado Perlmuter, Yvonne Lefébure — a sojourn at the Medici villa: these mark the stages of a highly distinguished career as an interpreter and composer, which began in the bosom of the family, under a paternal gaze.

"My father was very present, and in a very specific way," recalls Michael. "First of all, because he accepted the risk involved, a risk that he assessed and that, I must say today, I assessed too. And also because he supported me during a time when musical studies began at a very early age. I'm from an era when one entered the Conservatory in shorts, at the age of ten, something that's unheard of today. And when you entered the Conservatory at ten, it was natural to see parents waiting in the halls for tests to finish or even classes. So I was born into a family where I had a great advantage, on the cultural level, of course, but also on a musical one. During those years, my father would go with my mother to see all of my teachers in order to settle the central question each time: Should he pursue music? My father was one of those parents who could be found in the Conservatory halls, living with this anxiety which was quite acute for a child of ten. Today, the average age at the Conservatory is around twenty. That era is quite gone, you see."

For all that, Emmanuel Levinas hardly had a reputation for being a music lover himself. He said that he knew nothing about music — "except that of my son" he would hastened to add — that he did not have an ear for it, that he heard nothing in it.

"It's true," says Michael, "that he was not musical, but that was due to something exacting on his part."

I don't think he understood the concept of being a music lover. Not being a music lover is something that undoubtedly came from an entire culture, from an artistic, aesthetic environment that was his own. Having done his studies with Maurice Blanchot, he shared with him this superficial sensibility that made him so circumspect in the realm of aesthetics. He had extreme restraint when it came to an art to which he did not have technical access. But all the same, to deny any musicality whatsoever to someone who was, during my entire childhood, until the age of twelve or thirteen years, in the same room where I prepared for my exams — *Totality and Infinity* was written approximately one meter away from my piano — is equally difficult. On the other hand, as soon as I took up composition, that is to say, beyond the instinct for composition that I had from the age of five — because I improvised and combined styles as a young child, something that was very important in my father's decision — as soon as I began writing in a mature phase, when I entered Olivier Messiaen's class, my father's presence as a guide in aesthetic exactness, the relationship to writing, the relationship to the anguish of writing, proved very significant. It was then that I realized that this anguish over writing and creating in musical life was there, one could say, from a very young age. This presence of the writer, of the philosopher, in the same room, in the living room where musical labors took place, the torn papers, the terror at the end of a day that had been fraught with impasses, all of that obviously had a considerable musical presence. And then also, from early childhood, this adjective that I inherited from him, referring to pieces I was working on: "extraordinary." Meaning, there are extra-ordinary people, there are extra-ordinary creators. This somewhat romantic image of the genius, my father passed on to me.

Michael is a few months older than I. I remember him from the days I spent at the Enio. His blond curls. His appearance — always looking like he had just fallen out of bed. His red scarf — even then. His gangly adolescent demeanor. His joking around with the girls. His manner of walking around and bobbing his disheveled head in the way of one friend, then another, delivering his witticisms. And that day we heard his father, proud like never before, telephoning Jules Brunschvicg to announce the good news. "Michael won first prize at the Conservatory. . . . No, no, not at the Consistory, at the Conservatory!" A small event at the school, passed around by word of mouth, accompanied by the hapless telephone misunderstanding by the president of the Alliance, who had a talent for setting off giggles.

SCATTERED PAPERS

I lived at the Enio, in an ambiance that, I'd say, made up for much familial grief, since I was born into a family of survivors, like many Ashkenazi families where there is no extended family. There was my sister, there was my mother, and that's it. The Enio, fortunately, provided a context. It's something that allowed my father — I don't know if it can be put this way — to reconstruct himself. In this respect, it had a considerable role. But in this community, as I think back on it, my father made me experience many things, many anxieties, many difficulties with writing, a kind of suffering that terrified me, that was truly terrifying. And then also certain discoveries. I experienced the way in which a book is constructed, deconstructed, emerging sometimes in a manner similar to a point of departure. It wasn't as if there was an idea for a philosophical project that then gave birth to a text. There was a kind of emptiness, a vertigo, then, scattered elements, rough drafts and concepts that finally took shape on the back of a business card, on the back of a wedding invitation. It's a very peculiar relationship with paper. The vertigo of the blank page didn't exist, there were no blank pages, only the turning over of sheets of paper. If we looked through my father's papers, we'd find not only things stapled together, things crossed out, but a variety of paper bits from which the social life of the 1950s can be reconstructed. Invitations to weddings, to bar mitzvahs, birth announcements were turned over and became manuscripts. And effectively, what you find in *Totality and Infinity* or in *Otherwise Than Being*, certain concepts that are now part of the vernacular, I saw truly emerging from scratch amid pain, sometimes surprise, sometimes revelation. I wasn't spared anything.

The evidence abounds regarding Levinas's difficulties with writing, his anxiety about writing. What is not well known is the feeling of solitude that he struggled with for many years, to which Michael attests:

> There was a very particular solitude in my father's life, which could be easily misunderstood from a distance. It was the solitude of a man who arrived from Lithuania, who evidently had, I realize today, an absolutely exceptional cultural environment. But you know, in daily life things are not lived in that manner. My father did not experience his writing work as a protégé of an institution. He was the director of a Jewish school who incidentally had exceptional encounters, from time to time visits, conversations. But I am not talking about the years in which he was a university professor, I am essentially talking about writing, about the 1950s when he wrote *Totality and Infinity*, when his thinking was being worked out. And, well, he was not an academic. He was someone who presented a lecture at Jean Wahl's Collège, a lecture written in extreme pain — hence today we could say these texts are cast in bronze — always on the verge of annulment. But someone who was not integrated. As a result, daily life, Sundays, Mondays, Tuesdays, those days, I experienced them. He was a man, a father of a family who had a strange power, but, in the end, a lonely man, for whom a telephone call from an institution was, I'd say, like a kind of drug that would restore his confidence. And it had that effect, I often think, because we always talk about the despair of writing, but sometimes writing can be experienced as something that goes completely unrecognized, summoned to serve

nothing, and experienced like something belonging to anyone in daily life. And then, there was this general sadness in my father's life.

Writing — I return to it and persist — how was it carried out? Was intuition at the heart of the work, which was then unraveled? Or was it rather, following the idea he one day confessed to Jacques Rolland, that he preferred "short sprints" to "longer runs," a series of intuitions that ended up converging?

No, what Jacques Rolland is talking about is something by and large common to all true writers. What's it about? I am speaking here as a musician, drawing from my own experience — if you'll forgive me. The notion of the great form, of development, of the "long run" as you say, the grand thesis of a novel of two hundred pages, of a two-hour symphony, of a four-hour opera, is already something of the order of the unpredictable. That is to say that the system, the elaboration of a system, to return to the philosophical form, is not a programmed endeavor. It's a certain number of intellectual events that find themselves building something. In music, this is evident. I don't think, except perhaps in the last operas of Wagner or in Stockhausen's long opera, that the form and hypertrophy of time correspond to a premeditated intention. They are the result of a certain number of phrases. I think that *Totality and Infinity* and *Otherwise Than Being* are effectively long runs, to resume the expression. They constitute the elaboration of many lectures, of many works, of many accidents. I think I remember that when my father finished *Otherwise Than Being,* he said that he had more or less finished his work. Either he said it, or I wanted to hear it, or I sensed it; in any event, it seemed that the breathing that allowed for the system to come into being had been made up of a certain number of phrases. But I don't think this is peculiar to my father, it's one of the tests of writing and the very genesis of great forms and of long runs.

SON AND FATHER

Michael did not read his father's writings until much later. His initial contact with philosophy began at the age of seventeen. The first book that his father had him read was Granier's *Nietzsche.* After this, he discovered the *Talmudic Lectures* and *Difficult Freedom.* As for *Totality and Infinity,* he tackled it much later on. On the other hand, Michael was present on several trips. Not being a part of an academic institution, nor, later, being bound by any curriculum in traditional university studies, he was able to accompany his father to conferences held in the four corners of the world. In Holland. In Italy. In the United States. In Morocco.

> I was one of the parties, or one of the difficulties, in each of these experiences. I was with my father at Johns Hopkins. It's thanks to him that I was in Rome for the first time. I also made this somewhat strange trip to Iran, to a world that posed a problem for him, what one might call the "fascist" world of the Shah, where he felt so out of place in this luxury hotel completely under guard by the Savak. He did not salute the empress. Many academics, who were apparently more progressive than he, had done so. Then there was the visit into the sanctum of the Meshed Mosque where one could already see fundamentalism brewing and what frenzied belief could lead to, something to which my father was utterly opposed because of the violence that it could cause. I experienced all of that with him. Both of us fell ill, moreover, with a horrible fever, and that's how we spent *Rosh Hashanah,* in my opinion due to the shock of the Meshed Mosque.

Whenever he was invited somewhere, the philosopher would often ask if it was possible to provide a piano for his son — for example, on the trip to Tioumlinine in Morocco.

> I was eight years old, and I remember an ecumenical speech of the kind that was heard in the era of Moulay Hassan.

He claimed not to understand why the different religions fought with each other. And I got this saying as a child: "But he's lying, he's like Napoleon!" Nevertheless, since you want to know whether my father took charge of my musical life, well, before leaving for Morocco, he asked if there was a piano in the Moyen-Atlas. There wasn't a piano in the Moyen-Atlas. As it was a given that his son was more important than he, he wanted to cancel the trip. He inquired at the time, through pneumatic tube, to my professor Lazare Lévy, whether it was acceptable for me to desist from playing the piano for ten days. Official approval was given. And it was with this official approval that my father left for Morocco. We returned to this great anxiety over my musical life, or this great guilt. So much was intense for him: the idea that in the field of philosophy as in the arts only exceptional abilities could justify dedicating oneself to a vocation. I don't know if I have these abilities or not, but he made constant inquiries to my professors to find out whether the commitment he made to have me pursue a musical career was truly justified. And that went on until I was quite old, which often made my parents seem completely eccentric.

There were also trips to Germany, to which Michael traveled alone — in his father's name. In 1983, Emmanuel Levinas received the Karl Jaspers award from the University of Heidelberg. Jeanne Hersch was to present it to him, but Michael stood in as the recipient. He read the speech prepared by his father and spoke before a very attentive academic audience, from the height of Hegel's chair, in the university's great Aula. Levinas's vow to never return to Germany, where he had endured five years of captivity during the war, was something that went without comment, but was understood by his children.

He actually shared something with me on this subject. He believed that he was saved by the French uniform. My father was a lumberjack in the camps. He remained one for a while, I think that that gave him a lot of strength to go on living. It's terrible to say that, but that's how it was. He lived these five years of captivity in camaraderie. He declared himself a Jew right away. He met Eric Weil in one of these camps, who preferred not to declare his religion and went by the name Dubois. My father considered it unthinkable to lie, and he lived out these years of captivity with a full awareness, he told me, that in reality, this was the waiting room of deportation. He got up every morning at five o'clock, he went out to cut down trees, and the head lumberjack who guided them would comment every day, it seemed: "You'll see how this goes when you're in the hands of the SS." Something else that I know about this terrible scar on his life is that he and his fellow inmates regularly received letters in which some of them learned that members of their families were arrested and deported, usually in the encoded metaphor: "We're going to the wedding." That's how he was informed of my grandmother's deportation. The horrifying conditions in which his parents and his brothers were murdered he didn't know about, I think, until after the war. But, from what he told me later on, I think that he accepted it as a matter of fate, that essentially he himself was basically going to die, and that it was useless for Jews to think of escaping from a camp. In other words, whatever happened, it would all end with a firing squad.

"I should also say," Michael adds,

that when he was alive what I saw in my father's correspondences was a very great love for France, something that perhaps no longer exists today in the European mentality, a veritable patriotism, and also a fraternity with a number of great French citizens. I am thinking of people whom no one knows, friends who saved my mother, a woman named Suzanne Poirier, her husband, and Maurice Blanchot, of course. In this there was — without being anachronistic here — a French specificity in relation to the Nazi horror, and I do mean a "specificity," something extraordinary, something that made my father a Gaullist.

He had this filial relationship with de Gaulle that perhaps once again demonstrated a Napoleonic image of France against a Russia of pogroms. I believe that this carried a lot of weight, beyond my musical career, in his decision to remain in France until his death.

One particular image from the period of captivity stayed with him all his life, something he never evoked in his writings and confided only to those who were very close to him: the camp where he was detained was located not far from Buchenwald, and, one day, he saw the shadows of deportees. He became aware of the horror while passing by a column of deportees in the forest, with all that this could represent of physical tragedy.

SECULAR CRACKS

I remind Michael of this word he had once used: he had said to me that his father was a philosopher of cracks, an expression that, at the time, struck me as profound and accurate, and on which I had to meditate for a long time, without being able to decide how much it covered.

> I think that it goes back to what we said about the fragility involved in the act of writing, the noninstitutional nature of his work, as well as his navigating between his Jewish intellectual development and his purely philosophical development — I don't know if he would accept the expression "purely philosophical" — and his breathlessness that effected me so much musically. If you listen to his recordings, there are often unfinished phrases, with the *"n'est-ce pas?"* that cannot be attributed solely to his being a foreigner speaking French — a kind of instability in the elaboration of a concept, an extreme mobility, almost talmudic, in fact, in the conceptualization that really expresses the crack in the concept. This goes well beyond something dialectical, it belongs to the order of the fissure. The con-

cept is in the process of being born and it is put back into question at the very moment in which it is formulated. It results in, I was going to say, an oratory style that very much inspired me in my music.

Allow me this somewhat indecent analogy, but the presence of breathing, a fear in the way I approach sound, something of the order of a rustling of wings, an anxiety in the timbre, in the sound, comes from this aesthetic dimension of my father's work and from his oratorical art. And I'd say, I think that the role of erasure in work is not the result of chance. It's very strange because that's accompanied by an aspect we sometimes talk about but which we don't put in the foreground with regard to my father, because of course he is not really regarded as a philosopher of aesthetics. But my father is the one who said to me, in the course of composing, when I was at an impasse or felt it impossible to write, that it was ultimately necessary to accept incompleteness. Eventually, at the age of twenty, I took that to be a paternal approval to fail at something, but I didn't take it that way alone. He said to me, "Sometimes, the thing suffices in its incompleteness." He added that one could go see the works of a painter named Charles Lapicque, whom he had met at Jean Wahl's Collège, whose work consisted of presenting various states of incompleteness in a painting.

The last year of his life, I came across his essay on erasure, regarding Michel Leiris, and in reality, indirectly and in a very subtle manner, my father guided me toward a problem that belonged to his time, after the war: that of a work of art or a piece of writing that is not sealed, that is not formalized in an institutional manner, around which there is an enormous question mark or an enormous vertigo of incompleteness. And actually, it's not Lapicque that one should go see for this, but Giacometti. I made a kind of analogy between this crack so characteristic of my father's thinking and the manner in which the figures of Giacometti — who is basically his contemporary — appear threadbare, breathless. It wouldn't be expressionistic to say that these cracks could evoke these figures we've just been talking about, but it is essentially the humanity, or the body, or the shame of the body. He calls this the face, basically. The crack — that's the face.

How did he divide up his time, that which he devoted to philosophy and that which he dedicated to Jewish texts? Did it, or did it not, all blend together in reflection, in study, in writing? "I never had a very sharp awareness of that," Michael says,

> But I'd say one thing: he ceased all philosophical work between 1947 and 1952, from the time he received Chouchani at home. That's clear; he said so himself. He said that he spent as much time writing his dissertation as he did being trained by Chouchani. As for the rest, the time devoted to writing, I can't tell you what happened there. That began at five o'clock in the morning, and ended at midnight. When I was a child, he was a man who went downstairs to the first floor of the school, who kept his office hours, it's important to know that — watch out for people who tell you "I can't teach and write." We spoke about this anonymity in his life, this solitude; there was also this submission that I find impressive in the life of the office worker. Don't forget that before the war, my father was a minor employee in the offices of the Alliance, who, instead of writing a dissertation or completing an *agrégation,* still went on Sunday mornings to rue la Bruyère to post the mail to the AIU schools in Morocco. He never considered it to be inferior work. I also believe that this was very important, this acceptance of daily life. Then there was prayer in the morning. When there wasn't a bell yet, he would bang on the floor to wake up the student boarders who had to be at synagogue by seven-thirty. Until the end of his life, he was at the office at seven-thirty for morning office hours. Afterwards, he'd write until midnight — after classes, after school, he'd work. So you see, it's quite prosaic.
>
> At the same time, there was the preparation for the Saturday morning Rashi class. There was the daily contact

and exchanges with Dr. Nerson. Tuesday evening classes with Enio students. Sunday evening classes at the house with different people from the Jewish community. After Chouchani's departure, there was a course on the Talmud on Sundays, reserved for Nerson and a few others. And then, a constant and worn-in familiarity with texts. That's how it went. I really think that the Enio, teaching young people, was an important extension of his original way of life, I mean the life of a little Jewish community in Eastern Europe that kept everything that is *chol*, profane, on the outside. That stayed with him all his life. He was always a bit of a stranger to secular institutions and to secular life.

Indeed, the concern with school affairs never left him, but at what price, to the philosopher, for the meditation on essences, for the writing of commentaries?

I believe that my father had a true pedagogical vocation, a love of students, be it the Enio student to whom he gave direction, the seminar student, or someone who gave him a manuscript to read. So for example, in 1976 he named Pascal Quignard as someone destined to a great future. Before Jacques Derrida would become what he became, he was convinced that he belonged to the ranks of the important philosophers. Later on, it was Jacques Rolland and a few others. Allow me to add an anecdote. He had on his table a typescript on musicology and aesthetics, anonymously written. He said to me, quite moved: "This text shows a true pen and exceptional poetic feeling." The text belonged to the one who would become his daughter-in-law, Danielle Cohen-Levinas, with whom he had a very tight bond.

THE TORN MANUSCRIPT

Another vivid and surprising event that I learned about from Michael concerned an important moment in Levinas's life and work, the publication of *Totality and Infinity*. It was the book that disseminated his name, that launched his university career. The book almost never saw the light of day. It came close to being destroyed:

> *Totality and Infinity* was begun in a small house in Evian in 1955. I still have photographs of this time. And the manuscript was practically torn up. It was almost torn up because — I hesitate to say it — it was refused by Gallimard, by a fairly important man, Brice Parain, who telephoned one day, saying: "Bad news." That day, the book had to be taken from my father's hands, who truly wanted to cut it up into pieces. This book, therefore, nearly went unseen. Then, Father Van Breda came and took the book in order to publish it. Around that time, one fine morning, Jean Wahl telephoned to say, "Stop the publication immediately, you must defend it as a thesis." And there was this extraordinary oral defense; I was ten years old, I was in the room. There was Blanchot. A prestigious committee with Jankélévitch, Gabriel Marcel, Wahl and Blin. That basically marked my father's entrance into the university. As he put it, this entrance into the university was not born of youthful impatience. In 1961, my father was fifty-five or fifty-six years old. It was really not a precocious career.

And so, this book that was the glory of Levinas — he himself was going to tear into pieces after having shed blood and tears writing it. This illustrates his rapport with the book in another way. Sublimation, on the one hand: everything he could write under the inspired character of all the great books, confidence in books, the book more profound and more interior than consciousness; everything he did to push an entire generation of Jews to open their books. But books have a story, have a life. And their worth emerges only through this history and this life given to them. Hence, idealization on the one hand, and on the other hand, a tremendous demystification of the book. This decision to destroy a book, like the decision several years earlier to stop writing, from

1947 to 1952, shows an awareness of the possible vanity of books. He once appealed to these words by Rosenzweig from *The New Thinking:* "The book is not a goal that has been reached, not even a preliminary one. It itself must be answered for, instead of it carrying itself or being carried by others of its kind. This responsibility happens in everyday life."[3]

Books must justify life, but life must justify books. One cannot take leave of a book as soon as it is written. On the contrary, the work begins at that point. The book must be supported. One must stand behind it. It must be justified.

Three years later came the nomination to Poitiers, followed by Nanterre and the Sorbonne. "And for my father," Michael recounts,

> — something I never understood before — there was a kind of philosophical euphoria, "an exit from the desert," as they say in politics. This can be seen in *Otherwise Than Being.* It's clear that he experienced the writing of *Otherwise Than Being* in a constant state of anxiety over paraphrasing, and, at the same time, in the necessity of going to the end of something that had never been tackled until *Totality and Infinity.* But there was, I think, a courage of expression in *Otherwise Than Being,* and probably an elaboration of the theory of the face that abandoned a cautiousness that he may have had in *Totality and Infinity* and that perhaps consisted of masking certain Jewish or Talmudic roots. This mask, for that matter, was uncovered in a certain way by an alarming comment made by Gabriel Marcel at the oral defense. He asked my father: Why do you always say "the Other" when you know that the term exists in the biblical tradition, as the "neighbor"? And this element — we cannot say this inhibition — this complex geographical position of the work, between the spirit of *Difficult Freedom* and the spirit of a philosophy emancipated from this tradition, was lifted further in *Otherwise Than Being.*

Philosopher. Jew. Philosopher and Jew. Jewish philosopher? We know that Emmanuel Levinas did not like the expression. He refused to be defined in this way. He said so on several occasions. And Michael corroborates it:

> Let's put aside biographical conjecture and the extremely important and complex relationship that my father could have had with Jewish institutions. That's the story of daily life, I would say, and it's not for me to talk about. Can we talk about an identity that would explain itself through its origins? I think that my father experienced this tension in a very productive, originary manner in his work. Basically, I think that that's what was at stake, and in saying "Jewish philosopher," the tension is lifted and a system of thought is explained. The problem is not in the explanation, it's in the reduction. We are not going to stupidly contrast Judaism and universalism. We are not going to contrast, as some do, Greece and the Bible. These are what I'd call polygraphic statements. I think we'd make an error with that. Basically, I see something strange in relation to my father, in relation to his work, strange and agonizing. Right now I am talking to you about a man I saw get up, pray, put on *tefillin,* call the Enio students, bawl them out, encourage them, grade, eat, tear up a book, and I see a work that totally escapes all of that. That is to say, without a doubt, a Jewish work, a Jewish life from beginning to end. I remember how he had this visceral attachment to his cap in his last year. He kept it on until his last breath. He died on the eighth day of Hanukkah. It was in the morning. He didn't feel well. It was eleven o'clock, I lit the last Hanukkah candle, he took the prayer book, he kissed the book, he kissed my hand, we left for the hospital and he passed away a few hours later. The whole time, he never took off the cap, but not because of forgetfulness, that's unthinkable. He had never worn the cap. He wore it throughout the last year of his life. This element is indisputable, just like, incidentally, the attachment to Israel. To use Raymond Aron's phrase, if he had to witness this country disappear, he would have lost the will to live.

"At the same time," Michael continues,

> the philosophical work escapes all that. When it comes down to it, I no longer know very well what it will become,

it has its own life. I see something that is basically very Gogolian. It's Gogol's story of the nose that my father always interpreted as the fact that the body rebels against itself. I don't think that my father's work is either my nose, or the nose of who knows who. At a certain point, the work simply doesn't want to return to from whence it came. It has its uniform and goes around by horse-drawn carriage. And it's necessary to accept that; we should accept that the work has its own singularity. This is harrowing because at the time that he wrote it — we return here to the story of the crack — did the writer truly know what he wrote? And is it helpful to know? He wrote it, and the work lives, belonging to whoever wants it, on the condition that it not be distorted. I see this experience when I see my father's work as that of someone whom I absolutely did not know. It's something I cannot fully explain to you, something he wouldn't be able to explain to you either.

Tea

*Levinas and his wife. They offer me tea. They often offered tea.
Alain David has a lovely story on this subject. He is visiting in
the living room; there is a knock at the door. It is Mrs. Levinas's
physiotherapist. He greets everyone. And the philosopher invites
him to have a cup of tea. "If you're having some, I'd love to!"
The philosopher's response, with his big smile: "No, me, I already
had one, and I am a monotheist."*

*I once again delight in my conversation with him. They have
aged, both of them. They have changed. But the sense of humor is
always there, around each remark.*

*Music again and always. It comes back like a refrain. "You
never loved music, you never tried to understand, you know, you
don't have a bad ear, but you persist." Then, speaking about contemporary music, she adds, "Me, I don't like it, but I try to
understand it!"*

*The telephone rings. Someone notifies them that Mitterand is
on television. We burst out laughing, all three of us, and they
turn on the television. François Mitterand is talking about the
economy. "He really knows his stuff, it's quite accurate!" the
philosopher gets excited. I discover on this occasion that he did
not always like him, that there was a time when he found him
deceitful.*

*I take my leave, happy to have shared this moment, to have
watched television with them. As soon as I get back home, I*

receive a telephone call from him: "I am happy you came by. We had a very nice time!"

"Me too," I reply, and I think about how I don't know anyone who can be just as enchanting — is that the right word? — in a visit, in a private conversation, as in his courses and in his books. All those who had the privilege of these encounters around tea or Cointreau have the same memory.

A distant correspondent from Japan writes me that every year, on the same day, December 25, he meets with friends in Kyoto to drink a glass of the philosopher's liqueur of preference.

18 | RECOGNITION

The work of Emmanuel Levinas took root quite slowly. Beyond the circle of those who were near and those who were adherents, it took some time for it to meet up with its era. Was this due to his difficult language? To the peculiarity of his writing and the process whereby common words are divested of their common meaning in order to be rendered otherwise? To his violence, and the fascination that it provokes at the same time that it remains impossible to grasp? To his innovation as well?

Putting the Face at the center of his philosophy, describing the irruption of the ethical as turmoil, devastation, passion, resuscitating religion within the heart of the philosophical, clearing a new path into the depths of Judaism — this thinking was disruptive in more than one way. It provoked many caricatures, incited ire, but for the most part was quite simply ignored, or remained an inside interest among dedicated followers.

THE RETURN

Recognition was therefore late in coming. A genuine interest in Levinas's work in France did not emerge until the last
years of his life, practically after his retirement and departure from the Sorbonne. At the beginning of the 1970s, an
issue of *Magazine Littéraire* was dedicated to the top twenty
French philosophers. Levinas was not on the roster.[1] At
the end of this same decade, under the title "The Same and
the Other" — which title, in this case, covered the Aristotel-
ian, Hegelian, epistemological, and psychoanalytic perspectives, but which could have also included the Levinasian
one — Vincent Descombes prepared a panorama of forty
years of French philosophy from 1933 to 1978.[2] There he
explains the passage from the three H's — Hegel, Husserl
and Heidegger — to the three "masters of suspicion" —
Marx, Nietzsche and Freud. No mention of Levinas, neither
in the shadow of the former triad, nor in the wake of the
latter.

The month of May 1968 left Levinas on the sidelines, unknown to the battalions. According to one of his former students at Nanterre, he wrote his lectures on the blank backs
of pamphlets and, from time to time, turned over these sheets
to ask: "What are Margouilles?" — an allusion, presumably,
to some schemes concocted by the university and denounced
by the students. And Catherine Chalier, who was then his
student, before becoming a friend and one of his most faithful disciples, recounts how he often cancelled his classes during that period, and how he would not stop thundering every
time he saw "CRS-SS!" written on a public notice. It was a
time when, as Jean-Louis Schlegel puts it, if you wanted to
make people laugh, you spoke about religion, and when you

wanted to catch their interest, you spoke about politics. Twenty years later, the converse was true in some ways, and this reversal marked the beginning of Levinas's notoriety.

In 1980, a collection entitled *Textes pour Emmanuel Lévinas* was published, comprised of contributions by Maurice Blanchot, Jeanne Delhomme, Jacques Derrida, Mickel Dufrenne, Jean Halperin, Edmond Jabès, François Laruelle, Jean-François Lyotard, André Neher, Adriaan Peperzak, Paul Ricoeur and Edith Wyschograd. Philippe Nemo broadcast a series of radio interviews on France-Culture that ended up as a book.[3] Bernard-Henri Lévy published *Le Testament de Dieu*, which explicitly invoked the philosopher's name.[4] Alain Finkielkraut wrote a passionate acclamation which *Le Monde* placed in volume 1 of its literary supplement, accompanied by a portrait sketch by Charles Szlakman, the general approach of which was summarized in the single phrase: "Levinas places the definition of being human beyond every politics." In 1982, the same journal invited twelve French philosophers to contribute to its summer series. Each was entitled to a page. They were Jacques Derrida, Vincent Descombes, Michel Serres, Jean-Toussaint Dessanti, Clement Rosset, Élisabeth de Fontenay, and, taking part in the group for the first time, Emmanuel Levinas.[5]

What had happened in the meantime? Jean-Luc Marion observes that Levinas began his university career quite late in life, during the 1960s. He was already in his fifties. "I don't think there was any resistance to Levinas as a person or as a philosopher. It's something very simple, much more serious in one sense: it's that no one understood what he was saying. His philosophy was perceived to be very difficult because it was phenomenology in its purest form carried out by someone who knew it from the beginning. He was a thinker of the Other, yet a solitary thinker, who, in a sense, didn't have any followers and didn't seek any. He was not someone who kept a watchful eye out for the dissemination of his ideas. He was difficult to access intellectually. But, after all, let's be clear: how could you expect an original philosophy not to have a slow reception?"

For Marion, this philosophy, more than being original, has modified and continues to modify the landscape.

> It's important to appreciate Levinas's stature. He is, with Bergson, as I believe I said at the time of his death, the greatest French philosopher of the twentieth century. By great philosopher, I mean someone who introduces new analyses, who invents new approaches, who changes basic concepts; in other words, after him, the philosophical vocabulary is no longer the same, the lexicon is different. Bergson did it once, and Levinas did it a second time. The others, important as they may be, could have written brilliant things, but they don't make the cut. The general course of philosophy has undoubtedly been impoverished. But it hasn't been modified, the direction will remain the same. In France, there are only two men who attained these limits. Bergson, with an obvious suppleness, and Levinas, with the harshness and brutality found in his style, effected a redirection in the course of things. When it was declared that the ethical is the ultimate horizon of philosophy, a current was made to flow backwards.

This is why, Marion surmises, this thinking remains alive. Even more, in fact, it has yet to show its full force.

> I think that there is no purgatory for Levinas, and that we are only at the beginning of grappling in earnest with this thinking. We are at the beginning because the importance of Levinas cannot really be measured until Husserl is better understood — we haven't yet published everything, we haven't yet assimilated everything, and in particular everything that Husserl did on the question of the Other and on intersubjectivity — and when we have processed

Heidegger as well, then Levinas's work will be better under-stood. Levinas's thinking is very dense, strong, it's like a nuclear reactor that has just started to work. The emission of energy is not finished, far from it.

CONTRADICTIONS

Didier Franck teaches at Nanterre. He has a bitter memory of Levinas. It was 1989. Catherine Chalier and Miguel Abensour had just published a special edition of *Cahiers de l'Herne* devoted to the philosopher. And at Lyon, the review organized a soirée that would accompany the publication of the edition. They looked for someone who had not partici-pated in the anthology to open the evening. They approached Didier Franck, who accepted the invitation. Four hundred people crowded into the university's large amphitheater.

At this memorable soirée, over which David Kessler presided, and where Levinas was present, an enigmatic inci-dent took place. The philosopher, already quite old, had difficulty remaining in one place. Franck was accorded one hour to deliver his address. He had chosen *De l'existence à l'existant* as his topic. He hardly began his lecture when the philosopher who was to be honored broke into a violent out-burst of anger before a dumbfounded audience, exclaiming that he had "never been so poorly understood," and abruptly left the room.

Catherine Chalier, present at the conference, attributes this outburst to the philosopher's failing health. Didier Franck believes that the outburst was perfectly conscious and delib-erate: "A few days later, he sent me his apologies through Catherine Chalier, but I wasn't fooled. He had a keen eye. I had said no more than a few words, but he understood that criticism was to follow."

According to Franck, Levinas could be violent, experienced moments of blanking out that were quasi psychological, and knew how to be disagreeable when he wanted to be. This violence was already there in the work: "To equate being with evil, to say that you are guilty of being — that's colossal. It isn't even biblical, besides, since Creation is good. I don't see how we can affirm such a position. And at the same time, I can see very well how it supports the whole system for him."

Franck, nevertheless, had followed this man's journey with fascination. In 1974, he defended his dissertation on Husserl at Nanterre. Levinas had Jacques Colette ask him to come speak at the Sorbonne and invited him to his home.

"It's something that I find quite beautiful: the fact that he remained in the shadows for a long time. At the beginning, it's true, he was alone, no one understood anything, no one saw anything in him, he had an advantage of time over others." Then, at the beginning of the 1980s, he notes further, the movements at the time — the right to difference, the struggle against racism, human rights, the Jewish community which until then had been fairly well assimilated and was now rediscovering itself, the Catholic milieu in search of its sources and of revitalization — found, not just a representative in him, but also a symbolic and validating point of reference. For Franck, in that explosive moment at Lyon, Levinas crystallized all of these phenomena. But he adds immediately, "The confessional reading of Levinas is what has established his renown, but it's false. What commands is the philosophical."

The sociological explication is accurate, but insufficient. A philosopher of anti-ideology, Levinas became an established thinker during a time that saw the collapse of ideologies; a philosopher of ethics at the time of its return amid the rubble of the century. However, the circumstances surrounding his recognition do not fully account for the advent of an authentic thinking. Another question remains. A confessional reading? A philosophical reading? What is certain is that Levinas kept shifting the lines, including these ones, for everyone. He grew tense whenever one sought to categorize him as a "Jewish philosopher," and yet, philosophy and Judaism were intermingled in his life and remained so in his work. Most of his teaching career took place in a Jewish milieu and much of his writing concerns Jewish themes. And therefore? This intertwining should be analyzed without resorting to facile measures such as splitting the two aspects or, alternatively, blending them together. It is important to refuse to pit them against each other as if to distinguish them. To understand, even despite his own view, that he was a philosopher until the end, even in his confessional writings. And Jewish until the end, even in his philosophical writings. It is this infinite dialogue between philosophy and Judaism that constitutes Levinas's work, and accords him his universal power. His approach simultaneously gives his philosophy a distinctive tone because it is infused with Judaism, while giving his Judaism a particular resonance because it is infused with philosophy. The two worlds touch and sustain each other without merging.

"I don't see myself in any case as Jewish," he said, amazingly, one day to Burggraeve.[6] And what is no less true, according to Jean Halperin, Levinas still does not have the place in the Jewish world that he deserves:

> I think that he was heard, he was read. I think that *Difficult Freedom* and the *Talmudic Lectures* caused some important reverberations. But the thinker was still not received with the seriousness and attention that he warranted. In a paradoxical way, I would say that, sometimes, I have the

impression that the non-Jewish world is more attentive to
Levinas's thinking than the Jewish world. . . . Today Levinas
is someone who can best be understood by those who reflect,
whether they are Jewish or not, on what constitutes responsibility and on what freedom signifies for each person. These
words are commonplace, but in reality they play a very
powerful role in thinking and in interpretation. It's important
to not treat them like clichés. I believe that responsibility
and freedom are challenges, questions for the human being
who wishes to be worthy of his or her human condition and
who has something to say and to do, something to accomplish in this world. It's because of this that what strikes me
in his work is that, even though it sometimes gives the impression of being abstract, as some philosophies can be, in reality it always leads to, or wants to lead to, doing. The thinking
is never gratuitous. And Levinas warns us against what we
call a *berakha levatala,* an empty or wasted blessing. It's important that the prayers we utter and the lessons we give have
meaning, and that they lead to action. Otherwise, it would
be an abuse of language.

PREDECESSORS AND POSTERITY

Before Levinas, there were three great encounters between
philosophy and Judaism: in the first century of the Christian
era, in Alexandria, with Philo; during the Middle Ages, around
Cordova, with Maimonides, Yehuda Halevi and Ibn Gabirol;
and at the beginning of the twentieth century, stemming
from Berlin, with Hermann Cohen and Franz Rosenzweig.

In this respect, we can draw parallels between Levinas and
Philo of Alexandria, whose ambition was essentially to make
the Bible commensurate with Plato, to translate revelation
into the language of ideas, despite the risks, in order to affirm
its universal character. The connection with Cohen and above
all with Rosenzweig is explicit. Yet the proximity was greater
still with Salomon Ibn Gabirol, the poet and philosopher

whose texts fostered and continue to foster all of Jewish liturgy. His major work enjoyed much success in the Latin translation *Fons vitae,* once attributed to Avicena. It was for a long time considered to be of Christian or Muslim origins before Salomon Munk resolved the historical enigma. Duns Scotus and many scholastic theologians were inspired by it. It is perhaps strange that Levinas never wrote anything on this Neoplatonic thinker whom he resembled in so many ways[7] — whereas he wrote much on Maimonides, and that only because of his need to separate the philosophical work from the Jewish work; on the one hand, a reflection on faith and religious ideals, without any apparent relation to the tradition, and in a universal cast of mind, and on the other hand, a celebration of this same tradition in a brilliant, poetic work anchored in the sources.

Ibn Gabirol's major work, *Mekor Chaim* (the source of life), written originally in Arabic, preserved solely in its Latin version and rediscovered in the nineteenth century, had this astonishing career of being inserted into the Church's thinking, having no influence on Jewish thought, or certainly a marginal one, even when this same author's properly Jewish writings would come to enjoy a dazzling popularity! Will Levinas enjoy the same kind of Jewish posterity? A preservation of the *Talmudic Lectures* and *Difficult Freedom,* while *Otherwise Than Being* is left for the Catholic universities and the postmodern philosophers to deal with?

René Gutman, chief rabbi of Strasbourg, who had special access to Levinas through his father, a former comrade-in-captivity of the philosopher, does not shy away from the question. "I was very drawn to his philosophy, to the teaching of his humanism. I tried to familiarize myself with his work that always has been for me a source of inspiration, and that has had quite an influence on my life and my experience as a rabbi."

He confesses, nevertheless, that there was always a mis-understanding between Levinas and the religious world. From both sides, for that matter. The philosopher was readily ironic whenever the rabbinate was mentioned. And in the domain of religious Judaism, there was an inability to comprehend his work. "It's difficult for religious Judaism to go to the other side, to the point where Levinas went, without hazarding a certain erasure of its own identity. A spiritual and intellectual audacity is needed, and those who have it are few in number. The concept of hostage, or of substitution, is trouble-some. For a Jew who thinks by referring to accepted traditional norms, where the identity of the self is obvious, this idea that one can be rid of oneself, that one can be besieged by the other, the idea that one cannot belong anymore, is a philo-sophical boldness that is perhaps inaudible for a Jew who is used to a language that does not tolerate such an exposition. This face that commands me, this exposition of the other, this presents a vital choice."

The proof for this is that there are only a few rabbis who cite Levinas today. But would he be surprised, in his lifetime never having been invited to speak before any rabbinical con-gress, that, for example, at the Séminaire Israélite de France, his work is not taught, and that in the Jewish schools there is no anthology of his writings?

Yet, according to René Gutman, who is passionate about Levinas's work, it is a thinking that is deeply rooted in the Jewish tradition, and that is certainly viable. "The notion of the human in the Torah precedes difference. The interhu-man relationship is in a certain sense written down before the Law. I am obligated by the Other before he or she is obliged to me. Levinas's thinking returns to the chapter of Genesis where it says: 'It was then that men began to invoke the Lord by name' [Gen. 4:26]. It's after the death of Cain. Adam begets Seth and Seth begets Enosh. And the passage is found after the birth of Enosh, whose name in Hebrew signifies 'human.' Humanity, in Genesis, begins there." And Gutman concludes, "I have read and reread *Humanism and the Other Human Being*. It's my bedside book. I always have it with me. It always inspires me. Even if I don't quote it — the language is difficult — my references can be found there. Just like when it comes to Judeo-Christian issues. My perspective is inspired mostly by Rosenzweig on that question, but the two are connected. Both understand this relationship in a similar manner."

INFINITE READING

What does one do with all of the papers accumulated in a lifetime? What will become of all these "things," as Levinas put it, over which he struggled and which did not fit into the work, which remain in a state of disorganization, of sketch, of "remorse" or failure? The question obsessed him. He liked the comment by Rashi, which often came up in his courses, on the broken shards of the tablets of the Law which Moses was charged with preserving in the Sanctuary, the broken fragments of the first set of tablets next to the second set, as if the story of the first set was part of the second set, as if something would be missing in the second without the "scraps" of the first.

Levinas wrote a lot and published much of what he wrote. The essential is there, in his work. His speeches, his conferences, the colloquia in which he participated are found scattered here and there, and often gathered together by his own hand. What he did not wish to say, he did not say, and what he kept was no doubt kept deliberately.

The work has coherence. The life, too. Each of them is complete in and of itself. What else could one discover that might serve to alter the image? Short of finding the "fault"?

The Archimedean point? The moment from which we can regard the whole.

Levinas left behind many documents after his death. Course notes, drafts, essays with annotations, manuscripts, lecture notes, various philosophical developments, plans for seminars, correspondences with writers, thinkers, philosophers, theologians, translators, editors.[8] . . . The sheer inventory of these archives is illuminating. We find the thread running through his work, the habitual benchmarks, the familiar references, everything that marked the existence of the philosopher, of the Jewish thinker, of the educator.

Unpublished material? Surprises? Unknown texts? Going through them we find a good number of them on Maimonides. Course notes on Hassidism and Agnon. Old essays about prisoners of war. Journals from his imprisonment recorded in seven notebooks. Course notes on Judah Halevi. Course notes on Maimonides. A correspondence with Martin Buber. Handwritten course notes on Heidegger. A handwritten reading and translation of the Song of Songs. A fictional essay about Eros. A number of speeches given to the European Parliament on Europe, on peace, on the European citizen. A plan for creating a review for the United Jewish Social Fund in 1951, the name of which was to be "The New Bridge." A correspondence with Derrida, with a text and notes on the oral defense of his dissertation. A correspondence with Mario Soares, president of Portugal, in 1990, regarding plans for a conference — which in the end never took place.

In 1956, for the two hundredth anniversary of Mozart's birth, Heidegger apparently read a letter to his students in which the composer explained his creative process.[9] While walking, traveling, or during nights of insomnia, pieces took shape in his head. And then there was a moment — "a deli-cious moment" — when he was able to "see in a single glance" and to "hear everything at once."

A philosophical work is not a symphony, and Levinas is not Mozart. But was there a moment when the work crys-tallized? Was there a moment when Levinas took in his work entirely in one glance? Did he not refer to his three major works — *Totality and Infinity, Otherwise Than Being* and *Of God Who Comes to Mind* — in the preface to the German edition, as a "discourse begun twenty-five years ago constituting a whole"? And to Poirié, did he not say, regarding one of his first writings, *On Escape,* written in 1935, "I had perhaps the feeling of being tormented by something unique, which still torments me"?[10]

Where is this sturdy core of the work? This moment when the work is heard and seen in its entirety? Nineteen thirty-three and the rise of Nazism? Nineteen thirty-five and the discovery of Rosenzweig? Nineteen forty and imprisonment? Nineteen seventy-four and the completion of *Otherwise Than Being,* when he had the feeling, already, that everything was said?

It is the intimate secret of this work. And the only way, perhaps, of keeping it open.

François-David Sebbah is one of the youngest thinkers in Levinas's wake. Teaching at the University of Compiègne, director of programs at the Collège International de Philo-sophie, he devoted his dissertation to Levinas, Derrida and Michel Henry. Sebbah did not know Levinas very well while he was alive, attending only one or two of his courses, and does feel that he belongs among his disciples. In *Lire Lévinas et penser tout autrement,* nevertheless, a text from which he would transport certain ideas into a later work, reflecting on the subsequent, less impressive reception of Levinas, on the "saccharine" or "pious" readings — of which the philosopher himself was wary: "Ethics is always on the brink of inanity"[11] — on the way in which attempts are made to situate this disturbing thinking, he describes the thinking as follows: "A discourse that is, strictly speaking, untenable, that is no longer tenable, and that for this very reason, does not cease to return, never lets us settle down anywhere, refuses to be instituted. . . . No thinker can find any firm footing there, or the comfort of any dwelling for his or her thinking. The text is, strictly speaking, uninhabitable."[12]

As Jean Greisch confirms, Levinas himself was very belligerent with his work, anxious not to let anyone take up his thinking or his themes in order to make them into slogans. To be sure, his thinking shows itself to be uninhabitable. A thinking in which there is no last word, where nothing is definitive, where nothing is fixed, providing no tranquility. Might it be a work that simply bears witness to the infinite resourcefulness of exegesis? To the power that exegesis has to uproot mountains?

19 LEVINAS IN JERUSALEM

In May 2002, an international congress devoted to Emmanuel Levinas was organized for the first time at the Hebrew University of Jerusalem. The theme: "Philosophical Interpretations and Religious Perspectives." The sessions took place in the Maison de France Auditorium, with talks given in English, French and Hebrew. There were specialists, translators, and biographers from around the world. From France: Xavier Tilliette, Jean François Rey, Robert Redecker, Dominique Bourel, David Banon, Marie-Anne Lescourret, Jeffrey Barash, Georges Hansel, Enzo Neppi. From the United States: Richard Cohen, Annette Aronovitch, Peter Atterton, Edith Wyschogrod. From the United Kingdom: Simon Critchley. From Belgium: Françoise Mies, François Coppens. From Holland: Theodor de Boer. From the Baltics: Igor Dukhan. From Israel: Daniel Epstein, Ephraim Meir, Aviezer Ravitsky, Moshe Halberthal, Shmuel Wygoda, Gabriel Motzkin.

The registered attendants of the Congress were of diverse affiliations and walks of life. Religious and lay, young and old, students, professors or simply unaffiliated auditors. French immigrants or Israeli natives. There were also some Orthodox

Jews with long beards, some "Bnei Akiva" groups, a Zionist-religious crowd with crocheted *kippas,* some visitors from distant *kibboutzim,* and even some residents from the settlements, not to mention a good number of professionals from the education field.

This same kaleidoscope would be found in the crowd that squeezed into the Mount Scopus Auditorium for an evening reserved for the general public — close to a thousand people were present — with the agenda of conjuring up "Levinas the man." The ambassador of France extolled "a thinker who it is impossible to confine to one category, however broadly it may be defined, as he was able to fuse together and to open up a store of traditions onto a different dimension." And Labor representative Colette Avital enthusiastically praised a thinker who became "a leading figure of Israeli culture."

What happened with Levinas in Jerusalem? Whence did this sudden and belated keen interest arise, compelling the journal *HaAretz* — a leftwing daily that is highly regarded on the Israeli intellectual scene — to devote four pages of its weekly supplement to the French philosopher under the title, "The Levinas Fashion"? A surprising turnaround! This country that he had so cherished, and that had rebuffed him during his whole life and even afterwards, was suddenly throwing him a party! These universities, which had paid tribute to him half-heartedly on a few occasions, which had sometimes invited him to lecture to empty seats, were now celebrating him!

THE BOOK CLOSET

For anyone who is familiar with the Anglo-Saxon tropism of Israeli culture, its inherent distrust for "diaspora thinkers" — except when such thinkers decide, as did Buber or Scholem, to throw in their lot with the Jewish state and share in its dangerous existence, something Levinas did not do — its somewhat provincial taste for instances of short-lived fame, this development is noteworthy.

For a long time, Levinas's name elicited only a distracted and more or less polite interest on the shores of the Holy Land. At the beginning of the 1980s, when his star began to rise in Europe, his readers in Israeli universities were very few in number. Richard Cohen, an American translator of his works and author of several pieces on the philosopher, recounts how, during those years, when one of Levinas's works was being published in London and the editor had inserted a comment on the cover flap proclaiming, "After France and Israel, Levinas in England," he had to intervene and explain that Levinas was neither translated nor known in Israel. It was also around that time that Father Marcel Dubois, then chair of the department of philosophy at the Hebrew University, suggested that an invitation be extended to the French philosopher, to which his colleagues responded: "We don't need ideology here!" Dubois notes: "Anything that could pass for religion was categorized as ideological."

Levinas was nevertheless invited to give some seminars during the summer at the Hebrew University where he found himself before a sparse audience. A few religious Jews showed up out of curiosity, staying for a while as the speaker labored to express himself in a slightly exotic Lithuanian Hebrew. Then the guest moved to French, and the little group disappeared. It was during this time, moreover, that one of the bigwigs in the Department of Jewish Thought at this same university — whose name will not be mentioned out of kindness — could be heard saying: "Levinas? It's a joke!"

In 1995, *Ethics and Infinity,* a series of conversations with Philippe Nemo, was published in Hebrew, translated by

Ephraim Meir. For the first time, the French philosopher made his entry into Israeli bookstores, at a time when the themes that were dear to him — such as the humanistic message of Judaism, its universal import, its ethical demand — were undergoing a general examination. The prime minister, Yitzhak Rabin, had just been assassinated by a young fundamentalist militant opposed to the Oslo accords. The text went unnoticed. No one paid attention. Two years later, Ze'ev Levy, professor of philosophy in Haifa, living in a kibbutz affiliated with HaShomer HaTzair, a left-wing Zionist movement, published an original biographical essay, which hardly made a stir. Still, in the universities — where American fashions were undoubtedly at play — Levinas's name did begin to circulate, and his work began to be taught by Shalom Rosenberg in Jerusalem, Ze'ev Levy in Haifa and Ephraim Meir in Bar-Ilan. At the same time, Benny Levy, former secretary of Jean-Paul Sartre, who had made a "return" to the Jewish sources, first in a yeshiva, a talmudic institution in Strasbourg, then in Jerusalem where he settled down, launched — with the help of Alain Finkielkraut and Bernard-Henri Lévy — an Institute for Levinasian Studies, which organizes seminars and publishes a review.

To locate the origin of this change in Israeli society, we have to reach far back. Perhaps back to the Yom Kippur War of 1973 and the trauma of a people in prayer caught by a war who, suddenly discovering itself to be fallible, no longer sought its bearings from the right or the left, but reached back for origins, to places where the connection between the Israeli and the Jew could be made. Explorations were exacerbated by the assassination of Yitzhak Rabin. Study groups surfaced and spread throughout the country, secular and religious Jews mixed together in *batei midrash* in a common quest around what was called "the book closet." For an entire generation, there was an appeal to the father's or the grand-father's bookcases, which had been abandoned and even a bit mocked during the pioneer years, and were now turned to, not in the hopes of finding some nostalgic murmuring or the scent of things past, but for the sake of locating another viewpoint and uncovering new paths. Zionism wished to change the Jews, and in a certain sense succeeded in doing so. It seemed, to the eyes of the same movement, that it was also necessary to change Judaism itself. Some of the founding members were conscious of this, but they did not know how to do it, or did not want to, or could not. Their energies were spent elsewhere. And this is precisely how Judaism was reclaimed by history. Here and there throughout the country, the young and the not-so-young sought to restore lost connections with the Bible, which at school had often been taught to them as a history book or a moving relic, to reinvest a tradition stripped of all piety and of all orthodox religious practice. Was it surprising that this "fidelity without faith" joined up with a work that was written on the banks of the Seine, born from the European war, pitted against the war, and that, crossing over with a familiar breath and inspiration, was the bearer of an ancient and new desire to share Judaism's truths with humanity? Especially since this French philosopher, who was born in Lithuania and never considered making *Aliya* — a "return" to Israel — never ceased, throughout his life, to declare a visceral, carnal attachment to the Jewish state, to its rebirth, to its right to be, to its safety.

ZIONISM

"I believed Kovno was dead, I know that Kovno is eternal." These words would be attributed to him — the report is according to Alex Derczanski — during his first trip to Israel in 1952.

One year after the formation of the state of Israel, merely one year, in an essay flooded with emotion, entitled "When Words Return from Exile," Levinas writes: "I do not know whether the creation of the state of Israel amounts to the end of the diaspora. But already, it marks the end of the exile of words. It is not the renaissance of Hebrew that overly concerns me here. Ordering a sandwich in Mishnaic terms, being insulted in the market in the language of Isaiah, finding ancient words for new habits — this is all a question of convention and the dictionary. Something for philologists. But that ancient words that lost their referents, relinquishing all these ancient things, should suddenly raise up their buried thinking and their power — that is a wonder."[1] In the essay Levinas speaks of a "resurrection" and of his admiration for the work of the pioneers, invokes the teaching of the prophets, and begins to make use of the word "Zionism." Until this time, the philosopher seemed to have shared the Alliance's initial reticence concerning the Zionist movement. To trace the change of heart, this essay would have to be reread and compared to the kinds of things he wrote before the war, in the same bulletins of the institution, on the "diaspora as resignation."[2]

Following the war, in 1945, an official declaration by the AIU marked the turning point.[3] The text was drafted by Edmond Fleg. Its scope designed to equal the appeal of the founders, the manifesto emphasized: "The Alliance is resolute in asking, for the Jews who aspire to it, under the aegis of the United Nations and the responsibility of the Jewish Agency in Palestine, the right to enter Palestine. More than a refuge, what they will find there is a center of spiritual warmth, the only one in this world for which they are impatiently waiting, and from where, perhaps some day, the truths of Israel will once more radiate over the world." At the inauguration of the École Normale Israélite Orientale, Emmanuel Levinas declared, "Everything has changed in the East, everything has changed in Judaism, everything has changed in the world."[4]

Upon his return from his first trip to Israel, he would write, "When a Jew adheres to a great modern state in the West, or when he builds a just state on the ancestral land, he enters anew into the true tradition of thinking."[5] And in 1965, at a colloquium of Jewish intellectuals on "Promised Land, Permitted Land," he devoted his Talmudic lesson to the theme of the Spies, those twelve men sent by Moses to reconnoiter throughout the land of Canaan, which had been promised to the children of Israel. In passing, he brings to mind a society "such as the first founders of the *kibbutzes* wanted it — because they too built ladders to ascend to heaven despite the repugnance most of them felt for heaven."[6]

In 1967, for him as for many Jewish intellectuals, the Six-Day War was experienced in fear and despondency. The Arab armies surrounded Israel. General de Gaulle decreed an embargo on weapons destined for the Jewish state. The Jews in France demonstrated their solidarity in the streets of Paris. For the first time, they felt a deep unease. In the media, several articles would denounce the "double allegiance." Levinas took up his pen in the review *Esprit* in an impassioned essay in which he praised "the Zionist dream, which evolved from the most implausible nostalgia, going back to the very sources of Creation and echoing the highest expectation," and poignantly defended himself against all allegations of this sort. "Does being French," he wrote, "short of Euclidean space, mean moving only in one dimension?"[7]

In 1973, the Yom Kippur War provoked a similar dismay in him. The Egyptian army crossed the Suez Canal on the most sacred day of the Jewish calendar, a day called "awesome." Every male Israeli citizen of military age was summoned from his synagogue and had to exchange his prayer shawl for war gear and uniform in order to be mobilized to the warfront. The following year, the Jewish intellectuals of France devoted their traditional colloquium to "The Solitude of Israel." In a contribution to a roundtable discussion, Levinas asserted, "We return to the beginnings therefore. But this manner of losing any recognition from the outside, for our most intimate thoughts — for our truths that are ever young, but also most ancient and best demonstrated by the most secure and most verifiable principles — this manner of suddenly lacking external landmarks for certitudes, this is something that we have perhaps never experienced — this negativity on the part of the world with regard to us."[8]

Five years later, the Egyptian president Anwar Sadat surprised the world by deciding to land his plane at Ben-Gurion Airport to go speak in the Knesset, to shake the hand of Menachem Begin, the prime minister of the Jewish state, and to solemnly promise to the people of Israel: no more war. Emmanuel Levinas was deeply stirred by it. This time, he chose *Les Temps Modernes*, the review by Jean-Paul Sartre, to express his feelings. Bernard-Henri Lévy invited the philosopher, taking this opportunity to bring together the two men who, prior to this, had had occasion to meet only very briefly. They had crossed paths before the war, at Gabriel Marcel's home, at the Friday meetings on rue de Tournon. And one morning at the Israeli embassy in Paris, for a ceremony in which Sartre agreed to accept a doctorate *honoris causa* from the University of Jerusalem. There had also been, during the 1960s, a correspondence at the time that Sartre was offered the Nobel Prize. Levinas, who had never concealed his admiration for Sartre's manner — his very French manner — of being "alert," wrote to the laureate to tell him that his "refusal" of such honors henceforth gave him the right to speak. And he followed up by asking him to go see Nasser in Egypt: "You are the only one he'll listen to!" Receiving this note, Sartre asked his entourage: "But who is this Levinas?"

Levinas's text, entitled "Politics Afterwards," was therefore published in an edition of *Les Temps Modernes* devoted to the Palestinian question. In it the philosopher praised this "exceptional transhistorical event that one neither makes nor is contemporaneous with twice in a lifetime," whereby "peace had come by a path which led higher and came from further away than political roads."[9]

SABRA AND SHATILA

On September 14, 1982, in open war with Libya, a bomb exploded in east Beirut, in the building where Beshir Jemayel was to be found. The Libyan president was killed instantly, along with thirty-six of his family members. The next day, members of a Christian militia forced their way into the Palestinian camps of Sabra and Shatila and unleashed a massacre, without any intervention from the Israeli army occupying west Beirut. There were hundreds of victims. The response was outrage, an inquest commission was demanded. A hundred thousand Israelis took to the streets to demonstrate their disapproval.

Two weeks later, Levinas was invited to speak on a Jewish radio program in Paris alongside a young French intellectual, Alain Finkielkraut, who came to give a speech at the Memorial of the Jewish Martyr on what he called "the temptation of innocence." We recorded this discussion one summer afternoon at Levinas's home on rue d'Auteuil. Of the two philosophers, the first, the elder, was tense, always anxious in front of a tape recorder, even though the one lying on the table was the most old-fashioned type, while the second, the younger, excited, wrung his hands and twisted his fingers. Levinas called his junior "Monsieur Finkielkraut" and gave him, as was his habit, his full attention. He emphasized responsibility, even for that which one is not guilty, and immediately shifted the focus: "Perhaps that which is currently taking place in Israel creates the place where a confrontation occurs between the ethical and the political and where they seek their limits. Antinomies, like those that come into play between ethics and politics, unfortunately don't find their solutions solely in the reflections of philosophers."[10] But he did not avoid the question of "innocence": "In reference to the 'Holocaust,' to say that God is with us in every circumstance is just as odious as the *Gott Mit Uns* that was emblazoned on the executioners' belts." And Finkielkraut, in evoking at one point "the reflex of the beautiful soul, the luxury of a pure conscience removed from the quagmire of history," elicited this phrase from Levinas: "Out of fear of being beautiful souls, we become ugly souls."

This was one of the rare instances in which he surrendered to the event and agreed to react, quite hotly, without taking refuge in minimal commentary, as he did each time he was invited to speak publicly about current events. He did not avoid the Israeli-Palestinian conflict, nor even the blunt question: "Is the Other, for the Israeli, not above all the Palestinian?" "The Other," he says, "is the fellow human being, the neighbor, not necessarily the near one, but the near one too. And in this sense, being for the Other, you are for your neighbor. But if your neighbor attacks another neighbor or is unjust toward him, what can you do? There, alterity takes on a different character, there, in alterity, an enemy can appear, or at least gives rise to the problem of knowing who is right and who is wrong, who is just and who is unjust. There are people who are wrong." He did not go further.

Within the debate, everyone will find reasons in this text to attach the philosopher to one school of thought or another, and this cannot be avoided. Like the history of Levinas's reception in Israel, despite a delayed and surprising interest, it does not proceed without some conflict.

THE OLD AND THE NEW

The *Nine Talmudic Lectures,* collected and translated into Hebrew by Rabbi Daniel Epstein — who wanted to offer the reader a selection from different works by the author, as does the American edition — was published at the beginning of 2002 by Shocken. The book was quickly snapped up everywhere. For the following four months, it held first place on the bestseller list and enjoyed four subsequent editions. "It's quite exceptional for a work of this kind," the editor, Racheli Edelman, would remark. "In the last few years there's been a wave of lay curiosity in Judaism, and as the Talmud is generally not comprehensible to the lay reader, Levinas's book allows it to be grasped through a universal orientation. On the other hand, the interest for a religious audience that is liberal is evident."

The publication also sparked a lively debate in the columns of *HaAretz.* In it, one critic ironically mentions "tofu," the soybean food served in vegetarian restaurants that can take on the semblance of steak, veal, cheese, and virtually any other flavor. A way of saying that Levinasian exegesis, as inspiring and dazzling as it is, only finds in the talmudic text what was meant to be prefatory. The same critic jokes about those young yeshiva students who conceal light reading inside the jackets of the Talmud's austere folios.[11]

Another critic believes he has detected in the author an approach that Christianizes Judaism too much, provoking this reaction from Shalom Rosenberg: "The idea that Levinas had a Christian approach is an idiotic one. Christianity maintains that it represents grace and love where Judaism symbolizes justice. But whoever said that was true?"[12]

Aside from these few antagonistic reviews, the *Nine Talmudic
Readings,* appearing during the Intifada war in a country perpetually "on the alert," managed to raise essential questions.
Ephraim Meir makes no mistake about it: "Is there a chance
that, in this country, religion will step out of its narrowness
and closure and transform itself, after these 'Lectures' by
Levinas, into a challenge for our modern world? . . . Perhaps
there are profound elements in Jewish thought that philosophy neglected, perhaps it is also possible to enrich Judaism
by formulating the ancient Jewish message in philosophical
and universal terms!" And following up: "Will the meeting
between philosophy and Judaism interest the yeshiva students
who don't know Plato, Husserl, Heidegger, Spinoza, Freud
and Marx? And on the other hand, will it interest philosophers who don't know Abaye and Raba? Will historians and
philologists of the Talmud find in this book a challenge of
a different approach, a hermeneutic approach richer than
that of the 'science of Judaism'? Will the yeshiva students
find the material there to free them from their singular apologetic? Levinas was a Jew with vast horizons. His reception and
the reception of his writing are linked in large part to the
openness of the reader."[13]

For Rabbi Daniel Epstein, who teaches Levinas in "Matan,"
a *beit hamidrash* for women, the philosopher's revolutionary
contributions, the contributions proper to him, will take time
to become apparent. They will be more apparent still the
day that all his work will be accessible, in its coherence and
its necessity: "Judaism can speak the language of every human
being without renouncing its most profound claim, and universal thinking is not necessarily deaf to the voice coming

from Mount Horeb. The meeting place between Jewish thought and universal thought is none other than the very place that tears us away from every place that is easily found: the face of the Other that carries upon it the imprint of the Creator."[14]

Yom Kippur

Yom Kippur at school. The place is not a synagogue. There is no rabbi. It is a vast room that substitutes for a synagogue.

On the days of the High Holidays, and particularly on Yom Kippur, there are two services, one above, in the library room, the other below, in the basement, and the congregants split up according to their affinities or their conveniences. The philosopher usually prays downstairs. It is an old tradition. Quite naturally, the regulars of the Saturday class are found near him.

He is there, every year, in the first row, his son at his side. He mostly stands, not swaying back and forth like many of the congregants. He hums the tune of the liturgy in the Sephardic manner. After a while, he got used to the local melodies, although he had grown up in a very different tradition. There is hardly anything but the Kol Nidre *— the opening prayer of Yom Kippur — that the officiates concede to him and that he sings in the Ashkenazi manner, almost reciting it, in a hesitant and emotional voice.*

Most often he is riveted to his book and one can sense that he is savoring the texts of Ibn Gabirol and Yehuda Halevi, poets from the Andalusian period whose words are found scattered throughout the prayers of the Day of Atonement.

This year, his wife is absent. And he himself does not stay more than one hour. His son had accompanied him at the end of the morning. He was seen unfolding his tallit, *laying it a bit slanted on the shoulders. But then, everyone looks around for him. He is no longer there.*

No one dares to sit in his place. It remains unoccupied, with the prayer shawl rolled in a ball and the book on top of it.

The text from the prophet Jonah that follows the reading from the Torah, this text that he liked so much, no longer has the same flavor.

At the time of the final prayer, read from the Ne'ila, *a palpable shiver always runs through the assembled, as if in these last moments before the "closure," everyone wants to add an extra bit of soul, to redouble the fervor before the final verdict.*

And then the shofar sounds, blown as it is every year by Edmond Cicurel, who makes the to-and-fro between the high and the low, with a steady breath, in a succession of long sounds, short scansions and staccatos.

His place is empty, for the first time in so many years.

NOTES

NOTES TO TRANSLATOR'S NOTES

1. In his interview with François Poirié, *Is It Righteous to Be? Interviews with Emmanuel Levinas,* ed. Jill Robbins (Stanford: Stanford University Press, 2001), Levinas speaks of "the pathos of a well-written biography" (47). As we see from this substantial anthology of interviews from 1982 to 1992, Levinas was not indisposed to biographical investigations. It is only the prospect of a *well-written* biography, such as the present one, that struck him as an exercise in "pathos." (Yet a biographical interest in Heidegger's life is something he certainly deemed essential.) By the same token, it is not insignificant that *suffering,* even if only the drama of suffering, is what he sees as characterizing a methodical biography. As for the remark that such an account would be an *ideé stupide,* this, as the reader will presently find out, was made to no one less than Salomon Malka himself (see his introduction below).

2. Emmanuel Levinas, *Difficult Freedom,* trans. Sean Hand (Baltimore: Johns Hopkins University Press, 1990), 291.

3. *Is It Righteous to Be?,* 39.

4. Emmanuel Levinas, *Otherwise Than Being,* trans. Alphonso Lingis (Dordrecht: Nijhoff, 1974), i. It is significant that Maurice Blanchot, Levinas's oldest friend, saw in this dedication something that "traverses, carries Levinas's entire philosophy"; see Blanchot, "Notre compagne clandestine," in *Textes pour Emmanuel Lévinas,* ed. François Laruelle (Paris: J.-M. Place, 1980), 87.

5. Levinas, *Proper Names,* trans. Michael B. Smith (London: Athlone Press, 1996), 120.

6. The logic of this silence is analyzed at the beginning of Jean-François Lyotard, *The Differend,* trans. Georges Van Den Abbeele (Minneapolis: Minnesota, 1988).

7. Oona Ajzenstat, *Driven Back to the Text* (Pittsburgh: Duquesne University Press, 2001), notes how this heavy sentence by Levinas, reaching out simultaneously to both presentiment and memory, "plays with time" in diachronic fashion. "Why does it not appear in its place in the catalog or the later account? Because the Holocaust has no time of its own in Levinas's thought, no once-present; it is out of time; it does not 'appear'" (310). Anyone familiar with this chapter in Ajzenstat's book will readily note how the present note on translation follows closely behind her initiative.

8. Levinas calls Auschwitz "the paradigm" of radical evil, not an example of it. See "Useless Suffering," *Entre Nous*, trans. M. B. Smith and B. Harshav (New York: Columbia, 1998), 97. Just as "anti-Semitism" is not an example of hatred, as he says in the dedication to *Otherwise Than Being*, it is in fact, quite simply, the "hatred of the other man." "The injustice committed against Israel during the war, that one called the *shoah* . . . is the moment when humanity began to bleed through the wounds of Israel" (*Is It Righteous to Be?* 92).

9. *Is it Righteous to Be?*, 141.

10. Emmanuel Levinas, "Nameless," *Proper Names*, trans. Michael B. Smith (Stanford: Stanford University Press, 1996), 122.

11. Ibid., 119–20.

12. The philosophical nature of such thinking was already noticed and analyzed by Levinas in 1934, in "Some Thoughts on the Philosophy of Hiterism," *Unforeseen History*, trans. Nidra Poller (Urbana: University of Chicago Press, 2004), 13–21.

13. In "The Name of a Dog, or Natural Rights" (*Difficult Freedom*, 151–53), Levinas recalls a dog named Bobby in the stalag whose merit it was to remind the inmates that they were not apes. "For him, there was no doubt that we were men." Compare *Is It Righteous to Be?*, 41, 90.

14. Levinas, *Entre Nous*, 97.

15. *Is It Righteous to Be?*, 77–78, compare 260.

16. In "Useless Suffering" (*Entre Nous*, 91–101), Levinas rejects any assignment of meaning to human suffering, such as is typically found in theodicy.

17. Levinas, *Proper Names*, 122.

18. Levinas, *Otherwise Than Being*, 91.

19. Levinas, "The Trace of the Other," in *Deconstruction in Context*, ed. Mark Taylor (Chicago: University of Chicago Press, 1986), 356.

20. "A face does not function in proximity as a sign of a hidden God who would impose the neighbor on me." *Otherwise than Being*, 94.

21. Levinas, *Entre Nous*, 57.

22. Emmanuel Levinas, *Totality and Infinity*, trans. Alphonso Lingis (Pittsburgh: Duquesne University Press, 1969), 21.

NOTES TO CHAPTER 1, "KAUNAS"

1. Haïm Cohen, *L'Enfance des grands* (Paris: Plon, 1995), 95.

2. Marguerite Lena, *Honneur aux maîtres* (Paris: Criterion, 1991).

3. The Haskala, the Jewish "Enlightenment" beginning in the eighteenth century, was founded by Moses Mendelssohn. See Mendelssohn, *Jérusalem*, translated from the German by Dominique Bourel with a preface by Emmanuel Levinas (Paris: Les Presses d'Aujourd'hui, 1982); Moses Mendelssohn, *Jerusalem, or on Religious Power and Judaism*, trans. Allan Arkush (Lebanon, N.H.: University Press of New England, 1983).

4. See Henri Minczeles, *Histoire générale du Bund: Un mouvement révolutionnaire juif* (Paris: Editions Austral, 1995). See also Minczeles, *Vilna, Wilno, Vilnius, la Jérusalem de Lituanie* (Paris: La Découverte, 1993), and the edition of *Autrement* on the "Lituanie juive, 1918–1940," 1996.

5. See Minczeles, "Lituanie juive," 66.

6. Zev Birger, *Survivant de l'holocauste* (Paris: Odile Jacob, 1997), 37.

7. See Dov Lévin, *Lita, pinkas hakehilot* (Jérusalem: Yad Vashem, 1996), 523.

8. Ibid., 517.

9. Immanuel Etkes, *Rabbi Israel Salanter and the Mussar Movement: Seeking the Torah of Truth* (Philadelphia: The Jewish Publication Society, 1993).

10. Hillel Goldberg, *Israel Salanter, Text, Structure, Idea: The Ethics and Theology of an Early Psychologist of the Unconscious* (New York: Ktav, 1982).

NOTES TO CHAPTER 2, "STRASBOURG"

1. François Poirié, *Emmanuel Lévinas, qui êtes-vous?* (Lyon: La Manufacture, 1987), 69. English version in *Is It Righteous to Be? Interviews with Emmanuel Levinas*, ed. Jill Robbins (Stanford: Stanford University Press, 2001), 28.

2. Robbins, *Is It Righteous to Be?*, 84–92.

3. Maurice Pradines, *Le Beau voyage: Itinéraire de Paris aux frontières de Jérusalem* (Paris: Le Cerf, 1982).

4. Charles Blondel, *La Psychanalyse* (Paris: Félix Alcan, 1924), 9.

5. Poirié, *Emmanuel Lévinas, qui êtes-vous?*, 79.

6. *Études bergsoniennes* (Paris: Presses Universitaires de France), 16.

7. Robbins, *Is It Righteous to Be?*, 36.

8. Maurice Blanchot, "N'oubliez pas," *L'Arche*, no. 373 (May 1988).

9. Maurice Blanchot, letter to Salomon Malka, November 4, 1981.

10. Maurice Blanchot, *Textes pour Emmanuel Lévinas* (Paris: Jean-Michel Place, 1980), 80.

11. Emmanuel Levinas, "Some Reflections on the Philosophy of Hitlerism," *Esprit*, no. 26 (November 1934).

12. Christophe Bident, *Maurice Blanchot, partenaire invisible* (Seyssel: Champ Vallon, 1998), 97.

13. Blanchot, "N'oubliez pas."

14. Georges Bataille, "De l'existentialisme au primat de l'économie," *Oeuvres complètes,* vol. 11 (Paris: Gallimard, 1970), 293.

15. Bident, *Maurice Blanchot,* 47.

16. Marie-Anne Lescourret, *Emmanuel Lévinas* (Paris: Flammarion, 1994), 67.

NOTES TO CHAPTER 3, "FREIBURG-IM-BREISGAU"

1. Cited in Emmanuel Levinas and Jean-Luc Marion, *Positivité et transcendance* (Paris: Presses Universitaires de France, 2000), 52.

2. "Souvenirs de jeunesse auprès de Husserl," in ibid., 3.

3. Jean-François Lavigne, "Lévinas avant Lévinas," in ibid., 53.

4. Husserl, "La ruine de la représentation," first published in *Edmund Husserl 1859–1959,* a commemorative collection published on the occasion of the philosopher's hundredth birthday (Leiden: Martinus Nijhoff, 1959). Reprinted in Emmanuel Levinas, *En découvrant l'existence avec Husserl et Heidegger* (Paris: Vrin, 1967), 195.

5. See Rüdiger Safranski, *Heidegger et son temps* (Paris: Grasset, 1994), 120.

6. Marlène Zarader, *La Dette impensée: Heidegger et l'héritage hébraïque* (Paris: Le Seuil, 1990).

7. Pierre Aubenque, "The 1929 Debate between Cassirer and Heidegger," vol. 2, *Martin Heidegger: Critical Assessments,* ed. Charles McCann (London: Routledge, 1992), 208–21.

8. Toni Cassirer, *Aus meinem Leben mit Ernst Cassirer* (Hildesheim: Gerstenbeg Verlag, 1981); originally published privately in New York, 1950.

9. Maurice de Gandillac, *Le Siècle traversé* (Paris, Albin Michel, 1998), 134.

10. He did it in an indirect manner. Some years after the war, he told me one day that he met a friend in Rome who told him, after having seen Mme. Cassirer in Zurich, that she continued to be quite bitter over the soirée in Davos. Levinas asked him to tell her that he was sorry. Sometime later he saw this friend again in Rome, who told him that Mme. Cassirer heard his apologies before her husband's death. "I always say that these two trips to Rome were not without purpose," Levinas commented.

11. See Stephane Moses, *Système et révélation* (Paris, Le Seuil, 1982); *System and Revelation: The Philosophy of Franz Rosenzweig*, trans. Catherine Tihanyi (Detroit: Wayne State University Press, 1991).

NOTES TO CHAPTER 4, "PARIS"

1. Emmanuel Levinas, *Difficult Freedom*, trans. Séan Hand (Baltimore: The Johns Hopkins University Press, 1990), 291.

2. According to a naturalization file that I was able to consult at the National Archives, class BB11, file no. 24900X30.

3. Chouchani is the mysterious wandering Jewish genius and Renaissance man described in chapter 9. Elie Wiesel, who, like Levinas, was an elite disciple of Chouchani, paints a compelling thumbnail portrait of the master in his anthology *Legends of Our Time* (New York: Avon Books, 1968), 119–42 (translator's note).

4. Emmanuel Levinas, "L'actualité de Maïmonide," *Paix et Droit* 4 (April 1935): 6–7.

5. Emmanuel Levinas, "L'inspiration religieuse de l'Alliance," *Paix et Droit* 10 (October 1935): 4.

6. Emmanuel Levinas, *Paix et Droit* (October 1936).

7. Emmanuel Levinas, *Paix et Droit* (May 1938).

8. Emmanuel Levinas, "Un moment de la conscience humaine," *Paix et Droit* (March 1939).

9. Emmanuel Levinas, *Totality and Infinity: An Essay on Exteriority*, trans. Alphonso Lingis (Pittsburgh: Duquesne University Press, 1969), 28.

10. Franz Rosenzweig, *L'Étoile de la rédemption*, trans. Jean-Louis Schlegel and Alex Derczanski (Paris: Le Seuil, 1982).

NOTES TO CHAPTER 5, "CAPTIVITY"

1. Yves Durand, *La Captivité: Histoire des prisonniers de guerre français 1939–1945* (Paris: National Federation of Prisoners of War Veterans and Veterans of Algeria, Tunisia and Morocco, 1982), 119.

2. Ibid., 192.

3. Emmanuel Levinas, "Name of a Dog or Natural Law," *Difficult Freedom*, 153.

4. Ibid., 153.

5. Ibid., 12.

6. Charrette [Michel Caillau], *Histoire du MRPGD ou d'un vrai mouvement de résistance 1941–1945* (Paris: M. Caillau, 1987).

7. A short speech given in the autumn of 1945 by Rabbi Ernest Gugenheim at the time of the first ceremony of the reopening of the Séminaire Israélite de France. He would be appointed professor of the Talmud and of rabbinical law in this school before becoming director there (text passed along by his son, Chief Rabbi Michel Gugenheim).

8. Acronym from Psalm 142. Emmanuel Levinas, *Otherwise Than Being, or Beyond Essence*, trans. Alphonso Lingis (Pittsburgh: Duquesne University Press, 1998), v.

9. Durand, *La Captivité*, 531.

10. Vaclav Havel, *Lettres à Olga* (La Tour d'Aigues: Éditions de l'Aube, 1990), 347.

11. Ibid., 347.

12. Emmanuel Levinas, *Proper Names*, trans. Michael B. Smith (London: Athlone Press, 1996), 121–22.

NOTES TO CHAPTER 6, "THE ENIO YEARS"

1. Babylonian Talmud, Tractate Sota, 40a.

2. *Minha* (literally, offering) is the afternoon service, and *arvit* (from the root *erev*, evening) is the service that takes place after dusk.

NOTE TO CHAPTER 7, "THE RASHI COURSE"

1. The text of the Torah, or Pentateuch, is traditionally divided into fifty-four sections, each of which is called a *sidra* (an "order"; more colloquially known as a *parsha*), and each more or less corresponding to a week in the calendar year. The weekly *sidra* is chanted out loud during the Saturday morning *shabbat* service (translator's note).

NOTES TO CHAPTER 8, "THE TALMUDIC LESSON"

1. *Sugia:* an entire chapter, page or lesson in the Talmud.

2. Emmanuel Levinas, *Nine Talmudic Readings*, trans. Annette Aronowicz (Bloomington: Indiana University Press, 1990), 97.

3. Ibid., 8–10.

4. Emmanuel Levinas, *Nouvelles lectures talmudiques* (Paris: Minuit, 1996), 40; translated by Richard A. Cohen as *New Talmudic Readings* (Pittsburgh: Duquesne University Press, 1999).

5. *Yesh omrim:* literally, "there are those who say," a talmudic expression signaling a contradictory opinion.

6. Levinas, *Nine Talmudic Readings,* 13–14.

7. A work of compilation, synthesis and interpretation of Jewish laws.

8. Sanhedrin (36b–37a) in Levinas, *Nine Talmudic Readings,* 70–88.

9. Mishna: a legal treatise comprising laws and decisions. Gemara: a collection of discussions and controversies between sages. Together, the Mishna and the Gemara constitute the Talmud.

10. Emmanuel Levinas, *Beyond the Verse,* trans. Gary D. Mole (Bloomington: Indiana University Press), 1994, 13–33.

11. Shabbat (88a and 88b), in Levinas, *Nine Talmudic Readings,* 32–50.

12. Bava Metzia (83a–83b), in ibid., 94–119.

13. Bava Kama (60a–60b), in ibid., 178–97.

NOTES TO CHAPTER 9, "THE FERRYMAN AND THE METEOR"

1. Emmanuel Levinas, *Time and the Other,* trans. Richard A. Cohen (Pittsburgh: Duquesne University Press, 1987).

2. *Le Temps et l'autre* (Montpellier: Fata Morgana, 1979), 17.

3. Jean Lacroix, "Autrui et la séparation," *Le Monde,* January 19, 1961.

4. Shmuel Wygoda, "A Phenomenological Outlook on the Talmud, Levinas as a Reader of the Talmud," *Phenomenological Inquiry* 24 (October 2000): 117, published under the direction of Anna-Teresa Tyminiecka under the aegis of the World Institute for Advanced Phenomenological Research and Learning, Belmont, Massachusetts.

5. Salomon Malka, *Monsieur Chouchani: L'enigme d'un maître du XXᵉ siecle* (Paris: Jean-Claude Lattès, 1994).

6. Bulletin no. 497 of the Sdé Eliahu kibbutz, cited in Ze'ev Levy, *HaAher ve-haAhrayout* (Jerusalem: Magnès Press, 1996), 17.

7. Robbins, *Is It Righteous to Be?,* 78.

8. Ibid., 80.

NOTES TO CHAPTER 10, "THE BAD GENIUS"

1. Dominique Janicaud, *Heidegger en France* (Paris: Albin Michel, 2001).

2. Victor Farias, *Heidegger and Nazism,* trans. Paul Burrell and Gabriel R. Ricci (Philadelphia: Temple University Press, 1989).

3. Paul Ricoeur, *Réforme,* January 6, 1996.

4. Emmanuel Levinas, review of Victor Farias, *Autrement*, no. 102 (November 1988).

5. Emmanuel Levinas, "Comme un consentement à l'horrible," *Le Nouvel Observateur,* January 22, 1988.

6. Adriaan Peperzak, *Ethics as First Philosophy* (New York: Routledge, 1995), 123–31.

7. William J. Richardson, *Heidegger: Through Phenomenology to Thought* (Leiden: Martinus Nijhoff, 1963).

8. Emmanuel Levinas, *Existence and Existents,* trans. Alphonso Lingis (Pittsburgh: Duquesne University Press, 2001), 19.

9. Emmanuel Levinas, *Discovering Existence with Husserl,* trans. Richard A. Cohen and Michael B. Smith (Evanston, Ill.: Northwestern University Press, 1998).

10. Interview with Emmanuel Levinas, *L'Arche* (November 1981).

11. Emmanuel Levinas, *Difficult Freedom,* 232–33.

12. Janicaud, *Heidegger en France,* 202.

13. *Heidegger et la question de Dieu,* ed. Richard Kearney and Joseph Stephen O'Leary (Paris: Grasset, 1980), 239.

14. Reprinted in Levinas, *Entre Nous: On Thinking-of-the-Other,* trans. Michael B. Smith and Barbara Harshav (New York: Columbia University Press, 1998), 207–18.

Notes to Chapter 11, "The Double and the Opposite"

1. Jacques Derrida, "Violence and Metaphysics: An Essay on the Thought of Emmanuel Levinas," *Writing and Difference,* trans. Alan Bass (Chicago: University of Chicago Press, 1978), 79–153.

2. Geoffrey Bennington, *Jacques Derrida* (Chicago: University of Chicago Press, 1993).

3. *Textes pour Emmanuel Levinas,* ed. François Laruelle (Paris: J.-M. Place, 1980). Derrida's text, "At this very moment in this work here I am" can be found in *Re-reading Levinas,* ed. Robert Bernasconi and Simon Critchley (Bloomington: Indiana University Press, 1991), 11–50.

4. *L'Endurance de la pensée, pour saluer Jean Beaufret,* ed. René Char (Paris: Plon, 1968).

5. Levinas, *Proper Names,* 62.

6. François-David Sebbah, *Emmanuel Lévinas, ambiguités de l'éthique* (Paris: Les Belles Lettres, 2000).

7. Jacques Derrida, *Adieu to Emmanuel Levinas,* trans. Pascale-Anne Brault and Michael Naas (Stanford, Calif.: Stanford University Press, 1999), 5.

Notes to Chapter 12, "The Near and the Far"

1. Paul Ricoeur, *Critique and Conviction: Conversations with François Azouvi and Marc De Launay*, trans. Kathleen Blamey (Cambridge: Polity Press, 1998).
2. François Dosse, *Paul Ricoeur: Le sens d'une vie* (Paris: La Découverte, 2001), 443.
3. *Réforme*, January 6, 1996.
4. Dosse, *Paul Ricoeur*, 750.
5. Emmanuel Levinas, *In the Time of the Nations*, trans. Michael B. Smith (Bloomington: Indiana University Press, 1994).

Notes to Chapter 13, "The Archivist and the Precursors"

1. Roger Burggraeve, *Emmanuel Lévinas: Une bibliographie primaire et secondaire (1929–1985)* (Louvain: Peeters, 1986).
2. The text of the short speech given by the president of the Belgian group of investment banks is found in a brochure of the group published on the occasion of the twenty-fifth anniversary of the group, Brussels, 1987. See also Roger Burggraeve, *Emmanuel Lévinas et la socialité de l'argent* (Louvain: Peeters, 1997).
3. Salomon Malka, *Lire Lévinas* (Paris: Le Cerf, 1986).
4. Rabbi Hayyim de Volozhin, *L'Âme de la vie, Nefesh Hahayyim*, trans. Benjamin Gross, preface by Emmanuel Levinas (Lagrasse: Verdier, 1986).
5. Emmanuel Levinas, "Judaïsme 'et' christianisme," published in German in *Zeitgewium* (Frankfurt-on-Main: Joseph Knecht Verlag, 1987), and reprinted in *In the Time of the Nations*.

Notes to Chapter 14, "The Aristocrat and the Cardinal"

1. Enrico Castelli, *Diari* (Padova: L'Instituto di Studi Filosofici Enrico Castelli, 1997), 535–36.
2. Emmanuel Levinas, "Notes sur la pensée philosophique du Cardinal Wojtyla," *Communio*, no. 1 (July–August 1980).
3. Anna-Teresa Tyminiecka, "A Tribute to the Memory of Emmanuel

Levinas, a Great Thinker and a Friend," *Phenomenological Enquiry* 24 (October 2000): 15–17.

4. *Le Monde,* June 1–2, 1980.

5. Emmanuel Levinas, "Le Mystère d'Israël," *Le Figaro,* April 14, 1986.

NOTES TO CHAPTER 15, "RITUAL AND THE WORLD"

1. Levinas, *Totality and Infinity,* 278.

2. "La signification de la pratique religieuse," program broadcast on "Écoute Israël" on France Culture, April 9, 1937, and published afterward in *l'Univers israélite,* then in *Les Cahiers du judaïsme* (December 1999).

NOTES TO CHAPTER 16, "MONTAIGNE AND BOÉTIE"

1. Francine Lévy, *Le porte-clés ou la réminiscence* (Paris: L'Harmattan, 1997), 95.

2. Emmanuel Levinas, *Le Journal des Communautés* (May 1980).

3. Robbins, *Is It Righteous to Be?,* 75.

NOTES TO CHAPTER 17, "GOGOL'S NOSE"

1. Levinas, *Totality and Infinity,* 277.

2. Ibid., 268.

3. Franz Rosenzweig, *The New Thinking,* trans. Alan Udoff and Barbara E. Galli (Syracuse, N.Y.: Syracuse University Press, 1999), 100.

NOTES TO CHAPTER 18, "RECOGNITION"

1. *Le Magazine littéraire,* "20 ans de philosophie en France," no. 127–28 (September 1977).

2. Vincent Descombes, *Le Même et l'autre, quarante-cinq ans de philosophie française (1933–1978)* (Paris: Minuit, 1979).

3. Emmanuel Levinas, *Ethics and Infinity: Conversations with Philippe Nemo,* trans. Richard A. Cohen (Pittsburgh: Duquesne University Press, 1985).

4. Bernard-Henri Lévy, *Testament of God*, trans. George Holoch (New York: Harper & Row, 1980).

5. Emmanuel Levinas, "Religion et idée de l'infini," *Le Monde*, September 6, 1982.

6. Burggraeve, *Emmanuel Lévinas et la socialité de l'argent*, 96.

7. Levinas's only citation from Ibn Gabirol, this passage is from a text of poetry in which human beings "take shelter from God in God," in Emmanuel Levinas, *Sur Maurice Blanchot* (Montpellier: Fata Morgana, 1975), 13.

8. The archives are inaccessible for the time being.

9. "Heidegger et la curiosité biographique," by Sophie Foltz in a special edition of *Magazine Littéraire* devoted to Martin Heidegger, November 1986.

10. Robbins, *Is It Righteous to Be?*, 44.

11. Levinas, *Autrement qu'être ou au-delà de l'essence* (Leiden: Martinus Nijhoff, 1974).

12. François-David Sebbah, "Lire Lévinas et penser tout autrement," *Esprit*, July 1997. Reprinted in Sebbah, *Emmanuel Lévinas, ambiguités de l'éthique*.

NOTES TO CHAPTER 19, "LEVINAS IN JERUSALEM"

1. Emmanuel Levinas, "Quand les mots reviennent de l'exil," *Les Cahiers de l'Alliance Israélite Universelle*, no. 32 (April 1949): 4.

2. Emmanuel Levinas, "L'Inspiration religieuse de l'Alliance," *Paix et Droit*, no. 8 (October 1935): 4.

3. André Chouraqui, *Cent ans d'histoire, l'Alliance Israélite Universelle et la renaissance juive contemporaine (1860–1960)* (Paris: Presses Universitaires de France, 1965), 493.

4. Emmanuel Levinas, "La Réouverture de l'École Normale," *Les Cahiers de l'Alliance* (December–January 1946–1947), 23.

5. Emmanuel Levinas, *Évidences*, no. 28 (November 1952): 36.

6. Levinas, *Nine Talmudic Readings*, 66.

7. Emmanuel Levinas, "Space Is Not One-Dimensional," *Esprit* (April 1968); text reprinted in Levinas, *Difficult Freedom*, 263, 259.

8. Jean Halpérin and Georges Levitte, eds., *Solitude d'Israël: Données et débats* (Paris: Presses Universitaires de France, 1975), 9–11.

9. Emmanuel Levinas, "Politique après," *Les Temps Modernes*, no. 398 (September 1979): 521–28; reprinted in Emmanuel Levinas, *Beyond the Verse: Talmudic Readings and Lectures*, trans. Gary D. Mole (Bloomington: Indiana University Press, 1994), 193, 189.

10. A paper given by Emmanuel Levinas, September 28, 1982, on the radio program "Radio Communauté," reprinted under the title "Israël: éthique et politique," *Les Nouveaux Cahiers,* no. 71 (Winter 1982–1983): 1–8.

11. Yaïr Oron, *HaAretz,* March 22, 2002.

12. Shalom Rosenberger, "La mode Lévinas," *HaAretz,* May 16, 2002, supplement.

13. Ephraim Meir, *HaAretz,* March 22, 2002.

14. Rabbi Daniel Epstein, "Sur les traces du prochain oublié, réflexions sur la pensée d'Emmanuel Lévinas," in *HaAcher,* edited by Haïm Deutsch and Menachem Ben-Sasson (Jerusalem: Yediot Ahronot, 2001).

BIBLIOGRAPHY

Precision is imperative when taking into account the extensive publications by or about Levinas. We have included here only the philosopher's essential works and refer the reader to Roger Burggraeve's exhaustive bibliography. For the rest, we indicate some of the books that accompanied us in our actual work, without laying claim, of course, to any sort of inventory.

Works by Emmanuel Levinas

À l'heure des nations. Paris: Minuit, 1988.

L'Au-delà du verset: Lectures et discours talmudiques. Paris: Minuit, 1982.

Autrement qu'être ou au-delà de l'essence. Leiden: Martinus Nijhoff, 1974.

Beyond the Verse: Talmudic Readings and Lectures. Translated by Gary D. Mole. Bloomington: Indiana University Press, 1994.

De Dieu qui vient à l'idée. Paris: Vrin, 1982.

De l'évasion. Introduction and annotation by Jacques Rolland. Montpellier: Fata Morgana, 1982. Originally published as an essay in 1935.

De l'existence à l'existant. Paris: Vrin, 1986. First published 1947 by The Fontaine Review.

Difficile liberté: Essai sur le judaïsme. Paris: Albin Michel, 1963.

Difficult Freedom: Essays on Judaism. Translated by Séan Hand. Baltimore: The Johns Hopkins University Press, 1990.

Discovering Existence with Husserl. Translated by Richard A. Cohen and Michael B. Smith. Chicago: Northwestern University Press, 1998.

Du sacré au saint: Cinq nouvelles lectures talmudiques. Paris: Minuit, 1977.

En découvrant l'existence avec Husserl et Heidegger. Paris: Vrin, 1949.

Entre nous: Essai sur le penser-à-l'autre. Montpellier: Fata Morgana, 1979.

Entre Nous: Thinking of the Other. Translated by Michael B. Smith and Barbara Harshav. New York: Columbia University Press, 1998.

Existence and Existents. Translated by Alphonso Lingis. Pittsburgh: Duquesne University Press, 2001.

Éthique et infini: Dialogues avec Philippe Némo. Paris: Fayard, 1982.

Ethics and Infinity: Conversations with Philippe Nemo. Translated by Richard A. Cohen. Pittsburgh: Duquesne University Press, 1985.

Hors sujet. Montpellier: Fata Morgana, 1987.

Humanisme de l'autre homme. Montpellier: Fata Morgana, 1972.

Humanism of the Other. Translated by Nidra Poller. Chicago: University of Chicago Press, 2003.

In the Time of the Nations. Translated by Michael B. Smith. Bloomington: Indiana University Press, 1994.

New Talmudic Readings. Translated by Richard A. Cohen. Pittsburgh: Duquesne University Press, 1999.

Nine Talmudic Readings. Translated by Annette Aronowicz. Bloomington: Indiana University Press, 1990.

Noms propres. Montpellier: Fata Morgana, 1975.

Nouvelles lectures talmudiques. Paris: Minuit, 1996.

Of God Who Comes to Mind. Translated by Bettina Bergo. Stanford, Calif.: Stanford University Press, 1998.

On Escape. Translated by Bettina Bergo. Stanford, Calif.: Stanford University Press, 2003.

Otherwise Than Being, or Beyond Essence. Springer, 1981.

Outside the Subject. Translated by Michael B. Smith. Stanford, Calif.: Stanford University Press, 1993.

Proper Names. Translated by Michael B. Smith. Stanford, Calif.: Stanford University Press, 1997.

Quatre lectures talmudiques. Paris: Minuit, 1982.

Sur Maurice Blanchot. Montpellier: Fata Morgana, 1975.

Le Temps et l'autre. Montpellier: Fata Morgana, 1979. First published 1947 by Arthaud.

Théorie de l'intuition dans la phénoménologie de Husserl. Paris: Alcan, 1930.

The Theory of Intuition in Husserl's Phenomenology. Translated by Andre Orianne. Chicago: Northwestern University Press, 1985.

Time and the Other. Translated by Richard A. Cohen. Pittsburgh: Duquesne University Press, 1987.

Totalité et infini: Essai sur l'extériorité. Leiden: Martinus Nijhoff, 1961.

Totality and Infinity: An Essay on Exteriority. Translated by Alphonso Lingis. Pittsburgh: Duquesne University Press, 1969.

Transcendance et intelligibilité. Geneva: Labor et Fides, 1984.

OTHER WORKS

Agamben, Georgio. *Remnants of Auschwitz*. Translated by Daniel Heller-Roazen. New York: Zone, 1999. Paris: Rivages, 1999.

Aubenque, Pierre. *The 1929 Debate between Heidegger*. Vol. 2, *Martin Heidegger: Critical Assessments*. Edited by Charles McCann. London: Routledge, 1992.

Banon, David. *La lecture infinie, les voies de l'interprétation midrachique*. Preface by Emmanuel Levinas. Paris: Le Seuil, 1987.

Birger, Zev. *Survivant de l'holocauste*. Paris: Odile Jacob, 1997.

Blanchot, Maurice. *L'Amitié*. Paris: Gallimard, 1971.

———. *La Communauté inavouable*. Paris: Minuit, 1983.

———. *L'Écriture du désastre*. Paris: Gallimard, 1980.

———. *L'Entretien infini*. Paris: Gallimard, 1969.

———. *Friendship*. Translated by Elizabeth Rottenberg. Stanford, Calif.: Stanford University Press, 1997.

———. *The Infinite Conversation*. Translated by Susan Hanson. Minneapolis: University of Minnesota Press, 1992.

———. "Paix au lointain et au proche." In *De la Bible à nos jours*, a catalogue of an exposition at the Grand Palace, organized by the Society of Independent Artists, Paris, June–July 1989.

———. *Textes pour Emmanuel Lévinas*. Paris: Jean-Michel Place, 1980.

———. *The Writing of the Disaster*. Translated by Ann Smock. Lincoln: University of Nebraska Press, 1995.

Bennington, Geoffrey, and Jacques Derrida. *Jacques Derrida*. Paris: Le Seuil, 1991.

———. *Jacques Derrida*. Translated by Geoffrey Bennington. Chicago: University of Chicago Press, 1993.

Bernasconi, Robert, and Simon Critchley. *Re-Reading Levinas*. London: Athlone Press, 1991.

Bident, Christophe. *Maurice Blanchot, partenaire invisible.* Seyssel: Champ Vallon, 1998.

Birger, Zev. *Survivant de l'holocauste.* Paris: Odile Jacob, 1997.

Blondel, Charles. *La Psychanalyse.* Paris: Félix Alcan, 1924.

Buber, Martin. "The Early Addresses." In *On Judaism.* Translated by Eva Jospe. New York: Schocken Books, 1996.

————. *Two Types of Faith.* Translated by Norman P. Goldhawk. Syracuse: Syracuse University Press, 2003.

Burggraeve, Roger. *Emmanuel Lévinas: Une bibliographie primaire et secondaire (1929–1985).* Louvain: Peeters, 1986.

————. *Emmanuel Lévinas et la socialité de l'argent.* Louvain: Peeters, 1997.

Cassirer, Toni. *Aus meinem Leben mit Ernst Cassirer.* Hildesheim: Gerstenbeg Verlag, 1981. Originally published privately in New York, 1950.

Castelli, Enrico. *Le Temps invertébré.* Paris: Aubier, 1970.

Chalier, Catherine. *Figures du féminin: Lecture d'Emmanuel Lévinas.* Paris: Le Cerf, 1982.

————. *Judaïsme et altérité.* Lagrasse: Verdier, 1982.

————. *L'Utopie de l'humain.* Paris: Albin Michel, 1993.

Charrette [Michel Caillau]. *Histoire du MRPGD ou d'un vrai mouvement de résistance 1941–1945.* Paris: M. Caillau, 1987.

Chouraqui, André. *Cent ans d'histoire, l'Alliance Israélite Universelle et la renaissance juive contemporaine (1860–1960).* Paris: Presses Universitaires de France, 1965.

Cohen, Haïm. *L'Enfance des grands.* Paris: Plon, 1995.

Cohen, Richard. *Elevations: The Heights of the Good in Rosenzweig and Levinas.* Chicago: University of Chicago Press, 1994.

Collin, François. *Maurice Blanchot et la question de l'écriture.* Paris: Gallimard, 1971.

Davis, Colin. *Levinas: An introduction.* Cambridge: Polity Press, 1988.

Derrida, Jacques. *Adieu à Emmanuel Lévinas.* Paris: Galilée, 1999.

————. *Adieu to Emmanuel Levinas.* Translated by Pascale-Anne Brault and Michael Naas. Stanford, Calif.: Stanford University Press, 1999.

————. *L'Écriture et la différence.* Paris: Le Seuil, 1967.

————. *Writing and Difference.* Translated by Alan Bass. Chicago: University of Chicago Press, 1978.

Descombes, Vincent. *Le Même et l'autre, quarante-cinq ans de philosophie française (1933–1978).* Paris: Minuit, 1979.

Deutsch, Chaim, and Menahem Ben-Sasson. *HaAcher*. Jerusalem: Yedioth Ahronoth, 2001.

Dosse, François. *Paul Ricoeur: Le sens d'une vie*. Paris: La Découverte, 2001.

Durand, Yves. *La Captivité: Histoire des prisonniers de guerre français 1939–1945*. Edited by the National Federation of Prisoners of War Veterans and Veterans of Algeria, Tunisia (Morocco, 1981).

Etkes, Immanuel. *Rabbi Israel Salanter and the Mussar Movement: Seeking the Torah of Truth*. Philadelphia: The Jewish Publication Society, 1993.

Farias, Victor. *Heidegger et le nazisme*. Lagrasse: Verdier, 1987.

———. *Heidegger and Nazism*. French materials translated by Paul Burrell, with the advice of Dominic Di Bernardi. German materials translated by Gabriel R. Ricci. Philadelphia: Temple University Press, 1989.

Finkielkraut, Alain. *La Défaite de la pensée*. Paris: Gallimard, 1987.

———. *The Defeat of the Mind*. Translated by Judith Friedlander. New York: Columbia University Press, 1995.

———. *La Sagesse de l'amour*. Paris: Gallimard, 1984.

———. *The Wisdom of Love*. Translated by Kevin O'Neill and David Suchoff. Lincoln: University of Nebraska Press, 1997.

Forthomme, Bernard. *Une philosophie de la transcendance: La Métaphysique d'Emmanuel Lévinas*. Paris: La Découverte, 1984.

Frogneux, Nathalie, and François Mies. *Emmanuel Lévinas et l'histoire*. Paris: Le Cerf, 1998.

Gandillac, Maurice de. *Le Siècle traversé*. Paris: Albin Michel, 1998.

Geffre, Claude. *Profession théologien*. Paris: Albin Michel, 1999.

Gibbs, Robert. *Correlations in Rosenzweig and Levinas*. Princeton, N.J.: Princeton University Press, 1992.

Goldberg, Hillel. *Israel Salanter, Text, Structure, Idea: The Ethics and Theology of an Early Psychologist of the Unconscious*. New York: Ktav, 1982.

Greenberg, Irving. *La Nuée et le feu*. Paris: Le Cerf, 2000.

Grossman, Vassili. "*Life and Fate*. Translated by Robert Chandler. New York: Harper & Row, 1987.

Havel, Vaclav. "Lettres à Olga." Éditions de l'Aube, 1990.

Hersch, Jeanne, Xavier Tilliette, Emmanuel Levinas. "Jean Wahl et Gabriel Marcel." Paris: Beauchesne, 1976.

Janicaud, Dominique. *Heidegger en France*. 2 vols. Paris: Albin Michel, 2001.

———. *Phenomenology and the "Theological Turn": The French Debate.* New York: Fordham University Press, 2001.

———. *Le Tournant théologique de la phénoménolgie française.* Combas: Édition de l'Éclat, 1990.

Katz, Dov. *Tenouat Hamoussar.* Jerusalem: Édition Weiss, 1969.

Kearney, Richard, and Stephen O'Leary. *Heidegger et la question de Dieu.* Paris: Grasset, 1980.

Laporte, Roger. *Maurice Blanchot: L'Ancien, l'effroyablement ancien.* Montpellier: Fata Morgana, 1987.

Laruelle, François, ed. *Textes pour Emmanuel Levinas.* Paris: J.-M. Place, 1980.

Lena, Marguerite. *Honneur aux maîtres.* Paris: Criterion, 1991.

Lescourret, Marie-Anne. *Emmanuel Lévinas.* Paris: Flammarion, 1994.

Lévin, Dov. *Lita, pinkas hakehilot.* Jerusalem: Yad Vashem, 1996.

Levinas, Emmanuel, and Jean-Luc Marion. *Positivité et transcendance.* Paris: Presses Universitaires de France, 2000.

Levy, Benny. *Le logos et la lettre.* Lagrasse: Verdier, 1988.

Levy, Bernard-Henri. *Sartre: The Philosopher of the Twentieth Century.* Translated by Andrew Brown. Cambridge: Polity Press, 2003.

———. *Le Siècle de Sartre.* Paris: Grasset, 2000.

———. *Le Testament de Dieu.* Paris: Grasset, 1980.

———. *Testament of God.* Translated by George Holoch. New York: Harper & Row, 1980.

Lévy, Francine. *Le porte-clés ou la réminiscence.* Paris: L'Harmattan, 1997.

Levy, Zeev. *HaAcher ve-haAchrayut, Iyunim ba-Pilosophia shel Emmanuel Lévinas.* Jerusalem: Magnes Press, 1997.

Malka, Salomon. *Monsieur Chouchani: L'enigme d'un maître du XXᵉ siecle.* Paris: Jean-Claude Lattès, 1994.

Meir, Ephraïm. *Kochav MiYa'akov.* Jerusalem: Magnès Press, 1994.

Mendelssohn, Moses. *Jérusalem.* Translated from the German by Dominique Bourel. Preface by Emmanuel Levinas. Paris: Les Presses d'Aujourd'hui, 1982.

———. *Jerusalem, or on Religious Power and Judaism.* Translated by Allan Arkush. Lebanon, N.H.: University Press of New England, 1983.

Minczeles, Henri. *Vilna, Wilno, Vilnius, la Jérusalem de Lituanie.* Paris: La Découverte, 1993.

———. *Histoire générale du Bund: Un mouvement révolutionnaire juif.* Austral, 1995.

Mongin, Olivier. *Paul Ricoeur*. Paris: Le Seuil, 1994.

Moses, Stephane. *System and Revelation: The Philosophy of Franz Rosenzweig*. Translated by Catherine Tihanyi. Detroit: Wayne State University Press, 1991.

———. *Système et révélation*. Paris: Le Seuil, 1982.

Peperzak, Adriaan. *Ethics as First Philosophy*. New York: Routledge, 1995.

Poirié, François. *Emmanuel Lévinas, qui êtes-vous?* Lyon: La Manufacture, 1987.

Pradines, Maurice. *Le Beau voyage: Itinéraire de Paris aux frontières de Jérusalem*. Paris: Le Cerf, 1982.

Rey, Jean-François. *La mesure de l'homme: L'Idée d'humanité dans la philosophie d'Emmanuel Lévinas*. Paris: Michalon, 2001.

Richardson, William J. *Heidegger: Through Phenomenology to Thought*. Leiden: Martinus Nijhoff, 1963.

Ricoeur, Paul. *Critique and Conviction: Conversations with François Azouvi and Marc De Launay*. Translated by Kathleen Blamey. Cambridge: Polity Press, 1998.

———. *Lectures I*. Paris: Le Seuil, 1991.

———. *Lectures III*. Paris: Le Seuil, 1992.

———. *Temps et récit*. Vols. 1–2. Paris: Le Seuil, 1989.

———. *Time and Narrative*. Translated by Kathleen McLaughlin and David Pellauer. Chicago: University of Chicago Press, 1984.

Robbins, Jill. *Altered Reading*. Chicago: University of Chicago Press, 1999.

Rosenzweig, Franz. *L'Étoile de la rédemption*. Translated by Jean-Louis Schlegel and Alex Derczanski. Paris: Le Seuil, 1982.

———. *Foi et savoir: Autour de "L'Étoile de la rédemption."* Paris: Vrin, 2001.

———. *The New Thinking*. Translated by Alan Udoff and Barbara E. Galli. Syracuse, N.Y.: Syracuse University Press, 1999.

———. *The Star of Redemption*. Translated by William W. Hallo. New York: Holt, Rinehart and Winston, 1970.

Safranski, Rüdiger. *Heidegger et son temps*. Paris: Grasset, 1994.

Salanski, Jean-Michel. *Heidegger*. Paris: Les Belles Lettres, 1997.

Sebbah, François-David. *Emmanuel Lévinas, ambiguités de l'éthique*. Paris: Les Belles Lettres, 2000.

———. *L'Épreuve de la limite*. Paris: Presses Universitaires de France, 2001.

Seidengart, Jean. *Ernst Cassirer, de Marbourg à New York*. Paris: Le Cerf, 1990.

Stone, Ira F. *Reading Levinas/Reading Talmud*. Philadelphia: The Jewish Publication Society, 1998.

Towarnicki, Frederic de. *Martin Heidegger: Souvenirs et chroniques*. Paris: Payot-Rivages, 1999.

Volozhin, Rabbi Hayyim de. *L'Âme de la vie, Nefesh Hahayyim*. Translated and annotated by Benjamin Gross. Preface by Emmanuel Levinas. Lagrasse: Verdier, 1986.

Wall, Thomas Carl. *Radical Passivity: Levinas, Blanchot and Agamben*. Albany: State University of New York Press, 1999.

Zarader, Marlène. *La Dette impensée: Heidegger et l'héritage hébraïque*. Paris: Le Seuil, 1990.

INDEX